SHROPSHIRE TOWNS & VILLAGES

Julie Meech

Series Editor: Terry Marsh

Published by Sigma Leisure – an imprint of
Sigma Press, 1 South Oak Lane, Wilmslow, Cheshire SK9 6AR, England.

British Library Cataloguing in Publication Data
A CIP record for this book is available from the British Library.

ISBN: 1-85058-643-8

Series Editor: Terry Marsh

Typesetting and Design by: Sigma Press, Wilmslow, Cheshire.

Cover Design: MFP Design & Print

Cover photographs: main picture – The Feathers, Ludlow; smaller pictures, from top – Much Wenlock, Stokesay Castle, The Iron Bridge

Photographs: by the author

Map: Morag Perrott

Printed by: MFP Design & Print

Contents

Dedicated to all friends around the Wrekin and to all descendants of William Wycherley

SHROPSHIRE

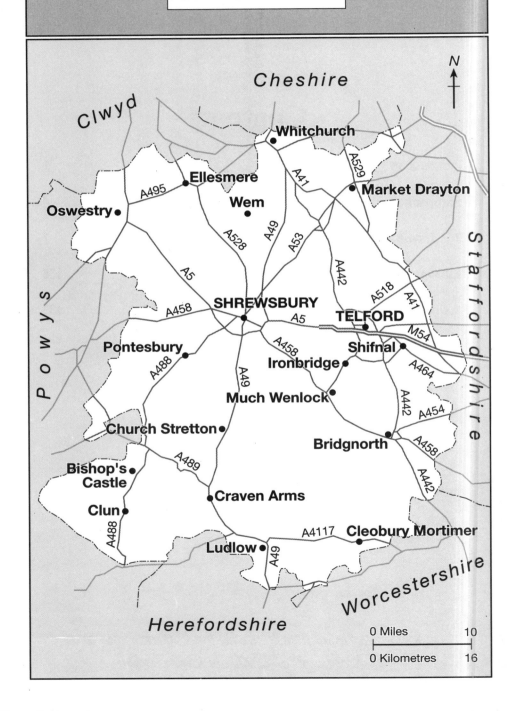

Introduction

The 'Towns and Villages of Britain' is a series of titles detailing a county-by-county approach to the many delights and fascinations of our country's cities, towns, villages and hamlets. There is much of interest and value throughout our towns and villages, but not all of it is widely documented, and some of it, particularly local customs, folklore and traditions, is in danger of being lost forever. By bringing all this information together, county-by-county, it becomes possible to build a unique and substantially comprehensive library of knowledge.

All of the books in the series are compiled to the same specification and in gazetteer format, and include information about the way or the reason a town or village evolved; references to anything associated with the preservation of the past, such as museums, heritage centres, historic or prehistoric sites, battle sites, places of worship and other locally or architecturally important buildings. Landscape features are also detailed, including important natural history sites, geological sites, water features, etc. as is information about important local people, and details of events or traditions, such as well-dressings and rush-bearing ceremonies. There are also notes about any significant present-day informal amenity/recreational features, like country parks, open access land, Areas of Outstanding Natural Beauty, nature reserves, and Sites of Special Scientific Interest. Finally, information is given on any significant Roman or prehistory context, and any anecdotal or endemic folklore references associated with the town or village which might illustrate a particular way of life or social development. The books are therefore eminently suitable for anyone interested in their own locality or in local history; students of history, folklore and related subjects; professional journalists wanting up-to-date and comprehensive information; public relations and similar businesses; photographers and artists, and, of course, the tourists and visitors to the counties.

Explanatory Notes

It has been suggested that to qualify as a village, a 'community' must possess a school, a pub, a post office and a church. Such a requirement, however, excludes a large number of places that are of immense interest, many having important historical associations, and which have played a vital part in the development of the county and its people. So, for the purposes of the books in this series, the criteria for inclusion have been kept deliberately simple: there must be something of interest about the place; or it must have associations with events and people of countywide or wider significance.

Often, the 'something of interest' will simply be the village church (its history, contents or architecture), or its green or a river bridge. In addition, the village may be important to the heritage of the county because it maintains the traditions, ways and beliefs of local culture, or has played a key role in the social, economic or political history of the county or the country as a whole.

Only occasionally, however, is the village pub of special interest in this context, and often the development of large supermarkets within easy travelling distance of the villages has, sadly, signalled the demise of the traditional village shop. Local schools have often been swallowed up by larger schools, and far too many post offices are proving difficult to sustain as viable concerns. So, while that 'classic' definition of a village has much to commend it, in reality it is today too restrictive.

Quite what makes a town is another, arguable, matter. But the precise definition is not too important here; it's the place and its people, not its status, that matters. As a very broad distinction, that no-one should take seriously, a 'hamlet' (a few of which appear in these books) is a distinct community, while a 'village' could be said to be a hamlet with a church, and a 'town' is a village with a market.

In many cases, the historical development of the community, whether a tiny village, a town or a city, is fascinating in itself, and so it is that each entry gradually builds up a picture of the county that is unique. That is what this book endeavours to portray, in a logical and easily accessible way, as well as being a source of reference.

Inevitably, there will be places that have been omitted that others might argue should have been included. But the value each community has to bring to a work of this nature has been carefully weighed; invariably, borderline cases have been given the benefit of the doubt and included.

It is equally clear that, taken to its logical conclusion, this book would be ten times larger, and there has had to be a considerable degree of selective editing to make it of manageable size. One day, perhaps, there could be one book that says everything there is to say about the county, but could we afford to buy it? Could we carry it? Would we want it, when part of the beauty of what does exist is the range of voices and shades of opinion so many different authors can bring?

Following the General Introduction, the book becomes a gazetteer, listing the towns and villages of the county in alphabetical order.

After each town or village name there appears, in square brackets, [ ], the name of the relevant district council (see below).

Next appears a two-letter, four-figure grid reference, which will pinpoint the settlement to within half a mile (one kilometre). This is followed by an approximate distance from some other, usually larger, settlement, together with an equally approximate direction indicator.

Those features or people 'of interest' directly associated with the settlement are highlighted in bold text, while an index lists other features or people only incidentally associated.

Where information is given about events, such as agricultural shows, or facilities, such as museums, details of dates and hours of opening are usually available from any of the Tourist Information Centres listed below.

County Information Centres

Bridgnorth, The Library, Listley Street, Bridgnorth WV16 4AW (Tel: 01746 763257)

Church Stretton, Shropshire Hills Information Centre, County Branch Library, Church Stretton SY6 6DQ (Tel: 01694 723133)

Ellesmere, Ellesmere Visitor Centre, Mereside, Ellesmere SY12 0HD (Tel: 01691 622981)

Ironbridge, The Wharfage, Ironbridge, Telford TF8 7AW (Tel: 01952 432166)

Ludlow, Information Centre, Castle Street, Ludlow SY8 1AS (Tel: 01584 875053)

Market Drayton, Information Centre, 49 Cheshire Street, Market Drayton TF9 1PH (Tel: 01630 652139)

Much Wenlock, Information Centre, The

Museum, High Street, Much Wenlock TF13 6HR (Tel: 01952 727679)

Oswestry Mile End, Information Centre, Mile End, Oswestry SY11 4JA (Tel: 01691 662488)

Oswestry Town, Heritage Centre, 2 Church Terrace, Oswestry SY11 2TE (Tel: 01691 662753)

Shrewsbury, Information Centre, The Music Hall, The Square, Shrewsbury SY1 1LH (Tel: 01743 350761)

Telford Town Centre, Information Centre, The Telford Centre, Telford TF3 4BX (Tel: 01952 230032)

Whitchurch, Information Centre, 12 St Mary's Street, Whitchurch SY13 1QY (Tel: 01948 664577)

District and Borough Councils

The relevant councils are:

Bridgnorth District Council, 22 Bradford Street, Shifnal (Tel: 01952 462545)

North Shropshire District Council, Normanbrook Court, Market Drayton (Tel: 01630 654435)

Oswestry Borough Council, Castle View, Oswestry (Tel: 01691 671111)

Shrewsbury and Atcham District Council, Guildhall, Dogpole, Shrewsbury (Tel: 01743 232255)

South Shropshire District Council, Stone House, Corve Street, Ludlow (Tel: 01584 874941)

Wrekin Council, Civic Offices, Telford (Tel: 01952 202100)

Shropshire on the Internet

If you ask your search engine to find information about Shropshire, you will get hundreds of "hits". To start with, try:

www.wiseword.demon.co.uk/shropshire

This claims to have been the first web site for the county. In addition to the interesting descriptive text, maps and pictures are just a click away.

A more comprehensive site is at: www.virtual-shropshire.co.uk

This one provides dozens of links to both commercial sites and to forthcoming events – which could be very useful if you are planning a holiday.

Shropshire

Shropshire first came into existence as a unit of government in the early 10th century, but many centuries before that the region that was to become Shropshire had already been inhabited by Stone Age, Bronze Age and Iron Age people. Large quantities of flint tools have been found in the county, especially in the valley of the Severn at places such as Alveley, Romsley and Worfield. It is also clear that by the Bronze Age an important trade route, the Clun-Clee Ridgeway, had been established from Anchor on the Welsh border across Clun Forest and the Clee Hills to the Severn, where the river was forded at what is now Bewdley (Worcestershire). Another trade route, the Port Way, traversed the Long Mynd, which, like much of South Shropshire, is scattered with Bronze Age tumuli and other earthworks. People didn't just trade, they settled too, finding the light, easily cultivated soils of South Shropshire much to their liking. Further north, the meres, mosses and marshes were a considerable impediment both to travel and to settlement.

In the 7th century BC the Severn Valley was settled by a Celtic people who left their mark on the land with the construction of numerous hill forts which were not merely defensive in purpose, but were also places where people lived and worked. These Celtic people brought with them the technology for making use of iron and they established a loosely organised society. Known as the Cornovii, they probably looked on the Wrekin hill fort as their "capital". These were the people whom the Romans encountered when they reached this area around AD50.

The Roman Conquest brought down the curtain on prehistory: from this time on written records have survived and we are no longer dependent on archaeological remains for our knowledge. Shropshire was important to the Romans for it was a centre of communications, a place where major roads met, and they established a town at Viroconium (Wroxeter) which was to grow into the fourth largest Roman city in Britain. Another important town developed at Mediolanum (Whitchurch). As the towns prospered, the countryside was cultivated, while in the west of the county the Romans were keen to exploit mineral reserves such as lead ore.

Rome's civilising influence came to an end when the legions withdrew and the next few centuries, as bands of invading Angles, Saxons and Jutes spread out across England, are known as the Dark Ages. Little is known about those years, though it seems likely that the hill forts were reoccupied and that strife became a way of life. It is also likely that what is now Shropshire formed the eastern part of the Celtic kingdom of Powys but by the 7th century the Anglo-Saxons had pushed this far west and were beginning to settle the land. Their penetration was peaceful for a while, owing to the good relations between King Penda of Mercia and the princes of Powys. However, after Penda's death in 654 war was the dominant theme, though things settled down a little after the frontier was defined by the great dyke built by King Offa of Mercia.

After the building of Offa's Dyke, the region was controlled by two Mercian groups, the Magonsaete and the

Wreocensaete, who were as concerned with defending their territories from invading Danes as they were about incursions from the west. It was in this period, some time between 900 and 925, that the shire was created, but no sooner had a modicum of organisation been imposed than a new wave of conquerors was sweeping into Shropshire. The Normans wasted no time in taking control. King William parcelled out the border country (the Marches) to his most trusted associates on the understanding that they were more or less free to carve out their own quasi-autonomous "kingdoms" as long as they kept the Celts and the Saxons in check. Shropshire was given to Roger de Montgomery, created Earl of Shrewsbury. Roger and the two sons who came after him ruled without reference to the monarch and it was only in 1102 that their power was curbed. They chose the losing side in a revolt against Henry I and afterwards Shropshire's government was more in line with that practised elsewhere in England. Nevertheless, the Marcher lords did retain considerable power and the castles that still dot the land today are testimony to this. There were great castles like Ludlow, of course, and middling castles like Clun, but there were also minor castles built by the most insignificant of landholders in the smallest of hamlets. Many of these castles can still be seen today, though in most cases there are only earthworks: usually a mound (motte), sometimes a moat and traces of a bailey. Castles could function simply as administrative centres but too often they were the strongholds of lordly oppressors who knew there was no better way to dominate the local population than to overawe it with symbols of military power and strength.

When they were not oppressing the Saxons or squabbling amongst themselves, the Marcher lords were very often to be found fighting the Welsh, and Shropshire (usually Ludlow) was the seat of the Council in the Marches of Wales, which sought to establish control over this turbulent area. It was only after Henry VII succeeded to the throne and the "Tudor Peace" succeeded the long years of the Wars of the Roses that the Marches began to enjoy calmer days. Legal union with Wales came in 1536 but was only a confirmation of what was by then the reality of peace (most of the time).

Peace brought further prosperity to an already flourishing county: while the barons had been making war the merchants had been quietly getting on with making money and Shrewsbury, for instance, was an important centre for the wool trade. The great monastic estates were hugely prosperous but already their days were numbered. The Dissolution of the Monasteries in the 1530s led to a massive transfer of land, influence and wealth to the gentry. New families rose to prominence but most of the old families survived.

The English Civil War of the 1640s brought great disruption to the county but already other changes, more important in the long term, were just beginning to suggest themselves. The 17th century was a time of industrial expansion, with forges and foundries established in numerous rural locations. However, it was not until 1709 that Abraham Darby's discovery that iron could be smelted with coke instead of charcoal set in motion the first real stirrings of the Industrial Revolution. From the 1750s onwards the large-scale exploitation of the smelting process gradually established Shropshire, specifically the region that is now Telford, as the greatest iron-making centre in the world.

Alongside iron and coal, new industries developed, and new transport systems were required. New roads were built, new canals were dug and Shropshire was fortunate to have the great Thomas Telford as surveyor of public works. The shepherd's son from Langholm was probably the finest civil engineer of all time and his contribution to Shropshire was a remarkable one.

When Telford died in 1834 the railway system was just beginning to make its presence felt, bringing further changes to Shropshire, but it was unable to provide the boost needed by the industrial towns of the coalfield, which had fallen behind in competition with the Black Country and South Wales. Shropshire's second Iron Age was all but over and dereliction and decay were the dominant themes in the former industrial areas. It was only in the 1960s that the Telford Development Corporation began to breathe new life into the dead and dying towns. It was a slow process at first but the former coalfield towns are now enjoying prosperity once again, while Shrewsbury and country towns such as the newly fashionable Ludlow are flourishing.

But not all the signs are good. Shropshire is largely an agricultural county and agriculture is going through hard times. As hill farmers struggle to make a living, farm workers in the villages are replaced by commuters, and tiny rural towns like Bishop's Castle have too many empty shops because too many residents would rather drive to a superstore at Shrewsbury than shop locally. There is a big question mark over the future. Fortunately, Shropshire folk are enterprising and adaptable, and they are beginning to realise the huge potential of their beautiful county, one of the most unspoilt in England, to attract tourists. Already there is an encouraging increase in the sort of small-scale, environmentally responsible initiatives that will help to attract the sort of visitor Shropshire needs. All the same, it will be hard to strike the correct balance and Shropshire really needs to get it right if it is not to be spoilt.

The Towns and Villages

ABDON [South Shropshire]

SO5786: 9 miles (14km) NE of Ludlow

A scattering of farms and cottages, Abdon burrows into the pastoral western slopes of Shropshire's highest hill, Brown Clee, and enjoys fine views of Wenlock Edge and Corve Dale. The Norman (heavily restored) **church of St Margaret** stands aloof from the modern village on a raised circular mound, indicating that it was probably a site of religious significance as far back as the Bronze Age. Adjacent earthworks reveal that Abdon was more extensive until the original village was abandoned in the 13th or 14th century. There are plenty of other deserted medieval villages in Shropshire but, unusually, this site was resettled for a time by miners and quarrymen in the 16th century.

Abdon lies due west of Abdon Burf, the higher of Brown Clee's twin tops. The other, further south, is Clee Burf, and both were formerly encircled by Iron Age forts long since destroyed by mining and quarrying. A lesser fort, Nordy Bank, is still intact.

ACTON BURNELL [Shrewsbury and Atcham]

SJ5302: 8 miles (13km) S of Shrewsbury

Nestling below wooded slopes, Acton Burnell is a village of considerable interest, with some 17th- and 18th-century houses, in a mixture of stone and timber-framing. **St Mary's Church** is Early English in style, cruciform in shape and was built c1270-80 by Robert Burnell, Bishop of Bath and Wells and Lord Chancellor to Edward I. Architecturally, it ranks as Shrop-

shire's finest 13th-century building. Among the many fine memorials the church contains is a remarkably sumptuous one to Sir Richard Lee (d1591). Another Lee memorial, to Sir Humphrey, was superbly carved in 1632 by Nicholas Stone, sculptor to Charles I. A memorial brass to Sir Nicholas Burnell (d1382) is equally impressive.

Acton Burnell Castle (English Heritage) is now just a shell, though a substantial one, and in reality not so much a castle as a fortified manor house, also built by Robert Burnell. Close by are two stone gable-ends which are all that remain of a barn which is believed to have been the meeting place of the first English Parliament at which the commons were fully represented, summoned by Edward I in 1283. It met in Shrewsbury first but then transferred to Acton Burnell, where it passed the Statute of Acton Burnell, regulating the process of debt collecting. However, the main parliamentary business was the trial of Dafydd ap Gruffydd, the last true Prince of Wales, subsequently executed in Shrewsbury.

The estate later passed into the hands of the Smythes, a Roman Catholic family, who built **Acton Burnell Hall**, a classical-style mansion, in 1814. Now functioning as a college, it stands in landscaped parkland. Adjoining the hall is a Catholic chapel built in 1846. From 1939, for 30 years or so, the hall served as a convent, with a school which was attended by the daughter of Charles de Gaulle in the 1940s. The park contains two lakes, overlooked from a rocky knoll by Sham Castle, a Gothic folly built in the 1780s. Acton Burnell Park is also known for its plentiful yew trees, including several of impressive girth, with some of the biggest on the line of the parish boundary.

ACTON ROUND [Bridgnorth]

SO6395: 3 miles (5km) SE of Much Wenlock

The tiny village of Acton Round lies just off the road from Bridgnorth to Much Wenlock, set amid fields on the wooded slopes of Spoonhill. The small **church** has a timber-framed porch and some 12th-century ironwork but has been over-restored. **Acton Round Hall** is an 18th-century mansion which was built as a dower house to Aldenham (see Morville).

One of England's largest oak trees, the **Acton Round Oak**, stands beside a track leading to Monkhall. It was probably a boundary marker in the Shirlett Forest, which once covered these hills, and may be over 800 years old.

ACTON SCOTT [South Shropshire]

SO4589: 3 miles (5km) S of Church Stretton

Beautifully set between the Stretton Hills and Ape Dale, the small village of Acton Scott stands on the site of a Roman settlement and was formerly known as Acton Super Montem. **St Margaret's Church** is medieval but was subject to extensive Victorian restoration, though it contains some good monuments. **Acton Scott Hall** is a 16th-century, gabled, brick mansion set in parkland and built by the Acton family who also owned Aldenham Park (see Morville). Of Saxon stock, the Actons have produced many notable characters. One such, **Sir John Acton**, served in the Royal Navy before entering the service of King Ferdinand IV of Naples. He reorganised the Neapolitan navy and became Generalissimo, Minister of Finance and ultimately Prime Minister. In 1806 King Ferdinand was overthrown and Acton was exiled to Palermo along with the royal family.

The hall's former Home Farm is now **Acton Scott Working Farm**, which shows visitors the reality of daily life before farming was mechanised. A team of heavy horses works the land with vintage machinery, while hand milking and butter churning take place daily. Blacksmiths and wheelwrights display their skills, and rare breeds of cattle, sheep, pigs and poultry are kept.

ADDERLEY [North Shropshire]

SJ6639: 4 miles (6km) N of Market Drayton

Formerly a medieval market town, Adderley has declined in importance to become a scattered village set in a pleasant, pastoral landscape. This is partly due to the Corbet family, who destroyed much of the town to landscape the grounds of Adderley Hall. The present village is largely modern, but the remains of a motte and bailey castle stand to the north-east, close to the Shropshire Union Canal. In 1086 Domesday Book recorded the castle as belonging to Nigel the Physician. The red sandstone **church of St Peter** was rebuilt in 1801; large and cruciform, it has a tower of 1712-13. It contains a notable 17th-century screen and interesting monuments to the Corbets and another local family, the Kilmoreys, who lived at nearby Shavington Hall. Built in 1685 and once described as the best house of its period in the county, it was demolished in 1958.

ALBERBURY [Shrewsbury and Atcham]

SJ3514: 9 miles (14km) W of Shrewsbury

A border village close to the River Severn and overlooked by the Breidden Hills, Alberbury has a long history. In 1942 a skeleton was uncovered in a nearby field, and proved to be the remains of a late Neolithic or early Bronze Age man (2500-2000BC). It is now in Rowley House Museum, Shrewsbury. Alberbury developed into a border settlement of some importance in the Middle Ages, but all that remains now of its ancient castle is an ivy-clad keep in a walled enclosure. Fulke FitzWarine built the castle in the late 12th or early 13th century.

St Michael's Church has a massive, late 13th-century saddleback tower and stands on the site of a Saxon collegiate church, of which no trace remains. Inside, notable features include a magnificent nave roof and the 14th-century Loton Chapel, with monuments to the Leightons of **Loton Park**, a red-brick mansion, partly Queen Anne and partly Jacobean, with a Victorian wing. A little to the north-east of Alberbury, the remains of an Augustinian priory founded in 1225 are incorporated into a farmhouse.

ALBRIGHTON [Bridgnorth]

SJ8104: 5 miles (8km) SE of Shifnal

Lying between Telford and Wolverhampton, the large village of Albrighton may yet be swallowed up by the latter and has already lost much of its character, though touches of Georgian elegance linger still. The red sandstone **church of St Mary Magdalene** is mostly of 1853 but the west tower is late Norman. The church contains some remarkable monuments, including one to Sir John Talbot (died 1555) and his wife. There is a plain tomb-chest, which may be that of the only Duke of Shrewsbury, who died in 1718, while a 13th-century tomb-chest with ornate heraldic decoration is possibly that of Andrew FitzNicholas of Willey, who died at the Battle of Evesham in 1265.

Now contiguous with Albrighton is the formerly separate settlement of Donington, where **St Cuthbert's Church** is set picturesquely by Donington Pool. The church dates from 1085 though the existing building is mostly much more recent. The churchyard contains the graves of airmen based at RAF Cosford, which is close by. Just below the church, hidden in woodland, is St Cuthbert's Well, reputed to be helpful for eye complaints.

ALBRIGHTON [Shrewsbury and Atcham]

SJ4918: 4 miles (6km) N of Shrewsbury.

Albrighton is a tiny village with timber-framed houses. The neo-Norman Victorian **church of St John the Baptist** (1840-41) contains a genuine Norman font. Just to the north of the church is **Albrighton Hall**, which is now a hotel. A short distance to the south-east is **Albright Hussey**, a timber-framed house of 1524, partly rebuilt in brick in 1601. There is no sign of a chapel that once stood beside the house. It fell into disuse when the church at nearby Battlefield was built.

ALDON [South Shropshire]

SO4379: 2 miles (3km) S of Craven Arms

A delightfully unspoilt hamlet of stone cottages and farms, Aldon clings to pastoral slopes above the Onny valley. Aldon Court, a substantial house, is just to the south, perched above the point where the land plunges into Aldon Gutter, a steep-sided, partially wooded coomb.

ALL STRETTON [South Shropshire]

SO4695: 1 mile (2km) N of Church Stretton

Though now seamlessly adjoining Church Stretton, the village of All Stretton still exists in its own right and is beautifully set between the Long Mynd and Caer Caradoc. **St Michael's Church** was built in 1902 by A.E. Lloyd Oswell, just below a prehistoric earthwork on a knoll christened Castle Hill. The 'All' of All Stretton is probably derived from an Anglo-Saxon personal name but the story still persists that James II, travelling from Ludlow to Shrewsbury, asked the names of the villages he passed through. At Little Stretton they told him Stretton, at Church Stretton they told him likewise, and when he received the same response at the third and most northerly of the Strettons he exclaimed, "It's all Stretton here!"

ALVELEY [Bridgnorth]

SO7684: 6 miles (10km) SE of Bridgnorth

A group of sandstone cottages marks the old centre of Alveley, but the village has been submerged in a sea of more modern housing built during its period as a mining town. The surrounding countryside is gently undulating, except to the west where the land falls steeply to the River Severn. **St Mary's Church** was heavily restored by Sir Arthur Blomfield in 1878-9 but remains an interesting building with work from several periods. The earliest part is the 12th-century tower, though even that has been restored. Founded c1140, the church has a fine nave, with Norman pillars and arches, and a 15th-century roof resting on unusual stone corbels.

There are two pubs in the village centre, with the Three Horseshoes Inn (first licensed 1406) claiming to be Shropshire's oldest, though it was largely rebuilt in the 19th century. The Bell Inn (licensed 1647) is believed to have been built with stone from a Saxon church which pre-dated the Norman one. Oliver Cromwell is said to have stayed at the Three Horseshoes.

About a mile to the north of the village is the **Butter Cross**, a wayside cross with a round head, both faces of which have a carving of a Maltese cross. Its original purpose is uncertain but it may mark the site of a medieval market. A more popular, if unproven, explanation is that it served as a place where food could be left in times of plague without the providers needing to enter the infected village.

Alveley and its counterpart on the west bank of the Severn (see Highley) lie at the northern limit of the Wyre Forest coalfield. Both coal mining and quarrying began in the Middle Ages but remained small-scale until the 19th century. Alveley stone was used in both Worcester Cathedral and Prior's Lodge in Much Wenlock. The quarries had been more or less worked out by 1912, but coal production peaked between 1879 and 1939, before finally coming to an end in 1969. A bridge, now known as Miners' Bridge, was built across the Severn in 1937 to facilitate the movement of coal from Alveley to the railway on the west bank. Today the bridge links the two parts of the Severn Valley Country Park, which straddles the river and has been created from the scarred landscape which was the legacy of mining.

To the north-east of Alveley, **Coton Hall** belonged to the Lee family, forebears of General Robert E. Lee of American Civil War fame. The existing house dates from c1820 and nothing remains of the original Elizabethan building. A ruined chapel stands close by.

APLEY [Bridgnorth]

SO7098: 4 miles (6km) N of Bridgnorth

Set in beautiful, well-wooded countryside, Apley consists of a scatter of buildings on both sides of the River Severn. There are just a few Victorian cottages at Apley Forge on the west bank, and it's hard to

The Butter Cross, Alveley

imagine that this peaceful place was once the scene of industry, with two forges in operation. Just a little way downstream are the remains of the riverside wharves that served the forge. The river trade decreased after the building of the railway, but this has itself been dismantled, though the former station house (for Linley) is still there, a short distance from Apley Forge.

Across the river, set in Apley Park, below the steep, wooded cliffs of Apley Terrace, stands **Apley Hall**, which was, until recently, used as a school and is now a retirement home. A castellated Gothic mansion of Grinshill stone, it was built for Bridgnorth MP Thomas Whitmore in 1811, incorporating an older Georgian house built on the site of a 14th-century fortified house. A private suspension bridge built c1905 spans the river and was possibly intended to link Apley Park with Linley Station.

AQUEDUCT [Wrekin]

SJ6805: 2 miles (3km) NE of Ironbridge

Now consumed by Telford New Town, Aqueduct has little of interest surviving other than the **aqueduct** from which it takes its name. This is a single-arched structure of grey limestone, which carried the eastern spur of the Shropshire Union Canal over the Wellington road. The canal was opened in 1792 to transport coal to the iron furnaces of Coalbrookdale.

ASH MAGNA [North Shropshire]

SJ5739: 2 miles (3km) SE of Whitchurch

This is a scattered and largely unspoiled settlement comprising Ash Magna and Ash Parva, with the brick-built, 19th-century **Church of Christ** by George Jenkin tucked away down a lane further north. **Ash Hall** is a splendid 18th-century brick house occupying a commanding position at the centre of Ash Magna. Other fine houses, some brick, some timber-framed, stand nearby.

A little way to the south-west of Ash is **Brown Moss**, an important nature reserve with a mixture of woodland, heath and wetland. Originally peat bog, it has been modified by past drainage.

ASHFORD BOWDLER [South Shropshire]

SO5170: 3 miles (5km) S of Ludlow

Unobtrusively tucked away in the lush Teme valley, Ashford Bowdler is a small village of mostly timber-framed (but also brick and stone) cottages, several of them thatched. There are also several more imposing houses, including The Grove, Manor Farm, Hall Farm, Yew Tree Farmhouse and 18th-century **Ashford Hall**, which lies to the north-west, beneath the slopes of High Vinnalls.

By the Teme stands the simple sandstone **church of St Andrew**, with just a nave and chancel and an oak-shingled broach spire. The churchyard contains headstones carved with appealingly primitive skulls and crossbones. St Andrew's is Norman but was restored in 1846 and again in 1904-7 after the chancel collapsed into the river.

ASHFORD CARBONEL [South Shropshire]

SO5270: 3 miles (5km) S of Ludlow

Ashford Carbonel is much larger than neighbouring Ashford Bowdler. It contains a number of modern houses but the original village is still much in evidence, with a variety of old houses in stone, brick and timber. The **church of St Mary Magdalene** occupies a commanding position on a knoll, with a good view of Titterstone Clee Hill. Built of local stone, it has a timbered belfry with a pyramidal roof, and a Norman doorway, windows, chancel arch and font. The windows are of particular interest, including one of a type that is rare in small parish churches: an almond-shaped vesica, related to the symbol of the fish that was used by early Christians. It is suggested that a vesica was a common feature in the churches of north-west France from whence came the eponymous Carbonel family. (Héoul Carbonel was one of William the Conqueror's principal captains.) The churchyard encloses five very ancient yew trees, and is also notable for its profusion of wild flowers. Most of the sandstone tombstones are badly eroded, but a cast-iron table tomb of 1806 in memory of Arabella Yate is in good condition. A tombstone of 1882 commemorates an unfortunate Mrs Lancett who was knocked over by a train near Ludlow while scavenging nuts that had fallen from an earlier train.

Between the two Ashfords is the ford from which they take their name. Before the bridge was built this must have been used by a great many travellers because it lay on an important trackway (probably a saltway) between Wales and the Midlands. The medieval single-arched bridge, rebuilt in 1877, overlooks a horseshoe weir next to a mill.

ASTERLEY [Shrewsbury and Atcham]

SJ3707: 2 miles (3km) NW of Pontesbury

A substantial village with some modern development, Asterley nestles among green fields which were mined for coal in the 19th century. There are still spoil heaps but they are small and have been absorbed into the landscape, many of them disappearing under tree-cover. The village church, brick-built and ivy-clad, is no longer in use, but there is also a stone-built Primitive Methodist Chapel of 1834. A little to the north of the village is a windmill, a rare sight in Shropshire.

ASTERTON [South Shropshire]

SO3991: 4 miles (6km) SW of Church Stretton

A mainly stone-built hamlet in a dramatically beautiful landscape, Asterton clusters about a crossroads immediately below the steep south-western slopes of the Long Mynd, on high ground overlooking the River West Onny. Perhaps the most notable building is a longhouse – cottage and adjoining barn or stable under one roof – a type not often found in Shropshire. Just to the north, Asterton Prolley Moor, now drained and put to pasture, was formerly a marshy wilderness where witches were said to meet.

ASTLEY [Shrewsbury and Atcham]

SJ5218: 5 miles (8km) NE of Shrewsbury

The original Astley is a compact and unremarkable village hidden away in the flat countryside north of Shrewsbury. Modern Astley is represented by housing at Upper Astley, just off the A53, and a few developments and commercial premises alongside the road itself. **St Mary's Church** is at the heart of the old village. It retains some Norman work but is mostly of the 14th century and was restored in the late 19th century. Close to the church is the surprising **Astley House**, a Georgian building in white stucco with a very Greek frontage.

ASTLEY ABBOTTS [Bridgnorth]

SO7096: 2 miles (3km) N of Bridgnorth

Just above the valley of the Severn and surrounded by rich agricultural land, Astley Abbotts is a village of timber-framed houses set amongst trees. A notable feature, next to the church, is the presence of what is probably Shropshire's only lavender farm. The **church of St Calixtus** was consecrated in 1138 and some Norman work does survive, though it was rebuilt in 1633 and partially rebuilt again in 1857. Bishop Thomas Percy (see Bridgnorth) served as curate at Astley Abbotts 1752-4.

In the north aisle hang a maiden's garland and a pair of gloves, in memory of Hannah Phillips who lived in the house next to the churchyard and died on the eve of her wedding in 1707. This is a reminder of a once widespread custom observed at the funeral of an unmarried, virtuous woman who was born, baptised and died within the parish. A rush or wooden frame supported a garland of ribbons and flowers, which was placed upon the coffin or carried by two young virgins, together with a pair of gloves or a handkerchief belonging to the deceased. After the funeral they were hung above her empty seat in the church. The custom started before the Reformation and in some places it continued into the 20th century. Surviving garlands are found in only a few churches today.

ASTON BOTTERELL [Bridgnorth]

SO6384: 8 miles (13km) SW of Bridgnorth

Situated in rolling farmland below Brown Clee Hill, Aston Botterell is a scattered parish based on a cluster of farm buildings round the church. The oldest part of stone-built **Aston Manor Farm** is 13th century and there is plenty of 16th-century work in evidence too. This was the home of the Botterells, while a moated site in an adjacent field is believed to be where the house of Tochil stood, the Saxon whom Domesday Book records as holding the manor before the Norman Botterells took over. **St Michael's Church** contains work from six centuries, though little survives of the original Norman masonry. St Michael's was restored in 1884 and the tower rebuilt, but the interior is unspoilt and full of interest, with a Norman font, Jacobean woodwork and good monuments from the 15th and 16th centuries.

ASTON EYRE [Bridgnorth]

SO6594: 4 miles (6km) W of Bridgnorth

Aston Eyre is a compact cluster of farms and cottages straddling the road between Morville and Monkhopton, surrounded by undulating mixed farmland and with the steep slopes of Aston Hill to the south. To the north of the road is **Hall Farm**, the best of several fine farmhouses in the parish. It incorporates part of a 13th-century manor

house. The Norman **church** is close by and has one of the oldest and finest stone sculptures in the county, a 12th-century tympanum representing Christ's entry into Jerusalem, on a strange-looking ass with enormous ears. It was probably carved by a member of the renowned Hereford School of sculptors.

ASTON MUNSLOW [South Shropshire]

SO5186: 6 miles (10km) SE of Church Stretton

Lying picturesquely on the edge of Corve Dale below the dip slope of Wenlock Edge, Aston Munslow is a stone-built village with some modern infilling. **Aston Hall** is a gabled stone house of the early 17th century. Of even more interest is the **White House**, which belongs to the Landmark Trust. Built of stone and timber, with cruck construction, it incorporates work from the Norman era to the Georgian. In the grounds is a range of farm buildings, including a dovecote, coach house, barns, granary, stable block and cider press.

ASTON ON CLUN [South Shropshire]

SO3981: 3 miles (5km) W of Craven Arms

A stone hamlet with an early 19th-century classical-style hall, two circular houses and a Gothic inn called The Kangaroo, Aston on Clun straddles a tributary stream close to its confluence with the River Clun. It is situated below the steep slopes of Hopesay Hill, Burrow (topped with an Iron Age fort) and Clunbury Hill. Aston is famous for a tree-dressing ceremony involving a black poplar known as the **Arbor Tree**. Sadly, this ancient tree fell in 1995, but a young tree has since replaced it and the old custom is still perpetuated when the tree is dressed with new flags on or close to Oak Apple Day (29th May) each year. The earliest written records of the ceremony are from 29th May 1786 when John Marston of

Oaker married Mary Carter of Sibdon. There are various versions of the story that connects their wedding celebrations with the tree, but its roots almost certainly lie in pagan fertility rites. Such celebrations were not limited to Aston on Clun, but in this case the custom was perpetuated because the Marston connection kept alive the practice, with the family continuing to fund the tree dressing until the 1950s when Hopesay Parish Council took over.

ATCHAM [Shrewsbury and Atcham]

SJ5409: 4 miles (6km) SE of Shrewsbury

A compact village of stone and brick houses, Atcham lies on the east bank of the Severn and on the edge of Attingham Park (National Trust). There are two bridges over the Severn at Atcham, a modern one (1927-29) and the elegant **Severn Bridge**, now used only by pedestrians. This was built in 1769 by John Gwynn, more famous for English Bridge at Shrewsbury, Worcester Bridge and Magdalen Bridge at Oxford. Gwynn's bridge at Atcham replaced a 16th-century structure which was insufficient to cope with increasing traffic in the 18th century on what was then the main Holyhead road.

Atcham's pub is the handsome, red-brick Mermaid, formerly the Mytton and Mermaid, a name which recalls one of Shropshire's more colourful characters, Mad Jack Mytton (see Whittington). After his death, his body lay here for a night before burial and his ghost is said to haunt the pub still.

On the riverbank stands the **church of St Eata**, the only one in England dedicated to this particular saint, who was consecrated Bishop of Lindisfarne in 678. The church spans the 13th to 15th centuries (though it originated in the 11th century) and is built partly of stones brought from the Roman city of Viroconium. It has been heavily restored but contains items of interest, mostly brought from elsewhere. For example, there is some 15th- and 16th-century glass

from Bacton in Herefordshire, transferred to Atcham in 1811.

The Anglo-Norman historian and writer **Ordericus Vitalis** (1075-1143) was born in Atcham and baptised at St Eata's. His most famous work is *Historia Ecclesiastica*.

Attingham Hall is famous for its magnificent Regency interior, and stands in spacious parkland dotted with clumps of trees. It was built in 1783-5 of Grinshill stone, for Noel Hill, the first Lord Berwick, to the design of George Steuart, a Scottish architect responsible for several houses and churches in Shropshire, though this is the only one of his houses to survive. In the early 19th century John Nash was commissioned by the second Lord Berwick to make alterations and to build a picture gallery. The ceiling of the gallery is the first in which cast-iron window frames were used. They were produced by the Coalbrookdale Company.

Originally part of a manorial estate, the parkland was designed in the late 18th century to complement the newly built hall. Humphry Repton modified an earlier layout and the trees he planted now stand as mature specimens, important for the insects and fungi they support. The house is seen at best advantage from the beautiful **Tern Bridge**, built in 1774 to the design of Robert Mylne. It carries the main road over the River Tern close to its confluence with the Severn, due south of Attingham Hall and due east of Atcham.

BADGER [Bridgnorth]

SO7699: 6 miles (10km) NE of Bridgnorth

Set on a gentle slope above the River Worfe, Badger is secluded and unspoilt, with a harmonious collection of stone, brick and timbered cottages. Sadly, Badger Hall has been demolished, but the chain of pools that was part of its landscaped grounds is still a delightful feature of the village. A little classical temple, probably by one of the Wyatts, also survives.

The heavily restored **church of St Giles** was originally Norman but now dates mostly from the 19th century and is rich in monuments by Flaxman, Chantrey and Gibson.

The novelist P.G. Wodehouse (see Stableford) was fond of Badger and used it in some of his books. Badger Dingle, for example, occurs as Badgwick Dingle.

BARROW [Bridgnorth]
SO6599: 2 miles (3km) E of Much Wenlock

A tiny village in lovely countryside, with a handful of houses, a school, a farm, a row of almshouses and a church, Barrow is sandwiched between Shirlett Park and Willeypark Wood, both remnants of the Forest of Shirlett.

The **church of St Giles** is one of the oldest and most interesting churches in the county. The square, stone tower is Norman, with brick battlements and a pyramidal roof added in the 18th century. The chancel is Saxon, from the early 11th century, and the nave is early Norman, with three deeply splayed windows. A classical brick and stone south porch was added in 1705 and the church interior was restored in 1852 and 1895. One of the best features of the church is its original main doorway, which was incorporated into the later tower and still retains its tympanum, distinctively carved with a design of lozenges and saltire crosses.

Outside, there is a fine cast-iron monument of 1807 and several cast-iron headstones, but these have been thrown in a rusting heap in the centre of the churchyard, while the stone ones have also been disturbed and now stand around the perimeter. One of Shropshire's best known characters, Tom Moody, the subject of songs, poems and paintings, is buried in the churchyard. Moody, who died in 1796, was a whipper-in for the local hunt and an accomplished horseman. His ghost, on horseback and accompanied by a hound, is said to roam the local fields and woods. Also buried in the churchyard is Thomas Turner,

who made china at Caughley. The Caughley works was later taken over by John Rose, the founder of Coalport porcelain. Another famous name in the field of pottery is Thomas Minton, who was also involved with Caughley before founding his own company at Stoke-on-Trent.

BASCHURCH [North Shropshire]
SJ4221: 8 miles (13km) NW of Shrewsbury

A settlement of some importance in Saxon times, Baschurch was already in decline by the 12th century. It stands in flat farmland close to the River Perry and mostly straggles along the main road, though the older part of the village forms a compact group around the red sandstone **All Saints' Church**. The church stands on a mound and has been much restored, although the 13th-century tower is unspoilt. Telford was responsible for work here in 1790.

About a mile to the north of the church is **The Berth**, a Celtic fort on a low hilltop, which may have been occupied by the 7th-century Welsh Prince Cynddylan. After the decline of Viroconium (see Wroxeter) it is possible that The Berth became the administrative centre for the region, before Shrewsbury rose to prominence in the 9th century.

BATCHCOTT [South Shropshire]
SO4970: 3 miles (5km) SW of Ludlow

A tiny, scattered village, with stone-built cottages and a Georgian brick rectory, Batchcott nestles in undulating countryside below High Vinnalls, the forested hill south-west of Ludlow. **All Saints' Church** was built in 1891 to the design of Norman Shaw and paid for by Mrs Johnston-Foster of Moor Park, a large house in spacious grounds just to the north of Batchcott. It once belonged to the Salweys, a prominent Shropshire family, and was very nearly purchased by the future Edward VII in 1861. In the end he chose Sandringham instead and Moor Park is now a Catholic prep school.

BATTLEFIELD [Shrewsbury and Atcham]

SJ5117: 3 miles (5km) NE of Shrewsbury

Modern Battlefield is a built-up area on the edge of Shrewsbury, but the place acquired its name in 1403 when Henry IV defeated Harry Hotspur at the Battle of Shrewsbury. The battle site is just to the west of the railway, reached by a lane off the A49. There is nothing there but the **church of St Mary Magdalene** and a couple of houses. Henry IV founded the church in thanksgiving for his victory, and decreed that eight chaplains should pray for the souls of those who died in the battle. The church later fell into disrepair and suffered the inevitable Victorian restoration in 1861-2, at the hands of S. Pountney Smith. However, it is relatively unspoiled inside and beautifully light and spacious. Fragments of the original glass remain in the vestry windows, and a statue of Henry IV stands in a niche at the east end. To the south of the church is part of the moat which surrounded the college in which the chaplains lived.

BAYSTON HILL [Shrewsbury and Atcham]

SJ4808: 2 miles (3km) S of Shrewsbury

Though now a modern suburb of Shrewsbury, Bayston Hill is a settlement of ancient origin. Its name is Saxon, but the parish was formed only in the 19th century from parts of Condover and St Julian's, Shrewsbury. **Christ Church** was built in 1843 by Haycock and overlooks the village green. Close by is **The Burgs**, the site of a Celtic fort. South-east of The Burgs is **Bomere Pool**, to which a number of legends attach. Today the pool is given over to leisure use, but until recently it was a quiet, almost isolated spot and it must have been easier then to believe in the Great Fish of Bomere, which guards Wild Edric's sword (see Stiperstones). Another legend has Bomere the site of a city during the Roman occupation. The inhabitants worshipped

pagan gods and were punished when a great flood engulfed the city, creating Bomere Pool. The Shropshire novelist Mary Webb (see Leighton), always sensitive to atmosphere, made Bomere into the Sarn Mere of *Precious Bane*. Just to the south of Bayston Hill is **Lyth Hill**, where Mary Webb lived at Spring Cottage from 1917 until her death in 1927. The cottage is still there, though much altered, but the magnificent views that Mary so admired are little changed.

BECKBURY [Bridgnorth]

SJ7601: 6 miles (10km) NE of Bridgnorth

Above the River Worfe, close to its confluence with Mad Brook, Beckbury's brick houses and cottages cluster around the 17th-century hall. A backdrop of yew trees sets off the pinky-grey sandstone **church of St Milburga**, which has a chancel of c1300. The nave and tower are Georgian and the north and south aisles Victorian. Though much restored, the interior is light and pleasant. A 19th-century schoolhouse stands nearby and a few timber-framed houses occupy the hill above the church. Lower Hall is said to be haunted by a phantom horse, possibly ridden by Squire Stubbs, a keen foxhunter who was born at the hall in 1671.

BEDLAM [South Shropshire]

SO5877: 5 miles (8km) NE of Ludlow

Also known as Titterstone Village, Bedlam is a Victorian quarrying settlement consisting of two rows of terraced houses, a war memorial, a corrugated-iron village hall and a Primitive Methodist Chapel, converted into a house. It's notable mainly for its idyllic location, high on the slopes of Titterstone Clee Hill. Apparently there was once a lunatic asylum here and this is how it acquired its name – from the notorious London asylum St Mary of Bethlehem Hospital, colloquially known as Bedlam.

A traditional county sign

BEDSTONE [South Shropshire]

SO3675: 10 miles (16km) W of Ludlow

Set in hilly country not far from the confluence of the River Clun and the River Redlake, Bedstone is a small village full of interest. The Norman **church of St Mary** has a timber-framed bellcote and a shingled spire. It was subject to 19th-century restoration but still retains some original windows and the Norman font. Nearby stand a few thatched cottages and a Victorian schoolhouse (converted to a private residence), while **Manor Farm** is a splendid timber-framed house partly faced in stone in 1775. Behind it stand two huge crucks, which are all that survive of the Old Hall, built c1350. To the south of the village is **Bedstone Court**, a flamboyant black and white mansion of 1884. It was designed by Thomas Harris for Sir Henry Ripley MP and is said to be a "calendar house" with 365 windows, 52 rooms and 12 chimneys. Just to the west of the village, on the slopes of Bedstone Hill, is **Castle Ditches**, a prehistoric camp.

BENTHALL [Wrekin]

SJ6602: 1 mile (2km) S of Ironbridge

Benthall straggles along a road on the edge of Broseley, of which it is now virtually a suburb. The main focus of interest is just to the north-west, where **Benthall Hall** (which belongs to the National Trust, but remains the home of Mr and Mrs Benthall) stands next to a farm and church. The hall is a superb building of grey stone built c1583 overlooking pastoral country. It has star-shaped chimney stacks, gables and mullioned windows, while inside its main features include a carved oak staircase, elaborate plasterwork and oak panelling. George Maw, of decorative tile fame (see Jackfield), once lived at Benthall Hall. A keen botanist, he filled the gardens with a wonderful display of plants. Next to the hall is **St Bartholomew's Church**, built in 1667 to replace a medieval chapel burnt down in the Civil War. It has a timber-framed belfry with a pyramidal roof and there is an unusual sundial on the south wall, featuring a mosaic representation of an eye. The church was restored in the 19th century, when the porch and gallery staircase were added.

To the north of Benthall the land falls away steeply to the Severn Gorge at Benthall Edge. The woods clothing the edge look ancient, but have actually regenerated over the last 150 years or so, since industrial production began to fall off. Benthall was first exploited for its coal in 1250 and by the 18th century was a busy industrial centre, almost cleared of woodland, with forges, furnaces, brickworks and wharves by the Severn. Today, the regenerated woodland is managed for its wildlife value and for public amenity by the Severn Gorge Countryside Trust, a consortium of local authorities and conservation groups.

BERRINGTON [Shrewsbury and Atcham]

SJ5306: 4 miles (6km) SE of Shrewsbury

Set in low green hills above the Cound Brook, the small, mainly brick-built village of Berrington is dominated by the pink sandstone tower of **All Saints' Church**. The church, which is approached over cobbles, was originally Norman, but only the font remains from that period. There is an unusual 13th-century oak effigy of a cross-legged knight in the south aisle. All Saints' used to be the annual venue for an Easter Day orgy known as the Love Feast. It is not known when this originated but it was already a longstanding tradition when the Bishop of Lichfield expressed his disapproval in 1639. The final Love Feast took place in 1713. Opposite the church is a timber-framed, gabled manor house, dated 1658.

Berrington stands about halfway along the chain of meres which extends south-eastwards from Bayston Hill. There are several around the village, of which Berrington Pool and Top Pool are the largest.

BETTON STRANGE [Shrewsbury and Atcham]

SJ5009: 2 miles (3km) S of Shrewsbury

The hamlet of Betton Strange occupies a secluded situation in pleasant countryside studded with small meres. It comprises little more than a house, a farm, a substantial hall and a church, all clustered round a "no through road". St Margaret's Church was built in 1858 in the Gothic style and is surrounded by trees. At the end of the road is Betton Alkmere, where a farm stands close to the largest of Betton Strange's meres. About a mile to the south is Betton Abbots, with just a farm and a few meres, including the large Betton Pool.

BETTWS-Y-CRWYN [South Shropshire]

SO2181: 6 miles (10km) W of Clun

This isolated hamlet stands high on a windswept hilltop in sublime border country where sheep outnumber people. Its name means the "prayer house of the fleeces" and it stands on a former drove road that developed on a much older route, the prehistoric Clun-Clee Ridgeway. The 13th-century St Mary's Church was restored in 1860 but retains a splendid 15th-century roof and a

finely carved oak chancel screen. The names of the local farms are still painted on the bench ends and there are some excellent 18th-century slate tablets by local craftsmen. Apart from Church Farm and a few cottages, there is nothing else at Bettws, except glorious views and buzzards overhead.

BICTON [Shrewsbury and Atcham]

SJ4415: 3 miles (5km) NW of Shrewsbury

There's not a great deal to see at Bicton, where an old yew-shrouded churchyard encloses the scant ruins of an 18th-century church next to Bicton Hall. A cluster of cottages and farms completes the hamlet, often known as Old Bicton to distinguish it from the modern village, which has grown up nearby around the Church of Holy Trinity, built in 1885. To the north of Bicton the Severn makes a spectacular meander, creating what is almost an island. Known as The Isle, it has a few houses, a farm, a large pool and the site of a moated medieval dwelling.

BILLINGSLEY [Bridgnorth]

SO7085: 5 miles (8km) S of Bridgnorth

Scattered haphazardly along a ridge above the Severn, Billingsley's main asset is the beauty of its situation. It's hard to imagine now, but this was once coal-mining country and traces of disused mines can be seen in places, as well as dismantled tramways which linked the mines with the Severn Valley Railway. St Mary's Church is Norman but was almost entirely rebuilt in 1875. However, it does retain its Norman font and an early 14th-century Easter Sepulchre.

BISHOP'S CASTLE [South Shropshire]

SO3288: 8 miles (13km) NW of Craven Arms

The documented history of Bishop's Castle begins in the late 8th century when it was part of the manor of Lydbury North, whose

Saxon lord, Egwin Shakehead, gave it to the Bishop of Hereford after he had been cured of the palsy at the tomb of St Ethelbert in Hereford Cathedral. The **castle** was built around 1100 by another Bishop of Hereford, on a site at the top of the present town, behind **Castle Hotel** (1719). It was referred to as Lydbury Castle at that time, and later as Newcastle, but it became Bishop's Castle in 1285. It was kept in good repair throughout the Middle Ages and into the Tudor period but became ruinous in the early 17th century. What little survives can be visited from Castle Street.

In the early Middle Ages the parish of Bishop's Castle was partly in England, partly in Wales, and often the subject of dispute. It was always a significant Marches township with people from both sides of the border making good use of its markets. It received its first charter in 1278 but in 1573 Queen Elizabeth I granted a new charter and from 1585 Bishop's Castle returned two MPs to Parliament. At one time it was the smallest borough in England, known as a "rotten borough" (one of many) because its small population didn't justify two MPs. In 1722 it was alleged that one of the elected MPs had bribed 52 of the 53 men who voted for him. In 1820 all four candidates polled 87 votes each, and in the absence of any other procedure all were duly elected. The Reform Act of 1832 put an end to this sort of thing and also to Bishop's Castle's political significance, though it remained a borough until 1967.

The Castle, as locals call it, has developed into one of the most charming small towns in England and retains many reminders of its long history, with a harmonious mix of architecturally diverse buildings in stone, brick and timber jostling for position. Most are simply pleasing and appropriate, rather than notable, but some, such as the Castle Hotel and the **Porch House**, are architecturally distinguished. The High Street rises steeply and narrows at the top, by the tiny **town hall**, which was built of brick and stone c1765. It has two circular windows in the basement, which served as the town lock-up for many years. The town hall is now the venue for the weekly Friday market. Next to the town hall is the **House on Crutches Museum,** an Elizabethan building with its gable-end supported on wooden posts. It now functions as a museum of local history. Other buildings of interest include a school of 1875 and an imposing 18th-century bank.

The **church of St John the Baptist** stands at the lower end of the town and was rebuilt in 1592, in 1648 (after Civil War damage) and again in 1860, to the design of the Hereford architect T. Nicholson. However, a church is known to have existed on this site by the 13th century and the characteristically sturdy border tower may be the original one.

Bishop's Castle was once a railway town, at the end of a line built in 1865 from Craven Arms and usually described as "eccentric" or "bizarre" because it had no chance of making a profit. Immensely scenic, the route was never financially viable and closed in 1935, though it is remembered affectionately at the town's **Railway Museum**.

The little town is also known for its real ale. **The Three Tuns** is a historic brew-pub that obtained its licence in 1642, though the present Grade II-listed tower brewery is Victorian. **The Six Bells,** a 17th-century coaching inn, also offers beer brewed on site and is owned by a trust formed to save it from redevelopment.

BITTERLEY [South Shropshire]

SO5677: 4 miles (6km) NE of Ludlow

The village of Bitterley slumbers among rich green meadows in the shadow of Titterstone Clee Hill. The village houses are a pleasing mixture of styles and materials, and there is a Victorian school, successor to a grammar school founded in the 16th century. **St Mary's Church** stands apart from the village centre but close to

St Mary's, Bitterley

Bitterley Court, a gabled house set in parkland. Part Jacobean, it has a Georgian facade. The church is mostly Early English, with a massive Norman tower topped with a little broach spire above a shingled cap. The churchyard is graced by a tall 14th-century preaching cross with a carving of the Crucifixion. The interior of the church has been heavily restored but there is a fine Norman font and interesting monuments, including one to Timothy Lucy, who died in 1616. He came from Charlecote Park in Warwickshire and was a grandson of the Sir Thomas Lucy caricatured by Shakespeare as Mr Justice Shallow in *The Merry Wives of Windsor*.

BONINGALE [Bridgnorth]

SJ8102: 5 miles (8km) SE of Shifnal

Though perilously close to Wolverhampton, Boningale remains an attractive village with a number of timber-framed houses, of which **Church Farm** is the most notable. Tree-shaded St **Chad's Church** is Norman but was rather harshly restored in 1861. Boningale produced one of Shropshire's more notorious characters, **Jonathan Wild,** who was born in the village in 1682 and became a hugely successful leader of organised crime in London. He was eventually caught, convicted and executed but John Gay used him as the model for Peachum in *The Beggar's Opera* in 1728.

BORASTON [South Shropshire]

SO6170: 7 miles (12km) SE of Ludlow

A remote and attractive little village, Boraston's red-brick Georgian houses and cottages are tucked away on the southernmost slopes of Titterstone Clee Hill, hidden down winding lanes. The church has two Norman doorways but was restored in 1884-7. The font (c1700) came from Buildwas.

BOSCOBEL [Bridgnorth]

SJ8308: 6 miles (10km) E of Shifnal

There's nothing much at Boscobel other than an unexceptional country house, built around 1600 as a hunting lodge in what was then Brewood Forest. However, **Boscobel House** (English Heritage) is famous as one of the places to which Charles II fled after his defeat at the Battle of Worcester in 1651. He stayed first at nearby **White Ladies Priory**, the site of an Augustinian nunnery established in 1186. He then spent a day hiding in the branches of a large, recently pollarded oak tree in Spring Coppice, just to the south of Boscobel House, followed by a night in the house itself. The so-called **Royal Oak** is now one of Britain's most famous trees, though it is actually an offspring of the original tree, which was destroyed by souvenir hunters. It stands in a field, the surrounding coppice having been cleared. Oak Apple Day is still celebrated on 29th May (the day Charles was restored to the throne), and thousands of pubs are named the Royal Oak after the Boscobel tree. The ruins of White Ladies Priory lie in a field about 1 mile south-west of Boscobel House.

BOURTON [Bridgnorth]

SO5996: 3 miles (5km) SW of Much Wenlock

Originally one of the estates held by Wenlock Abbey, Bourton is a charming, mainly stone-built village below Wenlock Edge in Corve Dale, with a brook running alongside the main street. **Bourton Hall Farm** is a splendid 17th-century stone house with star-shaped chimney stacks, while **Bourton Manor** is a rambling house designed by Norman Shaw in the 1870s, incorporating parts of an earlier building. It has half-timbered gables and a tile-hung first floor, a massive stone-arched doorway and a dramatic roof-line of 16 chimneys. The **church of Holy Trinity** stands close by, on a small knoll. Of Gothic appearance now, following extensive restoration in 1844, it retains a 12th-century nave, doorway and font, and some Jacobean woodwork. In 1857 Ann Williams, alias Morgan, alias Evans, otherwise known as "Nanny Morgan, the Wenlock witch" was buried in an unmarked grave in the churchyard, after apparently having been murdered.

The names of several village houses tell a sad but familiar story: The Old Inn, The Old Post Office, The Old Shoppe and The Old School can all be seen. The Old Manor is now a hotel.

BRIDGNORTH [Bridgnorth]

SO7192: 7 miles (12km) SE of Much Wenlock

The most dramatic of Shropshire towns, Bridgnorth is unlike anywhere else in Britain in the almost continental way it clings to the top of a sandstone cliff. It was in 912 that King Alfred's daughter Ethelfleda built a fortified township above the Severn, a township that was later to grow into Bridgnorth as we know it today. In 1101-2 Robert de Belleme, the son of Roger de Montgomery, replaced Ethelfleda's fortifications with a more substantial castle, which was later much altered and extended by Henry II. Henry granted a charter to Bridgnorth in 1157 and the High Street was probably laid out soon after.

The burgeoning town occupied an obviously strategic position, making it well placed to prosper as a centre of communications, a river crossing and a port. By the 13th century, the only Shropshire town greater in importance was Shrewsbury, though Bridgnorth was a busier port, with three dockyards and a flourishing boat-building industry. The more Bridgnorth prospered as a port, the more it attracted industry, particularly ironworks and carpet mills, as well as clothing, brewing, tanning and other trades.

By the mid-19th century Bridgnorth was declining as an industrial centre, and when the Severn Valley Railway opened in 1862, linking Shrewsbury and Bridgnorth with Worcester, it spelt the end for the river trade. Only a century later the railway was itself closed but a preservation society was formed and steam trains now run regularly between Bridgnorth and Kidderminster, contributing significantly to the tourist trade which is a vital part of Bridgnorth's economy today.

Bridgnorth is actually two towns: **High**

The cliff railway

Town, which crowns the sandstone cliff and clings to its sides; and **Low Town**, which occupies the riverside and the east bank. The two are linked by a road, with further pedestrian access provided by seven ancient stairways and a cartway cut into the sandstone. A remarkable **cliff railway**, with a gradient of 1:1½, has provided an alternative route since 1892.

The remains of **Bridgnorth Castle** still stand, but consist of no more than the keep, tilted at a crazy angle three times greater than the Leaning Tower of Pisa. The rest was dismantled after the castle was surrendered by its Royalist garrison to the parliamentarians in 1646. If you want to survey the surrounding countryside, **Castle Walk** provides an impressive view, said by Charles I to be the finest in his kingdom. Neighbouring **East Castle Street** is one of Bridgnorth's most elegant thoroughfares, with gracious Georgian buildings leading the eye to the classical-style **church of St Mary Magdalene**, built of locally quarried

white sandstone in 1792-4 to the design of Thomas Telford. It replaced the Norman chapel attached to Bridgnorth Castle. The design is simple but successful, light and spacious inside, and only slightly spoiled by Sir Arthur Blomfield's addition of an apse in 1876.

At the other end of town is the original parish **church of St Leonard's**, a commanding edifice of dark red sandstone towering over a calm little oasis of period buildings. It dates mostly from a restoration of 1860-2 but the tower, built in 1870, is a convincing replica of the 1448 tower built by Richard Horde. St Leonard's was almost completely destroyed during the Civil War when garrisoned by Royalist troops. Having been driven from the castle, they made the church their ammunition store, and when the Roundheads scored a direct hit the ensuing fire proved disastrous. St Leonard's is now maintained by the Redundant Churches Fund.

Steps descend from St Leonard's to the river, but of the ancient staircases and passageways linking the cliff-top with the riverside, it is **Cartway** that is the best known. For centuries it was the main route out of High Town and today it is still lined with attractive buildings, most notable of which is the gabled, timber-framed **Bishop Percy's House**, dated 1580. Several of Cartway's houses have heavy wooden shutters, designed for protection from the jostling of carts, wagons and horses. There are caves in the sandstone, which were used as homes until 1856, and there are more by the riverside, formerly used for storage as well as habitation. **Stoneway Steps** is a picturesque ancient stairway connecting with Cartway. Halfway down Stoneway the **Steps Theatre** occupies a former chapel and is said to be haunted.

The **High Street** is long and wide, lined with a superb array of 17th-, 18th- and 19th-century buildings, perhaps most notable of which is the **town hall** (1650-52). It stands in the middle of the road, its timbered upper storey resting on stone arches (now faced with brick). Nearby is the impressive **Swan Inn**, a 17th-century coaching inn. The top end of High Street is guarded by the **North Gate**, rebuilt in 1910 and the only survivor of five medieval gates into the town. Its upper storey now houses **Bridgnorth Museum**. At the southern end of High Street, on Postern Gate, is the unusual **Museum of Childhood and Costume** and just across the road is **Waterloo Terrace**, with a number of interesting buildings.

Connected to Castle Hill by a footbridge over the main road is **Bridgnorth Station**, now the northern terminus of the Severn Valley Railway. Beautifully maintained, the station house is a gabled, neo-Jacobean building of some character.

Low Town is neglected by visitors to Bridgnorth but is full of interest in its own right, with some charming buildings and a fine view of High Town from the bridge which spans the Severn. The bridge has been rebuilt several times since its original incarnation in the Middle Ages, and until 1538 it carried a chapel dedicated to St Osyth. Low Town was the site of Hazeldine's Foundry, where Richard Trevithick and John Rastrick built the world's first steam passenger locomotive in 1808.

Notable people born in Bridgnorth include **Thomas Percy** (1729-1811), a clergyman, antiquary and poet best known for editing and publishing a collection of medieval ballads under the title of *Reliques of Ancient English Poetry*. He was born in what is now known as Bishop Percy's House, at the bottom of Cartway, and was educated at Bridgnorth Grammar School before going up to Oxford. Percy became Royal Chaplain to George III and was later ordained as the Bishop of Dromore.

Francis Moore (1657-1715), the astrologer and creator of *Old Moore's Almanac*, was also born in Bridgnorth, probably in one of the cave dwellings.

On the eastern edge of Bridgnorth **Stanmore Country Park** has been established by Shropshire County Council on the site of a former RAF training camp, operational from 1939 to 1963. The mainly wooded site provides a valuable wildlife habitat. Close by is the **Midland Motor Museum** at Stanmore Hall.

BROCKTON [South Shropshire]
SO5793: 5 miles (8km) SW of Much Wenlock

Slumbering below Wenlock Edge, Brockton comprises a handful of houses, a school, post office and pub by a crossroads not far from the River Corve. One of the cottages is of cruck construction and a mound marks the site of a Norman motte and bailey castle.

BROCKTON [South Shropshire]
SO3285: 2 miles (3km) S of Bishop's Castle

On a tributary of the River Kemp, in hilly country on the edge of Clun Forest, Brockton is an unspoilt cluster of stone-built farms and cottages. About 1 mile to the south is **Lower Down**, a hilltop settlement with a couple of farms, a few houses and the remains of a Norman motte and bailey castle. Both Brockton and Lower Down are overlooked by **Bury Ditches**, a prehistoric hill fort on top of the forested slopes of Sunnyhill. One of the most formidable of the Shropshire hill forts, Bury Ditches dates from the 1st century BC and had two entrances defended by banks and ditches, which are particularly well defined on the north side. The view from the top is one of the finest in Shropshire and many of the surrounding hills also have ancient forts or settlements on them.

BROMFIELD [South Shropshire]
SO4876: 3 miles (5km) NW of Ludlow

Clustered around the junction of the A49 and A4113, by the confluence of the River Teme and River Onny, Bromfield is a handsome estate village with houses of stone, brick and timber. It stands on the edge of **Oakly Park**, a farming estate surrounding the home of the Earl of Plymouth, a Temeside Georgian house also known as Oakly Park.

St Mary's Church stands on a wooded promontory between the Onny and Teme. A notable avenue of 40 yew trees marks the approach to the east end of the church from the Teme, and the main part of the churchyard is a haven for native flowers, including the wild daffodil.

St Mary's contains much from the 13th and 14th centuries, though it was restored in 1890. The massive west tower has a 15th-century top but the lower courses are Norman. Inside is a painted plaster ceiling completed by Thomas Francis in 1672. Exuberantly vulgar, it is typical of its period with billowing clouds, fat cherubs and scrolling ribbons inscribed with texts.

The main entrance to the churchyard is guarded by a 14th-century stone and timber gatehouse which was once the entrance to a Benedictine priory, while St Mary's itself was originally the priory's chapel. After the Dissolution, part of St Mary's was made into a house, occupied by a Charles Foxe, and it was only in 1658 that it was returned to its proper function as a church.

A stone tablet in the church is inscribed to the memory of **Henry Hickman**, born in 1800 at a farmhouse in the nearby hamlet of Lady Halton. He became a member of the Royal College of Surgeons and practised locally, dedicating his spare time to the search for a suitable anaesthetic. He found that carbon dioxide offered the best hope but he was dismissed as a madman. He died at 30, some say of disappointment and frustration, and was forgotten for years until similar experiments recalled his memory. It was not until 1930, the centenary of his death, that the tablet was unveiled, celebrating him as "the earliest known pioneer of anaesthesia by inhalation".

Immediately to the north of Bromfield is the site of a Roman camp, though there are no obvious traces of it today. Just to the east is **Old Field**, now Ludlow's golf course and racecourse but also the site of several Bronze Age burial barrows.

BROSELEY [Wrekin]
SJ6701: 1 mile (2km) S of Ironbridge

Though only a small town today, Broseley has a long industrial history. Coal was mined there in the Middle Ages and by 1605 it was being exported on a wooden railway which provided a link with a wharf on the Severn at Jackfield. This was only the second railway to be built in Britain. By the end of the 18th century coal from Broseley and Madeley was the main downstream cargo on the Severn. Brick making also grew in importance, with the Broseley Brickworks established in 1754. The opening of the Iron Bridge in 1781 facilitated the export of iron ore, coal and limestone from Broseley to markets north of the river. The first iron furnace was built at nearby Coneybury c1786 and for a time iron founding was important, using local ironstone. But by 1830 all the ironworks had closed because it was considered more economic to export iron ore to the Black Country, which had a ready market and better communications. In the second half of the 19th century Broseley suffered such unemployment and poverty that it became almost derelict and remained that way for close on a century. Today, it thrives once again.

Bricks and tiles are still made at Broseley, though these industries were never more than locally important. Broseley tobacco pipes, however, were nationally famous, though only a small part of the local economy. Pipemaker Noah Roden (1770-1829) supplied most of the London clubs and coffee houses. The unusual **Clay Tobacco Pipe Museum** now occupies a former factory where Broseley's famous "Churchwarden pipes" were made until 1957.

Broseley sprawls haphazardly from

Ironbridge to Willey, but the old centre is at the south end by the imposing **church of All Saints**, built in 1845 by H. Eginton in Perpendicular style. Elaborate iron tombs in the churchyard remind us that Broseley was the place, in 1787, where the great ironmaster **John ("Iron-mad") Wilkinson** (1728-1808) made the first iron ship and launched it on the Severn. He had already had a forge at neighbouring Willey for some years and in 1776 had installed a steam engine made by Matthew Boulton and James Watt at their renowned Soho Works in Birmingham. This was the first of their engines to be used outside their own works.

There are many fine buildings in Broseley, with plenty of Georgian facades, a red-brick Methodist church of 1802 and a Gothic former school of blue bricks which is now a library and health centre. Some of the best houses are on Church Street, including **Broseley Hall**, a substantial brick mansion next to the church, and **The Lawns** (1727), with its splendid bow window. This was John Wilkinson's home from 1778 to 1800. When he left he rented the house to master-potter John Rose (see Coalport). Today it houses a collection of china and is open to the public.

At the north end of Broseley, Bridge Bank plunges steeply down to the Iron Bridge with a tangle of lanes known locally as jitties branching off it. These are lined with 18th- and 19th-century houses, many of which were originally squatters' cottages. The Benthall furnaces and potteries were situated near here and the famous **Benthall Mill**, known for its huge cast-iron waterwheel, was built near the bottom of the hill on Benthall Brook. It still stands (minus its wheel and partially derelict) amongst the trees of Ladywood.

BUCKNELL [South Shropshire]

SO3573: 5 miles (8km) SE of Clun

A relatively large and attractive village, Bucknell is situated on the River Redlake and just to the north of the River Teme, below towering and mostly forested slopes. To the south-east stands **Coxall Knoll**, one of many hills in the Marches suggested as the site of British leader Caradoc's famous "last stand" against the Romans. There is an Iron Age fort on top, but this proves nothing and we will never know where the battle took place.

The Norman **church of St Mary** was restored in 1870 but the font survives (it may even be Anglo-Saxon) and some of the original masonry has been re-used in the nave. The church, surrounded by huge yew trees, stands on a circular raised site with possible Bronze Age origins.

Stone and timber-framed houses, some of them thatched, form the nucleus of the village, and there is a Baptist Chapel of 1871 as well as a Methodist Chapel of 1849. The motte of a Norman castle still stands in the village and there is a Gothic railway station (1860) with "Tudor" chimney stacks.

BUILDWAS [Bridgnorth]

SJ6304: 3 miles (5km) N of Much Wenlock

Buildwas is where the Severn changes character, its oxbow meanderings coming to an abrupt end as it begins to sweep through the gorge towards Ironbridge. The village is by the road to the north of the river and consists mainly of a housing estate, though there are two old school buildings, a post office and village hall. The **church of Holy Trinity** was largely built with stone from Buildwas Abbey, and the present nave and south porch date only from 1720. The rest is of 1864.

The landscape is dominated by the enormous pinkish-grey towers of a power station on the south bank, downstream towards Ironbridge, but **Buildwas Abbey** (English Heritage) is better known, though now only a ruin. It was a Savignac foundation, but became Cistercian in 1147, and stands in meadows by the south bank of the river, next to an ancient crossing place (now bridged). Founded around 1135 by Roger de Clinton, Bishop of Chester, the abbey was a daughter house of Furness Abbey in Cumbria, and was built of Grinshill stone. The surviving buildings date from c1200 and the most substantial remains are of the church, famous for its superb nave arcades, among the grandest in the country, and the chapter house, with its fine vaulted roof. The 13th-century abbot's house, between the ruins and the river, is now incorporated into a private house. The abbey was a prosperous one, owning many outlying farms, and even had its own ironworks, a precursor of the later industrial development at Coalbrookdale and Ironbridge.

BURFORD [South Shropshire]

SO5868: 6 miles (10km) SE of Ludlow

The village of Burford stands in lush Temeside meadows on the southern edge of the county. Part of it, with housing, industrial premises and the impressive bow-windowed **Swan Hotel**, forms a suburb of Tenbury Wells (across the river in Worcestershire). Close to Teme Bridge stands a mound that marks the spot of a Norman motte and bailey castle built to defend the river crossing.

A mile to the west, possibly on the site of a Saxon fortification, is **Burford House**, at the point where the Ledwyche Brook joins the Teme. Burford House, a red-brick Georgian mansion of 1728, opens its gardens to the public and has the National Clematis Collection. The red sandstone **church of St Mary** stands nearby and is of the 12th century, though it was extended in the 14th and 15th centuries and restored in Arts and Crafts Gothic style by Sir Aston Webb in 1889. It contains a 15th-century panelled font and an excellent collection of monuments. The best are to the Cornwall family and include a 14th-century brass to Elizabeth de Cornewayle and a 15th-century alabaster figure of Princess Elizabeth, daughter of John of Gaunt, sister of Henry IV and wife of Sir John Cornewaile. Most

impressive and unusual is the large, painted triptych on the north wall of the chancel to Richard Cornwall (died 1568) and his parents. Signed by Melchior Salabuss, it is dated 1588.

BURWARTON [Bridgnorth]

SO6184: 9 miles (14km) SW of Bridgnorth

Sheltered below the tree-covered eastern slopes of Brown Clee Hill, Burwarton is a former farming village set in rich pasturelands. Built mainly of stone, the village has many substantial buildings, including the Georgian Boyne Arms, a school and the vicarage, a former dower house to **Burwarton Hall**, which lies above the village on the side of Brown Clee. It was designed in Italianate style by Anthony Salvin in 1876-7 and is the home of Lord Boyne. The surrounding parkland is noted for its fine trees and a commercial forestry scheme also operates, while footpaths lead to the top of Brown Clee. There are two churches, previously dedicated to St Lawrence, but the older one is an ivy-clad roofless ruin, and its replacement, also by Salvin in 1877, is now a private house.

CALVERHALL [North Shropshire]

SJ6037: 5 miles (8km) NW of Market Drayton

A small village, Calverhall is set in a characteristic north Shropshire landscape of rolling dairy country studded with numerous ponds. The **church of Holy Trinity** was built in the 1870s by Eden Nesfield and contains a stained-glass window by William Morris and Edward Burne-Jones. Nearby there stands a range of **almshouses** built of red brick in 1724. Nesfield destroyed one end of the range to make room for his church. The **Old Jack Inn** used to be famous for its "Jack of Corra", a leather flagon from which any traveller could drink as much as he liked for one penny until the flagon mysteriously disappeared around 1860.

CANTLOP [Shrewsbury and Atcham]

SJ5105: 5 miles (8km) SE of Shrewsbury

The hamlet of Cantlop consists of a scattering of farms and cottages in gentle countryside but it is famous for **Cantlop Bridge**, which carries what used to be the Acton Burnell-Shrewsbury turnpike road over Cound Brook. An elegant iron structure designed by Thomas Telford in 1812, the bridge is now closed to traffic and in the care of English Heritage.

CARDESTON [Shrewsbury and Atcham]

SJ3912: 6 miles (10km) W of Shrewsbury

A tiny place in gentle farmland, Cardeston stands on the edge of a breccia outcrop which used to be quarried for building stone and to fuel the local limeworks, which closed in 1817. **St Michael's Church** was built in the 12th century but little remains from that period. The nave and chancel were rebuilt in 1748 and an octagonal tower added in 1844.

CARDINGTON [Shrewsbury and Atcham]

SO5095: 4 miles (6km) NE of Church Stretton

Tucked away in a secluded location where the Stretton Hills meet Ape Dale, Cardington is one of Shropshire's loveliest villages. It is built mostly of stone but enlivened by a little timber-framing and some weatherboarded barns, one of which is dated 1558 and appears to be a rare example of a longhouse. **St James's Church** still retains its Norman nave and has an Early English tower with a Perpendicular upper stage. The church contains a Jacobean pulpit with curious carvings of mermen and there is a splendid memorial to William Leighton (see Plaish).

Just to the east of Cardington is a cluster of farms at **Gretton**, where the substantial earthworks of a long-gone manor house and its associated buildings extend over several fields.

CAYNHAM [South Shropshire]

SO5573: 3 miles (5km) SE of Ludlow

A small, rather scattered village, Caynham occupies an enviable position in hilly, well-hedged country above Ledwyche Brook. There are enticing views of Titterstone Clee Hill but closer to hand is Caynham's own hill, crowned with a prehistoric fort, **Caynham Camp**, believed to have first been settled c1000BC. It must have been a substantial and well-defended settlement, judging by the traces of stone ramparts which remain. The north slope is formidably steep and the fort commands an excellent view of Ludlow. Local tradition suggests that Cromwell used it as a base when besieging Ludlow Castle.

The most notable building in the village is **St Mary's Church**, approached along an avenue of fine yews interspersed with hollies. It has a Norman chancel arch of striking design but is mostly Victorian, having suffered over-zealous restoration in 1885. The square tower is topped with a pyramidal roof and dates from the 13th century. The shaft of a preaching cross with remnants of carving still discernible stands in the churchyard, which is maintained as a flower meadow.

Though there are several interesting old houses in the village, such as red-brick **Caynham Park** and a little stone-built school dated 1834, there is little to indicate that Caynham is one of the oldest villages in the county, believed to be one of the very first Anglo-Saxon settlements. The combination of fertile land and the mineral wealth of nearby Titterstone Clee must have made it the ideal site.

CHADWELL [Wrekin]

SJ7814: 4 miles (6km) SE of Newport

Tucked away in arable country, Chadwell is a small hamlet of red-brick houses. A working watermill, **Chadwell Mill**, is open to the public. The hamlet may take its name from St Chad, who is reputed to have blessed a well which can still be seen close to the mill pond.

CHAPEL LAWN [South Shropshire]

SO3176: 3 miles (5km) NE of Knighton

The setting for this tiny village could hardly be improved upon; Chapel Lawn hugs the banks of the River Redlake, overlooked by the high, rounded hills of Clun Forest. Immediately to the south is **Caer Caradoc** (not to be confused with its more famous namesake near Church Stretton), its steep slopes crowned with a substantial Iron Age fort. The village takes the first part of its name from a chapel that was attached to **Chapel Lawn Farm** (1600), while "lawn" means "a forest clearing". The chapel was replaced in 1844 by the **church of St Mary**, designed by Edward Haycock.

CHELMARSH [Bridgnorth]

SO7287: 3 miles (5km) S of Bridgnorth

The village of Chelmarsh straggles for some distance along the top of a narrow ridge overlooking the River Severn. It used to be orchard country, with the Severn Valley Railway facilitating the export of the fruit, but it is given over to mixed farming today and the orchards have gone. The coal mining which used to employ local people at Chelmarsh Common has also ceased, though ghostly miners are sometimes reported. The village overlooks **Chelmarsh Reservoir**, which is part of a Shropshire Wildlife Trust nature reserve but is also used for sailing.

The 14th-century **church of St Peter** is a splendid example of the Decorated style and also has a Norman doorway. Legend tells of a monk's heart interred in the east wall. The tower was built in 1720. Victorian **Chelmarsh Hall** is a building of considerable character, with 13th-century origins.

CHENEY LONGVILLE [South Shropshire]

SO4284: 2 miles (3km) NW of Craven Arms

Few hamlets are more unspoiled than Cheney Longville, its stone cottages and farms hidden away in pastoral countryside close to the River Onny. At the west end of the hamlet is a circular earthwork which is probably Norman in origin. Close by is **Cheney Longville Castle**, a former fortified house for which licence to crenellate was granted to Roger Cheney in 1395. Today, it's a substantial stone house with outbuildings, all much altered but retaining the basic 14th-century plan. Traces of a moat are still discernible. To the west of Cheney Longville a prehistoric settlement tops the tree-covered **Wart Hill**, while to the north-east an area of meadows and riverbank is open to the public under the Countryside Stewardship scheme. The dismantled Bishop's Castle railway runs through the site.

CHESWARDINE [North Shropshire]

SJ7129: 4 miles (6km) SE of Market Drayton

The old centre of Cheswardine occupies a slight hill in otherwise flat farming country close to the Shropshire Union Canal, while the rest of the village lies further down the slope to the south. The **church of St Swithin** may stand on the site of a prehistoric fortification, and the adjacent moated motte is probably the remains of a castle built by the Le Strange family some time after 1160. St Swithin's has an exceptional Early English chapel and an ornate Perpendicular tower. The exterior walls have some good 15th-century carvings: a lion, a dragon, a Talbot hunting dog and a Staffordshire knot (Cheswardine was once part of Staffordshire), which fortunately survived the restoration of the church by J.L. Pearson in 1888-9.

Cheswardine has much modern housing but there are still some older houses of charm and character, the best of which stand near the church. **Cheswardine Hall** is a neo-Elizabethan mansion, built of brick in 1875 with a four-storeyed porch tower. The village is fortunate in retaining a good range of facilities, including pubs, shops and a school, first built in 1738 but restored in 1877.

CHETTON [Bridgnorth]

SO6690: 4 miles (6km) SW of Bridgnorth

Beautifully situated on a hilltop in the undulating country between Bridgnorth and Brown Clee, Chetton is a small village with a mixture of old and new houses and the **Old Inn**, which is claimed to date back 800 years. The tree-shrouded **church of St Giles** is an 11th-century foundation with a 13th-century chancel but the nave was rebuilt in 1788 and the tower added in 1829. A thorough restoration took place in 1891. Before the Conquest Chetton belonged to Lady Godiva, Countess of Mercia, famous for her naked ride through Coventry, but it was subsequently given to Roger de Montgomery by William I.

CHETWYND [Wrekin]

SJ7321: 2 miles (3km) NW of Newport

Like Chetton, Chetwynd belonged to Lady Godiva until the Norman Conquest. It is a scattered settlement in attractive countryside below a tree-clad outcrop called **The Scaur**, a name which comes from the same Old English root as the modern word "scarp". Below the hill lies a large lake, part of the grounds of Chetwynd Park, an Elizabethan hall that was demolished in 1961 and replaced by a modern house. The buildings of the hall's **Home Farm** still stand, and include a dovecote. King Charles I is reputed to have stayed at the hall in 1649. The grounds of Chetwynd Park include a deer park but this was violated by the construction of the Newport bypass, and soon

after that most of the estate was sold for development. The large sandstone **church of St Michael** stands close to the bypass. It was built in 1865-7, with a broach spire and impressive interior carving. The churchyard and the deer park are said to be haunted by Madam Pigott, a one-time mistress of Chetwynd Park who died in the 1770s.

In 1981 part of a prehistoric dugout canoe was dredged from the River Meese, which runs just to the north of Chetwynd. The canoe is now in the National Maritime Museum at Greenwich.

CHILD'S ERCALL [North Shropshire]

SJ6625: 7 miles (11km) S of Market Drayton

A nucleated village of red brick which stands in flat countryside, Child's Ercall has few buildings of particular interest. The red sandstone **church of St Michael** has work from the 12th, 13th, 14th, 15th and 16th centuries but the chancel was built in 1879, though it incorporates a re-used Norman doorway.

CHIRBURY [South Shropshire]

SO2698: 3 miles (5km) NE of Montgomery

Chirbury is a relatively large village in a peninsula of Shropshire which projects into Powys. Just a couple of miles to the west, Offa's Dyke marks the border close to the Welsh town of Montgomery, while the dominant feature to the east, Corndon Hill, is also in Wales. The village must have seen some strife in the past, as the sturdy, obviously defensive tower of **St Michael's Church** confirms. An Augustinian priory once stood on this site, and the 13th-century nave and aisles are of the priory church. The tower was begun c1300 and added to in the 16th century, while the blue-brick chancel was added in 1733 and a full restoration was carried out in 1871. Local tradition suggests that if you walk 12 times round the church at midnight on

Hallowe'en you will hear the names of those parishioners who are going to die during the coming year.

Much of Chirbury is built of brick, but there are also stone and timber-framed houses, including the **Old Schoolhouse** (timber) of 1675, and the present school (stone), also a 17th-century building. **The Herbert Arms** is named after Lord Herbert (see Eyton), a distinguished Anglo-Welsh soldier, statesman, poet, historian and philosopher who became the 1st Baron Chirbury in 1629. He left a valuable collection of chained books to Chirbury, which were kept in The Old Schoolhouse until moved to the county archives at Shrewsbury.

On the western edge of the village are some rather indeterminate earthworks which are all that remain of **Chirbury Castle**, on a site believed to have first been fortified in 915 by Ethelfleda of Mercia. Chirbury stands within a large loop of the **River Camlad**, the only river to flow from England into Wales. To the east of Chirbury it forms the beautiful **Marrington Dingle**, near the southern end of which are the earthworks of two prehistoric camps, while **Marrington Hall** is an Elizabethan timber-framed house. On the slopes of Stapeley Hill above Chirbury is **Mitchell's Fold**, a small but atmospheric Neolithic stone circle.

CHIRK BANK [Oswestry]
SJ2936: 1 mile (2km) S of Chirk

Chirk (Y Waun) is in Wales but the red-brick village of Chirk Bank hugs the English side of the border, which coincides here with the River (Afon) Ceiriog. Most of Chirk Bank is enclosed within a bend of the Ellesmere branch of the Shropshire Union Canal and it is the canal which is the reason for the little settlement's main point of interest: the dramatic **Chirk Aqueduct**. It was built between 1796 and 1801 by Thomas Telford to carry the canal over the Ceiriog. Next to the aqueduct is an impressive **railway viaduct** built by Henry Robinson. Both structures are still in daily use.

CHURCH ASTON [Wrekin]
SJ7417: 1 mile (2km) S of Newport

Church Aston used to earn a living from mining limestone for smelting but has now become a modern suburb of Newport, and little of interest remains. The first church here was built in 1620 and was replaced by the **church of St Andrew**, designed by G.E. Street in 1867. It contains a stained-glass window by William Morris and Co.

CHURCH PREEN [Shrewsbury and Atcham]
SO5498: 6 miles (10km) SW of Much Wenlock

In lovely countryside between Wenlock Edge and the Stretton Hills, the secluded village of Church Preen stands on high ground with fine views. The **church of St John the Baptist** dates from the 13th century and adjoins the **Manor House**, which is an extension by Victorian architect Norman Shaw of a much older building. However, Shaw's house has since been partially demolished. Shaw also designed the local school (on the road to Hughley) in 1872. The most notable feature of the village is the **Church Preen Yew**, a magnificent tree which pre-dates the church by centuries.

CHURCH PULVERBATCH [Shrewsbury and Atcham]
SJ4202: 3 miles (5km) SE of Pontesbury

The village of Church Pulverbatch is unremarkable, but is set in beautiful countryside, on high ground itself, but overlooked by much higher hills such as Stiperstones and Long Mynd. The **church of St Edith** occupies a circular site and began life as a daughter church to Pontesbury before being destroyed by Welsh raiders around 1400. It was rebuilt at some point in the next century and in 1773 was substantially restored and provided with a square, stone tower. In 1853 further rebuilding was carried out. Close to the church is 17th-century **Lower House Farm** (the facade is later, probably early Georgian). Other buildings of interest include **Lower House** itself, **The Old Schoolhouse** in red and yellow chequered brick, and **The Old Rectory**, a rambling red-brick house which was built in 1806 especially to accommodate the large family of William Gilpin, rector for 42 years.

A short distance to the south-west is **Castle Pulverbatch**, with a cluster of modern houses, two pubs and a substantial motte on **The Knapp**, a superb defensive site where a Norman castle once stood. The castle moat and traces of two baileys are still evident.

CHURCH STRETTON [South Shropshire]

SO4593: 7 miles (11km) N of Craven Arms

In an architectural sense, Church Stretton has less to offer than many Shropshire towns, but in terms of its situation it is unrivalled. Squeezed into a narrow gap between the heathery bulk of the **Long Mynd** to the west and the shapely **Stretton Hills** to the east, no part of the little town is more than a few minutes walk from spectacular hill country. This makes it popular with tourists and walkers and it's no surprise to learn that in late Victorian times it was a minor spa. Long before that, however, it was already a market town, small but regionally important, as the large size of **St Lawrence's Church** indicates. The church is cruciform in shape, with a Norman nave. Most of the rest is Early English, but a Perpendicular stage was added to the top of the tower and additions and alterations were made in 1867 and 1883. On the exterior north wall, above the doorway, there is a sheela-na-gig, a Celtic fertility figure of a type widespread in Ireland but rare throughout the rest of the British Isles (see Holdgate and Tugford).

Church Stretton's older streets are lined with stone, brick and timber buildings of quiet charm. Sandford Avenue is Victo-

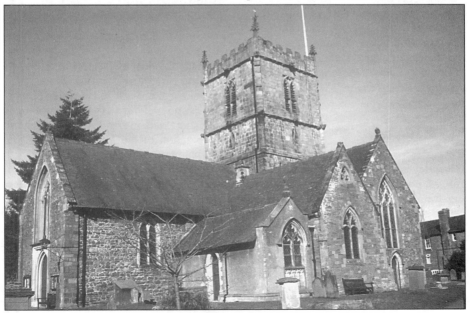

Church Stretton: St Lawrence's

rian, named in 1884 after the Reverend Holland Sandford, one of the main promoters of Church Stretton as a holiday resort. At the north end of town is the plant where Stretton Hills water from Cwm Spring is bottled by Wells Ltd. Just to the south of Church Stretton is **Brockhurst Castle**, the site of a once formidable motte and bailey castle.

The highest of the Stretton Hills is **Caer Caradoc**, crowned by a hill fort of the same name, yet another claimed as the place of Caradoc's last stand against the Romans. Other prehistoric sites in the Stretton Hills include two settlements on **The Lawley** and a field system on **Hope Bowdler Hill**. Nearby **Helmeth Hill** is entirely tree covered and belongs to the Woodland Trust, which also owns a small reserve on **Ragleth Hill**.

The **Long Mynd** is the largest semi-wilderness area in the Midlands and much of it is common land in the care of the National Trust. It's liberally dotted with prehistoric remains, including Bronze Age tumuli, settlements and dykes, and is traversed by a trading route known as the **Port Way**. Iron Age remains include a fort, **Bodbury Ring**.

Popular Victorian novelist **Hesba Stretton** (see Wellington) lived in Church Stretton for a time and there is a memorial window to her in the church. Her book *Jessica's First Prayer* (1866) sold several million copies worldwide.

CLAVERLEY [Bridgnorth]

SO7993: 5 miles (8km) E of Bridgnorth

Claverley is a delightful village with a cluster of cottages, a 15th-century timber-framed former vicarage, 12th-century **All Saints' Church** and a sandstone school. In the churchyard is a huge yew tree, at least 1500 years old, possibly much older. The imposing red sandstone church looks superficially Perpendicular but has work from many periods, and when restoration work was carried out in 1902 the foundations of a Saxon chancel were dis-

covered. The present church was founded by Roger de Montgomery some time between 1066 and 1094. The nave has an extremely rare, 13th-century painted frieze, almost in the style of the Bayeux Tapestry. It depicts armed knights on horseback, who are thought to represent the battle of the Pagan Vices and Christian Virtues. Among other items of interest is an alabaster memorial to Sir Robert Broke (d1558), his two wives and 18 children. Broke, who lived at nearby **Ludstone Hall**, was Speaker of the House of Commons and Chief Justice of Common Pleas. The churchyard is on a mound, indicating possible prehistoric origins, and Stone Age pebble-flint implements have been found in the parish.

Just downhill from the church is timber-framed **Pown Hall**, where William Gladstone used to stay when he was courting Catherine Glynne of Farmcote Hall. There is an unusually large number of other fine houses in the surrounding countryside, including **Woundale Farm** and **Gatacre Park**.

CLEEHILL [South Shropshire]

SO5975: 4 miles (6km) E of Ludlow

Few would claim that the quarrying village of Cleehill is attractive, but it stands high up on the shoulder of **Titterstone Clee Hill** with the benefit of stunning views which are among the finest in England. The village has no buildings of architectural merit but a short walk in any direction provides a combination of glorious scenery and the fascination of industrial archaeology.

Titterstone Clee and neighbouring Brown Clee are composed of Old Red Sandstone topped by coal measures and a capping of dhustone, the local name for a type of hard basalt used for road building. Coal, iron and stone have been worked since the 13th century but the primary industry was always coal until quarrying began a dramatic increase in the 1870s. Two tramway inclines were built to serve the quarries and a branch line linked them with the main railway line to Ludlow, enabling dhustone to be transported all over the country. Over 2000 men moved in to take up employment in the expanding quarries and Cleehill village grew rapidly, but remained an isolated community which evolved its own customs and dialect. In the 1950s new road-building techniques put an end to dhustone's dominance but quarrying still continues on the southern slopes of Titterstone Clee, though at a reduced level with the works well hidden within a dip in the hill. The summit of Titterstone is marked by a craggy outcrop of dhustone, the Devil's Chair. A large hill fort once occupied the entire flat top of the hill but was destroyed by quarrying. A radar station now stands within its former ramparts.

CLEE ST MARGARET [South Shropshire]

SO5684: 7 miles (11km) NE of Ludlow

Hidden down quiet lanes on the western slopes of Brown Clee Hill, Clee St Margaret is remote and tranquil, with Clee Brook running along the village street like a linear ford. Two huge beeches and a yew shelter the **church of St Margaret**, which has been restored but retains a 12th-century nave with an original north window and an 11th-century chancel with remnants of herringbone masonry and two Norman windows. The Iron Age fort of **Nordy Bank** is just a short walk from the village, the only one of Brown Clee's forts that is still intact.

CLEETON ST MARY [South Shropshire]

SO6078: 5 miles (8km) NW of Cleobury Mortimer

An unremarkable and mainly Victorian village, Cleeton St Mary enjoys a beautiful if lonely setting on the north-east slope of Titterstone Clee Hill. It comprises a handful of houses, a red-brick former school (1872) and a row of almshouses (1883), both paid for by George and Elizabeth

Pardoe, and the **church of St Mary**, built by T. Nicholson of Hereford in 1876. On lower ground nearby is a moated site at the deserted medieval village of **Cleeton**, close to **Cleeton Court**, a timber-framed, gabled house.

CLEOBURY MORTIMER [South Shropshire]

SO6775: 10 miles (16km) E of Ludlow

More than a village, yet not entirely convincing as a town, Cleobury Mortimer is a thoroughly charming place spread along the Ludlow to Kidderminster road, with the Clee Hills providing an impressive backdrop. There is just one main street but this is lined with attractive buildings in a harmonious mix of sizes and styles, though the emphasis is on the Georgian period. One of the finest buildings is the red-brick **Manor House** (c1700) which lies at the west end of town. The **church of St Mary** is built of a grey-green sandstone and is famous for its fine horseshoe-shaped tower arch of the late 12th century and for its twisted spire, a landmark for miles around. The twist is due to warping of the timbers. In 1999 Cleobury was accepted into the European Twisted Spires Association, which has 150 members (the only other British one is Chesterfield). Much of the rest of the church belongs to the 13th and 14th centuries and was subject to restoration by Sir Gilbert Scott in 1874-5. Close by the church is 18th-century **Childe's School**, built of stone on the site of a castle probably built by Hugh de Mortimer in the 12th century.

Though rural enough today, Cleobury has a long industrial tradition and is at the centre of an area where forges and mills were common features beside the River Rea and its tributaries. In the late 16th century Robert, Earl of Dudley, built a charcoal furnace for smelting the locally mined iron ore, and iron smelting, together with coal mining and paper making, remained locally important well into the 19th century. There are some 16th- and 17th-century forge sites on the nearby Mawley Estate, the best known of which is **Old Forge** beside the River Rea, accessible by public footpath. Nearby is **Castle Toot**, a Norman motte on which a modern house now stands. It dominates an early crossing point of the Rea and was probably the site of a castle built by Ralph de Mortimer in the 11th century. **Mawley Hall**, standing on a hill above the River Rea, was built in 1730 for Sir Edward Blount, and though the exterior is a model of restraint the interior is said to be magnificent, the best of its date in the county.

St Mary's Church has a memorial window to **William Langland** (c1331-1400), the author of the famous allegorical poem *Piers Plowman*. Though Cleobury claims to be Langland's birthplace, the same claim is made, possibly with more justification, by Ledbury in Herefordshire. What is not in dispute is that Cleobury was the home of a more modern poet, Simon Evans, who sought tranquillity here after his experiences in the First World War. He became a postman and his daily walk in peaceful countryside inspired several volumes of poetry before he died in 1940. In the 18th century Maisie Bloomer, a notorious witch who dealt in curses and love potions, was born in Cleobury.

CLEOBURY NORTH [Bridgnorth]

SO6287: 7 miles (11km) SW of Bridgnorth

A small village in the quiet countryside to the east of Brown Clee, Cleobury was until recently almost entirely owned by Lord Boyne (see Burwarton) but properties are now sold as they come available. The **church of St Peter and St Paul** occupies a well-wooded churchyard and has a Norman nave and a Norman tower with a later top storey of brick. The 13th-century chancel was largely rebuilt in 1890-1. Though the surrounding countryside is now almost entirely agricultural, the economy used to be based on mixed farming and mining.

Coal was mined locally as early as 1260 and small bell pits are scattered all over Brown Clee. A former mineral railway from Ditton Priors to Cleobury Mortimer, long since dismantled, passes through the village.

CLIVE [North Shropshire]

SJ5124: 3 miles (5km) S of Wem

Clive is a delightful village, its stone-built cottages clustering prettily on the slopes of Grinshill Hill around **All Saints' Church**, whose spire is a landmark for many miles around. A Norman foundation, which was rebuilt 1885-94, All Saints' has a steep and utterly charming churchyard that is awash with daffodils in spring. It shelters the bones of **William Wycherley** (1640-1716), the Restoration dramatist whose best-known work is probably *The Country Wife*. He was born at **Clive Hall**, an Elizabethan (possibly earlier) manor house. From the church a steep path known as The Glat leads uphill to the village school, built in 1873. An intriguing network of tunnels under the village is a legacy of the days when copper was mined here, from Roman times until 1886. The main shaft now holds water which is pumped up to provide the local supply.

CLUN [South Shropshire]

SO3080: 5 miles (8km) S of Bishop's Castle

Set in the most beautiful pastoral countryside, Clun is enfolded by enticing green hills on all sides. Its stone houses slumber beside church and castle and close to the confluence of the lovely River Clun with its tributary, the Unk. The surrounding area has a long history of human occupation, with Stone Age people known to have been present at least 5000 years ago.

Clun itself may have been settled as early as the Bronze Age. There are two parts to the town, with the original settlement based around **St George's Church**, just to the south of the river. The roughly circular churchyard is an indication that the site may have had pre-Christian religious significance, and there may later have been a Celtic church here. Clun is a Celtic name, related to the Welsh "llan", which means "sacred place" or "church". There is known to have been an Anglo-Saxon church, but St George's was built by the Normans and over-restored by Street in 1877, though he used much of the original stone. The square, sturdy, 12th-century tower, topped with a truncated pyramidal roof, is characteristic of border churches and probably served as a place of refuge from raiders. Parliamentary soldiers occupied the church in the Civil War, when it was partly burnt in a Royalist attack. The people of Clun were impressed by neither side and formed an association, the Clubman's Society, to defend their town against Roundheads and Royalists alike.

Across the 15th-century **Clun Bridge** is the "new town", itself 900 years old and laid out by the Normans in a regular grid pattern which still survives. On its western edge are the ruins of **Clun Castle**, built by Robert (better known as Picot) de Say

around 1099, and obviously intended to dominate the surrounding countryside. It was rebuilt in stone in 1140, and later passed by marriage to the FitzAlans, and then, in the early 16th century, to Thomas Howard, Duke of Norfolk. It was besieged and damaged on several occasions but became largely redundant after peace came to the Marches, especially as the FitzAlans preferred their considerably grander home at Arundel. Still owned by the Duke of Norfolk, and managed by English Heritage, it's freely accessible to visitors.

Clun may look and feel like a village, but it was granted its town charter in the 14th century, with the right to hold a weekly market and two annual fairs. For centuries it prospered, but decline set in during the 19th century after Clun was bypassed by the railways.

As well as the obvious ones, such as church and castle, Clun is full of interesting buildings. These include the single-storeyed **Trinity Hospital Almshouses**, founded in 1614 by Henry Howard, Earl of Northampton, for 12 poor men, who were summoned to prayer by a

Clun Castle

bell and subject to a curfew. Today, the almshouses accommodate 15 residents of both sexes under rather less strict conditions. The town hall was built by Lord Clive in 1780 and is now the home of a small **museum** that has a good local collection, including flint arrowheads, knives and scrapers. A little way out of town to the north **Clun Mill**, a good example of a watermill, is now a youth hostel.

Literary connections abound in Clun. E.M. Forster visited the town, which subsequently featured as "Oniton" in *Howard's End*. The castle is said to have been the inspiration for "Garde Doleureuse" in Sir Walter Scott's novel *The Betrothed*, published in 1825. Scott is believed to have stayed at the Buffalo Inn while working on the book. More recently, playwright John Osborne lived near Clun and now lies buried in the churchyard.

CLUNBURY [South Shropshire]

SO3780: 4 miles (6km) E of Clun

A small, tucked-away village, Clunbury has no particularly notable buildings but is quite beautiful nonetheless, totally in harmony with its setting below green hills by the River Clun. Most distinctive of the hills is Clunbury Hill, where sphagnum moss used to be harvested in the early 20th century for dressing wounds. Built largely of grey stone, with some Elizabethan and Jacobean timber-framed houses, the village is of Anglo-Saxon origin. **St Swithun's Church** has a Norman nave, chancel and font and a 13th-century battlemented tower.

CLUNGUNFORD [South Shropshire]

SO3978: 4 miles (6km) SW of Craven Arms

The village of Clungunford stands by an old ford over the River Clun, the property of a Saxon named Gunward in the 11th century. **The church of St Cuthbert** dates from about 1300 but was much restored in 1895, when the tower and porch were added. On the churchyard wall a plaque displays the level of The Great Flood of 1795 when the River Clun rose to unprecedented levels. To the north-east of the church is the motte of a Norman **castle**. One of the best houses in the village is **Clungunford House**, a Georgian brick mansion surrounded by parkland. It was built by the Rocke family and stands on the site of an earlier manor house. At nearby Abcott, a former pub, the Rocke Arms, is now a tearoom called **The Bird on the Rock**. A carving of a bird on a rock can be seen over the door of this unspoilt black and white building. This illustrates a rather obscure pun, based on the fact that John Rocke created a museum of British birds.

CLUNTON [South Shropshire]

SO3381: 2 miles (3km) E of Clun

An unremarkable village on the main road, Clunton does have the benefit of the Crown Inn, which was bought by an enterprising consortium of local people a few years ago to save it from closure. **Clunton Coppice** is a nature reserve belonging to Shropshire Wildlife Trust and forms a superb example of sessile oak coppice, which is managed in the traditional way.

COALBROOKDALE [Wrekin]

SJ6604: 1 mile (2km) NW of Ironbridge

Coalbrookdale was known for its coal long before the Industrial Revolution but that is not the reason for its name, which derives from Caldebrok. The steep valley of the "cold brook" was where, in 1709, Abraham Darby perfected the method of smelting iron with coke instead of charcoal. It sounds a small thing but it sparked a revolution that changed the world. Suddenly iron could be made cheaply in large quantities, instead of being dependent on the slow, laborious process of charcoal production. Darby's work was continued by his descendants and it was his grandson, Abraham III, who constructed the world's first iron bridge (see Ironbridge), which still spans the Severn just south of Coalbrookdale. By 1785 the Coalbrookdale Company was hugely prosperous and when John Wilkinson set up in competition this small valley and its environs became the foremost industrial area in the world, only to decline eventually in the face of competition from the Black Country and South Wales.

The Darby family needed to be close to the works to oversee any crisis which might arise so they built houses for themselves just a short distance away. **Rosehill** was built c1730 and has been carefully restored and furnished with items that belonged to the family. Next door, **Dale House** was built a few years earlier for Abraham I and is currently being restored. Further up the hill, **The Chestnuts** (private) belonged to Abraham III. Most of the family were Quakers and had a paternalistic attitude towards their workforce. They built decent houses for them and the terrace named **Tea Kettle Row**, built in 1746, is a characteristic example. Nearby is the **Quaker Burial Ground**, an unostentatious little place shaded by sombre pine trees. Simple memorials to local Quakers lean against two of the enclosing walls, with those to the Darby family on the left towards the top end.

Holy Trinity Church was built by Reeves and Voysey in 1850-54 with money given by Abraham Darby IV on his conversion to Anglicanism from Quakerism. He and his wife are buried in the churchyard and there is also a memorial to **Captain Matthew Webb** (see Dawley). Another plaque inside commemorates **Thomas Parker**, born in the dale in 1843, who was responsible for the first electric tramway and underground railway. Nearby is the blue-brick **Literary and Scientific Institute** (1858), now a youth hostel but originally built by the Darbys for their workers and claimed to be the first college of further education in England.

After industry declined the area fell into decay, which allowed the industrial scars to heal while a mantle of green slowly spread over the gorge again. Since the 1960s those industrial relics which do survive have been transformed into a fascinating collection of museums by the Ironbridge Gorge Museum Trust, while there are several delightful woodlands managed by the Severn Gorge Countryside Trust. **The Museum of Iron** relates the story of iron from the earliest days and includes the furnace where in 1709 Abraham Darby I pioneeered the technique of smelting iron ore with coke. The neighbouring Coalbrookdale Works still functions as part of the Glynwed Foundries group, making Aga and Rayburn cookers. A short walk from the works is **Upper Furnace Pool**, which powered Darby's original furnace. Apart from its historic value, it has also been designated a Site of Special Scientific Interest for its natural history.

COALPORT [Wrekin]
SJ7002: 2 miles (3km) SE of Ironbridge

There is much of historical interest in the red-brick village of Coalport, which was planned as a canal-river interchange port by ironmaster William Reynolds. Between 1788 and 1796 he built quays, warehouses, cottages and factories on former agricultural land by the river and Coalport soon prospered. Today, a stop lock and a short stretch of water are all that remain of the **Coalport Canal**, which Reynolds built between 1788 and 1792 to link local mines and ironworks with the Severn. Close by is the **Hay Inclined Plane**, a major industrial monument, and now part of the acclaimed **Blists Hill Open Air Museum** where a recreated town vividly portrays life in a 19th-century industrial community. The Inclined Plane was the means by which boats were transferred between the Coalport Canal and the Shropshire Canal – they were carried up and down the 1-in-3 gradient on wheeled cradles. Nearby is the

Tar Tunnel, where a rich spring of natural bitumen was discovered by miners in 1786. Part of the tunnel is open to the public.

John Rose took over the Coalport Porcelain Works in the 1790s after having learned his trade at Caughley (see Barrow). By 1820 the company was winning awards and went on to become one of the greatest names in porcelain (while one of Rose's apprentices from Caughley, Thomas Minton, was later to achieve almost equal fame when he set up his own company in Stoke-on-Trent). John Rose lived at **Hay House Farm,** an impressive 18th-century brick house of seven bays. The porcelain factory is now closed. Since 1926 Coalport china has been made by the Wedgwood group in Stoke, but the **Coalport China Museum** brilliantly recalls the former industry.

COCKSHUTT [North Shropshire]

SJ4329: 4 miles (6km) SE of Ellesmere

A small village on the main road, Cockshutt has red-brick **St Helen's Church** (c1777), a few timber-framed cottages and a lot of new housing. **Cockshutt House Farm** is open to the public with a display of small-scale farming techniques and a conservation trail. Just to the north is **Whattal Moss** (privately owned), one of only a few peat mosses now surviving in north Shropshire. A dugout canoe built c700BC was found in the peat and is on display at Shrewsbury Museum. Close by are **Crose Mere** and **Sweat Mere,** but these are also privately owned with no public access.

COLD WESTON [South Shropshire]

SO5583: 5 miles (8km) NE of Ludlow

A farm, a cottage and a church make up the tiny settlement of Cold Weston in a lonely, exposed but beautiful setting below Brown Clee Hill. The restored Norman **church of St Mary** is surrounded by faint holloways and house platforms, all that remains of a village which was already in decline before the Black Death.

COLEBATCH [South Shropshire]

SO3187: 1 mile (2km) S of Bishop's Castle

The stone-built cottages which constitute much of Colebatch cluster round a cross-roads below beautiful wooded hills. Timber-framed cottages, weatherboarded barns and a Norman motte border a lane branching east beside a tiny brook. A 14th-century timber-framed house stands in the middle of the village and is believed to have been part of the complex attached to the old manor house, which has not survived. Later in its history it served as a reading room and a venue for congregational services.

COLEMERE [North Shropshire]

SJ4332: 3 miles (5km) SE of Ellesmere

The hamlet consists of a group of thatched cottages and more modern farm cottages of brick with steeply pitched roofs, near the southern shore of **Cole Mere.** This is not only a SSSI, but also part of a country park, where wildlife has to co-exist with leisure use. Woods and hay meadows surround the mere, which is used for sailing. The **church of St John** stands among trees on raised ground and was built in 1870 to the design of Street. It replaced an older church on the same site, a bell from which is said to have been thrown into the mere by a parliamentarian soldier in the Civil War. It is claimed that the bell can still occasionally be heard ringing. To the east of St John's Church an avenue of chestnuts leads to the hamlet of Lyneal, with brick and timber-framed cottages and, just to the north, a wharf on the Shropshire Union Canal.

CONDOVER [Shrewsbury and Atcham]

SJ4905: 4 miles (6km) S of Shrewsbury

Well-wooded rolling country around Cound Brook provides the pleasant setting for the interesting village of Condover, which was the administrative centre for the Condover Hundred in the Middle Ages.

Condover Hall, built of pink sandstone for Thomas Owen, Justice of Common Pleas, in the 1590s, is considered the finest Elizabethan house in the county. With its towers, gables, bay windows and elaborate chimneys it simply can't fail to charm. Naturally, such a splendid building is haunted, with an indelible bloody handprint and a powerful curse both featuring in the story. Among the hall's many residents has been Clive of India who rented it for a time, while Mark Twain stayed here as a guest of Reginald Cholmondeley in 1873 and 1879. Today it's a school for the blind.

Many of the brick houses in the village are actually timber-framed beneath the brick cladding, some of them of early cruck construction. The pink sandstone **church of St Mary and St Andrew** is Norman but was largely rebuilt after the tower collapsed into the nave in 1660. There are notable monuments to local families inside and a much-admired hammerbeam roof.

Richard Tarleton (c1530-88) was born a farmer's son in Condover and became an actor and Court Jester to Elizabeth I. Some think that Shakespeare's Yorick in *Hamlet* is modelled on him.

CORELEY [South Shropshire]
SO6173: 4 miles (6km) SW of Cleobury Mortimer

Coreley is a tiny hamlet in pleasant country on the southern slopes of Titterstone Clee. The **church of St Peter** stands on a hilltop, surrounded by quietly grazing sheep, and has a squat 13th-century tower with a shingled broach spire and a brick nave and chancel of 1757. The porch, vestry and windows are Victorian.

CORFTON [South Shropshire]
SO4984: 5 miles (8km) NE of Craven Arms

On the edge of Corve Dale, below Wenlock Edge, the hamlet of Corfton extends either side of the main road, with a string of cottages along steep-sided Corfton Bache to the north, and a cluster of farms and cottages around a "no through road" to the south. The mound of a Norman motte and bailey castle stands just to the west of the road.

COSFORD [Bridgnorth]
SJ7905: 3 miles (5km) SE of Shifnal

The former village of Cosford has been taken over by the Royal Air Force, with not only an air base but also the **Royal Air Force Museum**, devoted to aviation history. Founded in 1979, the museum has one of the largest aviation collections in the UK, including a Second World War Lincoln bomber which is said to be haunted.

COUND [Shrewsbury and Atcham]
SJ5504: 6 miles (10km) SE of Shrewsbury

The village of Cound, bisected by Coundmoor Brook, lies off the main road behind **Cound Hall**, an imposing house built of red brick in 1704 for the Cressett family by John Prince of Shrewsbury. **St Peter's Church** dates from the 13th century, with considerable Victorian restoration and a Norman font. Some good 18th-century memorials include one to Dr Edward Cressett, Bishop of Llandaff, who died in 1755.

CRAVEN ARMS [South Shropshire]
SO4382: 7 miles (11km) NW of Ludlow

Craven Arms is a young town which owes its existence in its present form to the building of the railways, before which it consisted of little more than a hotel by a road junction and a huddle of cottages at the hamlet of Newton, by the River Onny. The hotel, the Craven Arms, stands by the junction of the A49 Hereford to Shrewsbury road and the B4368 which runs east to Much Wenlock and west through the Clun valley to Wales, and was used by cattle drovers at one time. Just to the west of Craven Arms is the Roman Watling Street. It seems likely, from this conjunction of roads, that the present hotel must occupy the site of a much older inn, built to serve the needs of travellers many centuries ago.

In the 1840s the Hereford to Shrewsbury railway was built, followed by the Knighton line to Wales, the Buildwas line to the coalfields and the Bishop's Castle line, making Craven Arms a major railway junction. The cattle and sheep that had travelled the drove roads now came by train and plenty of other transport opportunities were opened up. Local landowner Earl Craven recognised the potential for profit and responded by building a new town. For a while it seemed as though it might grow into a major centre but this never happened, though there are still huge livestock sales at The Arms, as locals call it. The most impressive building in town is still the Craven Arms Hotel and opposite this there stands an unusual milestone, in the form of an obelisk, with numerous towns and their distances from Craven Arms inscribed on it. Its age is unknown but the distances given indicate that it was built before Telford began work on improving the Holyhead road in 1811. The old hamlet of Newton still exists as a pleasant enclave of cottages at the south-east corner of town. Apart from this there is some light industry, a few shops, plenty of new housing, a Baptist chapel (1871) and a Methodist chapel (1880).

Two of the railway lines have gone but the Hereford-Shrewsbury line (part of the Cardiff-Manchester route) is still busy and the Knighton line is now known as the Heart of Wales line, which runs through glorious countryside all the way from Craven Arms to Swansea. During the Second World War a secret train was kept hidden in the sidings at Craven Arms, ready to be used as a mobile control centre for the whole rail network, should it prove necessary.

CRESSAGE [Shrewsbury and Atcham]

SJ5904: 3 miles (5km) NW of Much Wenlock

Now dominated by modern housing, Cressage is an unremarkable village, except for a notable view of the Wrekin from the bridge spanning the River Severn. A Norman castle commanded the ford close to the present bridge but only a slight mound survives today. The bridge was built in 1913 to replace a timber toll bridge built c1800 by Thomas Telford.

It is claimed that the Pope's emissary, St Augustine, preached to the Welsh bishops in AD584 under the Cressage Oak (originally Christ's Oak, from which the village name derives), which stood for centuries on the spot now occupied by the war memorial. A descendant of the original tree still stands in a nearby meadow. However, other places along the Severn make the same claim.

A stone marks the position of the old church of St Samson, which was pulled down in 1841 and replaced the same year by **Christ Church**, designed by Edward Haycock. It has a Norman font from the old church and a gallery supported by cast-iron columns.

CRUDGINGTON [Wrekin]

SJ6317: 4 miles (6km) N of Wellington

Dairy Crest has a large factory at Crudgington which dominates the landscape. It developed from a dairy farmers' co-operative established in 1921. Milk Marque has its research and development establishment here too. Other than that the hamlet, which stands on a small rise near the confluence of the River Strine with the River Tern, has several timber-framed cottages, including one of cruck construction, and some modern houses. The **church of St Mary** was built in 1863, and re-opened in 1970 after a period of closure.

CULMINGTON [South Shropshire]

SO4982: 5 miles (8km) N of Ludlow

Corve Dale provides a lovely setting for this attractive village of stone and timber-framed houses. The **church of All**

Saints has a 12th-century nave with herringbone masonry, a 13th-century chancel and a 14th-century tower with an incomplete broach spire topped by a modern aluminium cap. Not far to the north-east of the church is **Camp Ring**, the earthworks of a substantial Norman motte and bailey castle.

CWM HEAD [South Shropshire]

SO4288: 4 miles (6km) N of Craven Arms

Just a handful of houses at the head of a wooded valley constitutes Cwm Head, where **St Michael's Church** was built in 1845 in neo-Norman style to the design of H.C. Whitling. A coach house and stable were built nearby for the use of a peripatetic vicar when he came to take services, for the hamlet was too small to have a resident vicar.

DAWLEY [Wrekin]

SJ6807: 1 mile (2km) S of Telford

Though well and truly consumed by Telford, the former village of Dawley retains some character and plenty of green space. It was carved out of the forest in Saxon times and has a long industrial history as it overlies the Shropshire coalfield. Mining was small-scale until the 19th century, when Dawley grew rapidly, not just from mining but from iron working, brick making and associated industries. Like the rest of the Severn Gorge area, however, Dawley declined in the face of competition from the Black Country, the Potteries and South Wales. By the middle of the 20th century it was little more than an industrial wasteland, but the development of Telford New Town (originally intended to be Dawley New Town) brought it back to life.

There was once a stone castle at Dawley, which was held by the Royalists in the Civil War until it fell to Cromwell in 1645. Its ruins were later quarried for building stone and then what remained was buried under slag from Castle Furnaces. The castle was close to the site of the Perpendicular-style **church of Holy Trinity** (1845), which contains an elaborately decorated Norman font. There are several Nonconformist chapels and further south, at Little Dawley, the brick-built **church of St Luke**, which also dates from 1845.

Captain Matthew Webb, the first man to swim the English Channel, was born at Dawley in 1848.

DETTON [Bridgnorth]

SO6679: 3 miles (5km) N of Cleobury Mortimer

Lost in quiet country beside the River Rea, the hamlet of Detton consists only of the magnificent 17th-century **Detton Hall Farm** and a cottage in an adjacent field. Two footpaths across the field allow a close look at the earthworks of a **deserted medieval village**, which is believed to have been abandoned as early as 1300.

DEUXHILL [Bridgnorth]

SO6987: 4 miles (6km) SW of Bridgnorth

Pronounced "dukeshill", this is a tiny hamlet of two farms on high ground above Crunells Brook, with good views over the rolling fields and woods to the south. The scant remains of an old church are hidden at the back of Georgian **Church Farm**. Timber-framed **Hall Farm** is a particularly fine house and bears the date 1601.

DHUSTONE [South Shropshire]

SO5876: 1 mile (2km) N of Cleehill

The rather decayed hamlet of Dhustone takes its name from the hard basalt, locally known as dhustone, which caps the Clee Hills. Built for quarrymen and miners, it hugs the southern slope of Titterstone Clee, not far from Cleehill village, and consists of Victorian terraced houses among sheep pasture and spoil heaps, most of them now grassed over.

DIDDLEBURY [South Shropshire]

SO5085: 5 miles (8km) NE of Craven Arms

Locally known as Delbury, Diddlebury is a village of considerable charm which occupies a pleasant position in pastoral countryside below Wenlock Edge, near the River Corve. Old stone houses cluster beside **St Peter's Church**, next to a stone bridge over a brook. The church has a Saxon nave, its north wall entirely constructed of herringbone masonry. The north doorway is typically Saxon too and there is a Saxon window. The chancel is Norman but experts can't agree about the tower, though the lower part is probably Saxon and the upper part Norman. St Peter's is an exceptionally fine example of the Saxon building style.

Delbury Hall stands in parkland nearby and is a restrained red-brick house built in the 1750s. A mile to the east the earthworks of **Corfham Castle** stand in a field not far from the River Corve. At the Conquest, Diddlebury was part of the manor of Corfham, which had belonged to King Edward the Confessor. It was given to the Clifford family and they built the castle some time before the 12th century. It is claimed that Henry II's lover, Rosamund Clifford, was born here, but the same claim is made for other Clifford properties in Herefordshire and Gloucestershire.

DITTON PRIORS [Bridgnorth]

SO6089: 9 miles (14km) SW of Bridgnorth

Remote and secluded, the former mining and quarrying village of Ditton Priors huddles below the northern slopes of Brown Clee Hill. A small industrial estate on a former Royal Navy armaments depot provides employment now for those villagers who are not farmers or commuters. The village houses are a mixture of stone, timber and brick. The **church of St John the Baptist** dates mostly from the 13th century, though its weatherboarded broach spire is later and was rebuilt in 1831. The village has several

useful shops and a pub, the **Howard Arms**, said to date from 1301. Ditton Priors used to be the terminus of a mineral railway, opened in 1908, which ran to Cleobury Mortimer. From Ditton Priors a steep incline linked the railway with the quarries on top of Brown Clee. A limited passenger service also operated and munitions were transported from the armaments depot during the Second World War. The line closed in 1965.

DODDINGTON [South Shropshire]

SO6176: 4 miles (6km) W of Cleobury Mortimer

Doddington consists of little more than a scattering of buildings alongside the main road which crosses the flank of Titterstone Clee Hill. Many of the houses were originally squatters' cottages but have now been modernised. The **church of St John** was built in 1849. Old quarries and bell pits scar the slopes above Doddington but the views from here are quite spectacular.

DONNINGTON [Wrekin]

SJ7013: 3 miles (5km) N of Telford

Donnington used to be a farming hamlet but was industrialised in the 19th century. Today, it is part of Telford New Town and consists almost entirely of suburban housing. The most distinctive buildings are some dormer-windowed cottages which were part of the Duke of Sutherland's Lilleshall Estate until it was sold in 1917. There is also a modernistic Roman Catholic church. The Anglican **church of St Matthew** was built to the design of Sir George Gilbert Scott in 1843. A pub, the Champion Jockey, is named after **Sir Gordon Richards** (1904-86), who was born in nearby Oakengates and was champion jockey 26 times between 1921 and 1954, riding a total of 4870 winners.

Adjoining **Donnington Wood** used to be a village but was consumed by mining operations. The last mine closed in 1979 and reclamation is well underway, with **Granville Country Park** the centrepiece of the scheme. There are valuable, naturally regenerated areas of heathland, wetland and scrub, together with plenty of industrial relics of considerable interest, including the dry bed of the former Donnington Wood Canal and the remains of Muxton Bridge Colliery.

DORRINGTON [Shrewsbury and Atcham]

SJ4702: 5 miles (8km) S of Shrewsbury

A brick, mainly 19th-century, village with a few much older timber-framed houses, Dorrington inhabits undulating mixed farmland with good views of the hills to the south. The timber-framed **Old Hall**, now a restaurant, dates from c1670 and the **Old House** from 1588. The Anglo-Catholic **church of St Edward the Confessor** was built in 1845 by Edward Haycock on land given by John Thomas Hope of Netley, for whom **Netley Hall** was built in 1854-8, also by Haycock. It stands in parkland just to the south of the village. Dorrington lies adjacent to the Cardiff-Manchester railway and before the station was closed in 1958 there used to be regular cattle sales at the Railway Inn (now the White House).

DUDLESTON [North Shropshire]

SJ3438: 4 miles (6km) NW of Ellesmere

A peaceful hamlet of brick cottages, Dudleston occupies a hill in rolling country not far from the Welsh border. The **church of St Mary** seems to have been rebuilt in the 18th or early 19th century but stands on an ancient site, possibly within a defensive earthwork, surrounded by venerable yew trees. Nearly two miles to the south-east is Dudleston Heath, also known as Criftins, a scattered, thinly-spread settlement which extends over a considerable area and has developed from squatters' cottages built on former common land. **St Matthew's Church** was built of brick in 1874 to a de-

sign by W.G. McCarthy. Nearby is the hamlet of Gadlas where there is a medieval moated site close to **Gadlas Hall**, which was rented by the wife of Charles de Gaulle in 1940.

EARDINGTON [Bridgnorth]

SO7291: 2 miles (3km) S of Bridgnorth

A scattered settlement above the Severn, Eardington has some fine houses, such as Georgian **Eardington House** and the partly 17th-century **Hay Farm**. Just to the south is **Upper Forge**, a former iron-working site at the edge of a wooded dingle carved out by Mor Brook. The forge ceased operation in 1889 and today there remain some overgrown industrial buildings and a waterfall over a concrete dam. The site is now part of Astbury Falls Fish Farm. There is another former forge by the river at **Lower Forge**, where the workers' cottages are still lived in. The Severn Valley Railway runs between the two forges and there is a halt at the former Eardington Station.

To the north of Eardington is **Daniel's Mill**, a beautifully restored and fully operational watermill that is open to the public. The huge iron waterwheel was cast at Coalbrookdale in 1854 and is said to be the largest working waterwheel in England. There has been a mill on this site since at least the 11th century but the present buildings date from around 1700 or later.

To the west of Eardington is **Moor Ridding**, a timber-framed house with a curious custom attached to it. In 1281 Edward I gave land here to Earl Roger de Montgomery. In return Roger had to provide armed knights to protect the king on hunting trips on the earl's estates. As a reminder of this duty the earl had to deliver to the king each year at Michaelmas an "item of war", usually a pair of daggers. In later years hedging tools were presented instead. This ceremony is still carried out each autumn in London by the Queen's Remembrancer in the Law Courts, though the

Shropshire landowner is no longer required to be present.

EARDISTON [Oswestry]

SJ3624: 6 miles (10km) SE of Oswestry

A hamlet of stone houses in rolling country, Eardiston nestles between two areas of wooded parkland, with the Pradoe estate to the west and the Tedsmore estate to the north. **Pradoe House** was built by the Reverend Pritchard in the 18th century but he was ruined by the cost and was never able to live there. His ghost is said to have been resentfully haunting the house ever since. On the edge of the park is a **chapel** built in 1860 by Rhode Hawkins.

EASTHOPE [Bridgnorth]

SO5695: 6 miles (10km) SW of Much Wenlock

A small, secluded village, Easthope has a few buildings of great interest, including **Manor Farm** (rebuilt c1600) and, opposite it, a cruck-framed cottage. **The Malthouse**, built from oak timbers infilled with locally made brick, retains a 14th-century hall, altered in the 15th century, which is believed to be the only Shropshire example of the medieval cross-wing type of building, and is of great architectural importance. **St Peter's Church** is small and simple, with immensely thick limestone walls. Inside there is an hourglass beside the pulpit, a reminder of an old and tactful tradition which sought to discourage the delivery of long sermons. The date on its bracket is 1662 but it is a replica of the original, which was destroyed in a fire in 1928. Though St Peter's has a 12th-century nave and a chancel from about 1300, most of it was rebuilt after the fire. The circular shape of the churchyard probably indicates that it was a site of pre-Christian significance. It seems a peaceful place but is said to be haunted by three ghosts. One of these was Will Garmston, a vicar of the church who murdered its patron, John de Easthope, in 1333. The other two were monks who killed each other in a drunken fight. Their bodies are said to lie in two graves under a yew tree, each inscribed only with a cross.

To the south of Easthope the land rises steeply and the trees of Mogg Forest conceal the ramparts of **The Ditches**, a prehistoric fort built in the 1st or 2nd century BC. The Ditches overlooks **Lutwyche Hall**, a gabled mansion built in 1587 but substantially altered in the 18th century and again in the 19th century. Like many houses of its vintage, Lutwyche Hall is said to be haunted, both by the ghost of Sir Edward Lutwyche, a 17th-century judge, and by that of an unidentified woman who moves the furniture around. The novelist **Stella Benson** was born at Lutwyche Hall in 1892.

EATON CONSTANTINE [Shrewsbury and Atcham]

SJ5906: 5 miles (8km) NW of Much Wenlock

Below the Wrekin, overlooking the Severn, the village of Eaton Constantine has few buildings of particular interest other than **Baxter's House**, built of timber in 1645. Richard Baxter, the 17th-century Puritan theologian and chaplain to Oliver Cromwell, lived here for a time as a boy. Overlooking the village is **St Mary's Church**, which was built in 1841 but has a Norman font.

EATON-UNDER-HEYWOOD [South Shropshire]

SO4990: 4 miles (6km) SE of Church Stretton

It must have been more important once, for in 1219 it was granted a market charter, but today Eaton is a tiny, remote hamlet perched on the edge of Ape Dale, just where the land starts to rise steeply to Wenlock Edge. Eaton Brook flows past the handful of cottages which make up the hamlet, overlooked by the tree-shrouded **church of St Edith of Wilton**, which has a Norman nave, a 13th-century chancel and a chunky Norman tower with 15th-century battlements. The chancel contains a 14th-century oak effigy and there is some good Jacobean woodwork. St Edith was a Saxon saint and there was previously a Saxon church on this site, a daughter church of Wenlock Abbey. A mile to the south-west, **New Hall** has a rare 16th-century wall painting of a deer hunt.

Eaton was not always so isolated as it is today: it used to have a station on the dismantled Much Wenlock to Craven Arms railway and local farmers would join forces once a year to hire a special train to take their stock to Wellington market. In the severe winter of 1946, the railway was Eaton's only link with the outside world for six weeks. With the roads completely impassable, goods were hauled across the fields to and from the railway by horse-drawn sledge.

EATON UPON TERN [North Shropshire]

SJ6523: 7 miles (11km) S of Market Drayton

Hidden away down quiet lanes, Eaton is a peaceful hamlet with a variety of architectural styles, including Georgian and Victorian, and an unusual abundance of horse chestnut trees. The crumbling remains of a wartime aerodrome, RAF Peplow, lie to the north-east.

EDGMOND [Wrekin]

SJ7219: 2 miles (3km) W of Newport

Only the Strine Brook and a few fields separate Edgmond from Newport but it remains a pleasant residential village with a good range of facilities. The mainstays of the local economy are the Harper Adams Agricultural College and the National Poultry Institute. The sandstone **church of St Peter** stands on high ground and was founded c1080. It was rebuilt in the 14th century, has a 15th-century tower and inside there is an early Norman font. The chancel contains an early William Morris window. An ancient and once very wide-spread custom still takes place in Edgmond on the Sunday after St Peter's Day (June 29th). This is "clipping the church" and involves clergy, choir and congregation encircling the church and singing a hymn. On every Rogation Sunday the clergy, choir and congregation process from the church to the top of Edgmond Hill to participate in a blessing of the crops and the village. To the west of the church is a 14th-century building, **Provost's House**, which is the former rectory. It was much altered in the Georgian and Victorian periods but remains a fine house of considerable interest.

EDGTON [South Shropshire]

SO3885: 5 miles (8km) SE of Bishop's Castle

The gorgeous hilly country which unfolds to the south-east of Bishop's Castle is the setting for Edgton's stone and half-timbered farms and cottages. The number of footpaths and minor roads that converge on the village (including one along Ridgway Hill – almost certainly a prehistoric route) indicates a past importance greater than its present modest size suggests. **St Michael's Church** is of ancient foundation but was rebuilt in 1895, with only some 13th-century windows surviving from its predecessor. Many of the village buildings have been modernised, but there are a few charming black and white houses which look much as they must always have done.

EDSTASTON [North Shropshire]

SJ5131: 2 miles (3km) N of Wem

Edstaston is a nondescript village in flat country, but for some reason it was a favourite of the playwright George Bernard Shaw, who was a frequent visitor. It does have what is regarded as one of the county's finest churches, that is the **church of St Mary the Virgin**, which clearly displays its Norman origins in the elaborate carvings around its three doors. The south doorway is magnificent. The ironwork on the doors themselves is also impressive, and probably original. Inside are some sensitively restored but rather indistinct wall paintings. A little to the north of St Mary's, **Edstaston Bridge**, designed by Thomas Telford, carries the road over the (long since infilled) Prees branch of the Ellesmere Canal (part of the Shropshire Union system).

ELLERTON [North Shropshire]

SJ7125: 7 miles (11km) SE of Market Drayton

A tiny farming hamlet, Ellerton occupies a slight rise between Wagg's Brook and Goldstone Brook. The main focus is **Ellerton Hall**, a gabled brick house built in 1836. At Ellerton Mill the old waterwheel is still in place though the mill ceased operation as long ago as 1909. The most curious building at Ellerton is the stone **Round House**, which looks like a truncated windmill with a pitched roof.

ELLESMERE [North Shropshire]

SJ4034: 7 miles (11km) NE of Oswestry

Ellesmere is an attractive little market town and the unofficial capital of Shropshire's "Lake District", where depressions in glacial boulder clay have filled with water to create meres. Ellesmere stands on the western shore of the largest and best known, simply called **The Mere**. Despite all the human visitors who flock to The Mere, it still attracts large numbers of waterbirds, and is especially important for winter migrants such as wigeon, pochard, goosander and teal. It also has a heronry, one of only two in north Shropshire. The Mere and adjoining Cremorne Gardens were given to the public by Lord Brownlow in 1953. The gardens were created from a former industrial site – there were tanneries on the lakeside here for many years, with the last one closing in 1855.

Ellesmere itself is of Saxon origin but the Norman Roger de Montgomery planned a new town when he built a motte and bailey castle here in the late 11th century, on the

site now known as **Castlefields**. Nothing remains of the castle itself but the earthworks are clearly visible. There is a superb view of The Mere from this vantage point and the field is managed as a hay meadow. A little further along the lane is **Plantation Wood**, managed by Shropshire Wildlife Trust.

Ellesmere is well endowed with period buildings, including some fine timber-framed ones such as the **White Hart** in Birch Road, but the town centre is dominated by the pedimented, ashlar-faced **town hall**, built in 1833. There are several Georgian brick houses on Church Street, while the **Savings Bank** (c1840) on Scotland Street and **Fullwood House** (also c1840) on Victoria Street are both impressive.

The 12th-century **church of St Mary** stands on high ground overlooking The Mere. It was largely rebuilt in 1849 by Sir George Gilbert Scott but some original work remains, including the tower (Early English below, Perpendicular above) and two chapels, one of which has a superb carved roof.

The Llangollen branch of the Shropshire Union Canal runs just to the south of Ellesmere, with an arm branching off to serve the town centre wharves. The canal was constructed by the Ellesmere Canal Company between 1793 and 1805, supervised by Thomas Telford from offices in Beech House in Ellesmere. This is now the main British Waterways yard, a place of some character that has recently been refurbished.

On the far side of The Mere is **Oteley Hall**, built in 1963 to replace a neo-Elizabethan house of 1826-30. This had itself replaced an older house where the poet **Francis Kynaston** (1587-1642) was born. He was well known at the court of Charles I, while an earlier Francis Kynaston was also prominent at court, serving as Royal Cupbearer to Elizabeth I. A Prayer Book which the Queen gave to him is still kept at the house and there is an alabaster memorial to him in St Mary's Church.

Just to the south of Oteley Hall is The Lyth, a house of 1819 which was the birthplace of **Eglantyne Jebb** (1876-1928), a co-founder of the Save the Children Fund in 1919.

EUDON GEORGE [Bridgnorth]

SO6889: 3 miles (5km) SW of Bridgnorth

Eudon means "hill of the yew trees" but there are not many yews today in the lightly wooded country round the small farming hamlet of Eudon George. The second part of the name comes from the lord of the manor in 1242 who gloried in the impressive name of William de Sancto Georgio. There are two excellent timber-framed houses in the hamlet: **North Eudon Farm** and the splendid **Eudon Grange**, dated 1618 and restored with unusual sensitivity in the 1980s. Less than a mile to the east, but a long way round by road, is another farm at Eudon Burnell, while Eudon Mill lies to the north in the valley of Borle Brook.

EYTON ON SEVERN [Shrewsbury and Atcham]

SJ5706: 6 miles (10km) SE of Shrewsbury

The hamlet of Eyton comprises a small cluster of brick farms and timber-framed houses standing close to the Severn in the shadow of the Wrekin. The unusual **Eyton Tower**, now a holiday let, is said to have been intended as a summer house. It is all that remains of the demolished Eyton Hall, birthplace of the distinguished soldier, statesman, poet, historian and philosopher **Edward Herbert** (1583-1648), who was created Baron Chirbury in 1629. Just to the south-east of Eyton and next to another tiny hamlet, Dryton, is the rather unexpected **Eyton on Severn National Hunt Racecourse**.

EYTON UPON THE WEALD MOORS [Wrekin]

SJ6514: 2 miles (3km) N of Wellington

It would be hard to find more low-lying country than the Weald Moors, but Eyton is pleasantly situated on a very slight rise on the southern edge. Weald derives from "wild" and this was once marshy country, but it has been steadily drained from the 16th century onward. This drainage has caused the land to sink, with lanes standing above the surface almost like causeways, creating an unusual landscape that is now put mostly to arable use.

St Catherine's Church was built of brick in 1743, its tower topped by a little pyramid roof. A polygonal apse was added in 1850. A few houses and **Eyton Hall** make up the rest of the village, which is bordered to the north by a stretch of the disused Shrewsbury branch of the Shropshire Union Canal. The remains of locks are still apparent and there was formerly a busy canal junction at nearby Wappenshall.

FARLOW [Bridgnorth]

SO6380: 4 miles (6km) NW of Cleobury Mortimer

On high ground above Farlow Brook, the tiny village of Farlow is enviably situated in mixed farming country in the shadow of Brown Clee Hill. The village is split into two, with the **church of St Giles,** a school and a handful of brick and stone houses occupying a hilltop position well above the village shop and another cluster of houses towards the bottom of the slope. The church was rebuilt in 1858 in Early English style, and very little remains of the original Norman masonry. Farlow was in Herefordshire until 1844, having been an outlier of Leominster in the Middle Ages.

FAULS [North Shropshire]

SJ5832: 7 miles (11km) SE of Whitchurch

Though an unremarkable hamlet on the whole, and largely modern, Fauls does boast one of the oldest houses in the county. This is timber-framed **Moat Farm**, parts of which are thought to date from the 11th century. The moat has been filled in but its former position is still discernible. The **church of Holy Immanuel** was built of brick, with a shingled spire, in 1856.

FITZ [Shrewsbury and Atcham]

SJ4417: 5 miles (8km) NW of Shrewsbury

Lying in the flood plain between the River Severn and the River Perry, next to some of the Severn's craziest meanderings, Fitz is a small village, remarkable only in that it is almost entirely unspoiled. The brick **church of St Peter and St Paul** replaced a medieval building in 1722, was restored in 1878, and then again by Sir Aston Webb in 1905. There are some 13th-century tiles inside. The sandstone Old Schoolhouse, the brick Old Vicarage and the largely timber-framed Old Manor are all buildings of some character.

FORD [Shrewsbury and Atcham]

SJ4113: 5 miles (8km) W of Shrewsbury

Ford is disappointing at first glance, a nondescript modern settlement of no particular interest. However, further exploration reveals that the old part of the village still survives, separated from the modern development by a brook. The ford from which the village took its name is no longer there but the bridge which replaced it has some very attractive cottages for company. Above them, on top of a bank, is the **church of St Michael**, pleasing but over-zealously restored in 1875. Very little remains to show that this was a Norman foundation. Close by is 18th-century **Ford House**, an imposing brick edifice with a Tuscan porch. The nearby **Mansion House** (1779) is almost as splendid.

FRODESLEY [Shrewsbury and Atcham]

SJ5101: 8 miles (12km) SE of Shrewsbury

Just one street of stone and brick houses constitutes the unspoiled village of Frodesley which lies just off the Roman road Watling Street as it runs north-east to Viroconium (see Wroxeter). The **church of St Mark** was built in a simple style in 1809 but added to ham-fistedly in 1859, when an incongruous extension was stuck, lean-to fashion, on one side. Inside, however, St Mark's is flooded with natural light and appears as a rare and unspoiled example of a very early 19th-century church, with a beautifully panelled sanctuary. Sadly, the church is threatened with redundancy.

The village street ends at **Frodesley Lodge**, a gabled house with tall chimneys and a semi-circular stair tower built of grey stone in 1591. It stands on a slight hill and enjoys excellent views. The **Frodesley Oak** stands nearby, a huge tree which looks as though it will not survive many more years. The house may have been built as a hunting lodge for Frodesley Park. In places the stone wall which once enclosed the park can still be seen. The parkland was made into fields in the 18th century.

GLAZELEY [Bridgnorth]

SO7088: 3 miles (5km) S of Bridgnorth

In the undulating country between Bridgnorth and Cleobury Mortimer, the hamlet of Glazeley lies close to the top of a hill above the lovely wooded valley of Borle Brook and consists of little more than a farm, a couple of cottages, a manor house, a vicarage and the **church of St Bartholomew**, rebuilt in 1875 to a design by Blomfield.

GOBOWEN [Oswestry]

SJ3033: 3 miles (5km) N of Oswestry

Gobowen is an unremarkable place in gentle country below the Welsh hills, but it does have a fine Italianate **railway station**, built in 1848 and recently restored after a period of disrepair. The station is on the main line and there used to be a branch line to Oswestry: there are some hopes that this might be reopened in the near future. Not far away is the **church of All Saints**, built in the Perpendicular style in 1928, with a tower added in 1945. A slight mound nearby, almost certainly the remains of a castle, indicates that Gobowen is older than it looks.

GREAT BOLAS [Wrekin]

SJ6421: 7 miles (11km) N of Wellington

Great Bolas is a pleasant village in low-lying country close to the confluence of the River Tern and the River Meese. The village's 14th-century **church** was replaced in the 17th century and added to in 1726-9, when it was provided with a brick tower and nave. The box pews inside are thought to come from the original church. Great Bolas has no particularly memorable buildings and is best known for the story of the Cottage Countess. This was Sarah Hoggins, a miller's daughter, who was courted by the aristocratic Henry Cecil. He came here incognito, under the name of John Jones, in 1789, after leaving his home at Hanbury Hall, Worcestershire, following the break-up of his marriage to Emma Vernon, who had run off with the Hanbury curate. He was not divorced from his wife but this didn't stop him from entering into a bigamous marriage with the teenaged Sarah. He later did obtain a divorce, however, and married Sarah legally. They lived at Bolas Villa, a substantial house just to the west of Great Bolas, until Cecil inherited the family estates on the death of his uncle, the Earl of Exeter. Only then did Sarah find out who her husband really was and they went to live at the spectacular Burleigh House in Lincolnshire. Sarah, however, was apparently snubbed by so-called "polite" society and must have longed to return to a simpler life at Great Bolas. Sadly, she died at the age of 24, following the birth of her fifth child. A not entirely accurate version of her story was the subject of a poem by Tennyson.

GREAT NESS [Shrewsbury and Atcham]

SJ3918: 8 miles (12km) NW of Shrewsbury

In undulating countryside beneath the sandstone outcrop of Nesscliffe Hill, the tiny village of Great Ness has some good houses of Georgian brick, the best of which is Great Ness House. The sandstone **church of St Andrew** has an Early English nave and tower and a Decorated chancel.

GREAT RYTON [Shrewsbury and Atcham]

SJ4803: 4 miles (6km) S of Shrewsbury

Rolling pastoral country provides the perfect setting for the pleasant village of Great Ryton which sits on a slight rise. Several of its houses are of 16th-century origin and **Ryton Grange** is particularly attractive. The former Ryton Manor has become Yew Tree Cottages. There is a **church** of c1720, a pub, some cottages and barns and not much else.

GREAT WYTHEFORD [North Shropshire]

SJ5719: 6 miles (10km) NE of Shrewsbury

Set in flat country by the River Roden, Great Wytheford is a substantial farming hamlet which stands on a former industrial site where there was a watermill and iron was worked at a forge. Today, only Forge Cottages by the river serve as a reminder of those days. Behind the cottages is imposing **Wytheford Hall**. A little further on, Little Wytheford is another impressive farmhouse. Just to the south-west, across the Roden, is Poynton, where the scant remains of an old chapel have been incorporated into the wall of a farm building at **Poynton House**. A Perpendicular window and part of the medieval west wall are all that survive.

GREETE [South Shropshire]

SO5770: 3 miles (5km) NW of Tenbury Wells

Greete is a charming, scattered village lost in the hills which tumble down to the River Teme and the borders with Worcestershire and Herefordshire. The nucleus of the settlement is just above Greet Brook, around the **church of St James**, with its Norman doorway and mixture of Early English and Perpendicular windows. Opposite the church is the original manor house, **Greet Court**, which is mainly brick but partly timber-framed and has a priest hole in a chimney stack.

GRINDLEY BROOK [North Shropshire]

SJ5242: 2 miles (3km) NW of Whitchurch

A settlement on the Llangollen Canal, Grindley Brook has no feature of interest other than the canal itself, though the surrounding dairy lands are green and pleasant. The Llangollen Canal started life as the Ellesmere Canal and was constructed by the Ellesmere Canal Company between 1793 and 1805, under the supervision of Thomas Telford. It enters Shropshire here at Grindley Brook via a flight of six locks, with the top three in a triple staircase.

GRINSHILL [North Shropshire]

SJ5223: 3 miles (5km) S of Wem

The hard sandstone ridge of Grinshill Hill is part of the discontinuous semi-circle of New Red Sandstone that outcrops here and there throughout the north Shropshire plain and it makes a suitable backdrop for Grinshill, a village of considerable charm which nestles at its foot. Its houses are built from Grinshill stone, quarried from the ridge since Roman times and used in many a town and city throughout the country, and even in America. Some of Grinshill's houses are built of carefully dressed stone, others of massive blocks, fairly roughly hewn. **The Manor** is an imposing gabled house bearing the date 1624 and there is a handsome Georgian pub, the **Elephant and Castle Hotel**. The rather incongruous **All Saints' Church** was built in 1839-40, in neo-Norman style, with an Italianate tower. Just to the east of the village is **Stone Grange**, a fine building known locally as the Pest House because it was acquired as a country refuge for times of plague by

Cottages at Grinshill, built with enormous blocks of Grinshill stone

Shrewsbury School in 1617. There is still a working quarry on Grinshill Hill but much of the summit is open common land, renowned for its fine views, and there is also plenty of woodland, the result of regeneration on former quarry sites. **Corbet Wood** is an attractive nature reserve owned by the county council.

HABBERLEY [Shrewsbury and Atcham]

SJ3903: 2 miles (3km) S of Pontesbury

Set in gorgeous countryside below the foothills of Stiperstones, Habberley is an agricultural village of some charm. The **church of St Mary** tops a raised mound and is Norman, but was rebuilt in 1864 using much of the original masonry. Tree-shrouded **Habberley Hall** is timber-framed, with stone and brick gables and star-shaped chimney stacks. The earliest parts date from 1593. In the 18th century it was the home of historian William Mytton.

HADLEY [Wrekin]

SJ6711: 2 miles (3km) E of Wellington

Now part of Telford New Town, Hadley originated as a forest clearing where people earned a living from agriculture and small-scale coal mining. During the early years of the Industrial Revolution it developed as a social and shopping centre for the industrial areas which encircled it. Most of these are now redeveloped as housing estates, though there are still brick and tile works and a factory at Hadley Castle making parts for cars, trucks and tractors. The centre of Hadley has plenty of facilities and a few interesting buildings but nothing of particular note. The **church of Holy Trinity** was built in 1856 of red and yellow brick with lancet windows.

The remains of the Trench branch of the Shropshire Union Canal can still be traced in the northern part of Hadley, and **Hadley Park Lock** has unusual guillotine gates, the only ones of their kind to have retained their complete working mechanism. Nearby **Hadley Park** was once the home of the great ironmaster John Wilkinson. Adjacent **Hadley Park Mill** was built as a battlemented, brick windmill c.1750 but was later converted to operate by water-power. It remained in use until the early 20th century. From a distance it looks like a castle, inspiring Birmingham screwmakers Nettlefold and Chamberlain to sell goods under the brand name "Castle" when they set up here in 1871. Their factory became Castle Works and now the area is known as Hadley Castle.

HADNALL [North Shropshire]

SJ5220: 5 miles (8km) NE of Shrewsbury

A large, sprawling village, Hadnall contains no buildings of outstanding interest. The **church of St Mary Magdalene** is partly Norman with a 14th-century nave but was largely rebuilt in the 19th century. It contains a monument to **Viscount Hill** (1772-1842) who fought with Wellington at Waterloo. He was a leading general throughout the Peninsular War and Commander-in-Chief of the British Army from 1828 to 1842. Hill lived much of his life at Hardwicke Grange to the north of Hadnall. The house has been demolished, but the stables survive and are now used as industrial units. To celebrate his military exploits he built **Waterloo Windmill**, a replica of one near the battle site. The replica still stands on the northern edge of the village.

HALFORD [South Shropshire]

SO4383: ½ mile (1km) NE of Craven Arms

Below the southernmost slopes of Wenlock Edge, and separated from Craven Arms only by the River Onny, the hamlet of Halford comprises a few houses of grey stone, a mill, a school and a church, restored and altered in 1848 and 1887 but still retaining a Norman doorway. High above Halford, on top of Callow Hill, is **Flounders' Folly**, a dilapidated tower built for a local landowner and merchant in 1838. Quite why he wanted it no one knows, but one of several explanations suggests that Mr Flounders believed that from the top of the tower he could watch his ships sailing up the Mersey.

HAMPTON [Bridgnorth]

SO7486: 4 miles (6km) SE of Bridgnorth

Enviably situated on the west bank of the River Severn, the village of Hampton comprises little more than a pub and a handful of cottages, chalets and caravans beside the river, along with a few outlying farms. Of more interest is the beautifully restored **railway station**, still in regular use by steam trains on the Severn Valley Railway. Great wicker baskets of damsons used to be loaded onto the trains here and transported to Manchester to be made into dyes for the cotton trade. Today the railway carries only leisure passengers, but is probably busier than ever before. Across the river is **Hampton Loade**, the second part of its name derived from a Saxon word usually taken to mean a "ford". From 1796 until 1866 there were forges at Hampton Loade, where Papermill Brook joins the Severn, but today it is a popular spot with anglers, picnickers and walkers. There are a few cottages and another pub. A pedestrian ferry still operates between the two Hamptons.

HANWOOD [Shrewsbury and Atcham]

SJ4409: 3 miles (2km) SW of Shrewsbury

Hanwood is a substantial modern village along the busy A488, with commuters now replacing the industrial workers of the past, when Hanwood was the site of a brick works, limekilns, a coal mine and a number of other industries. The brick **church of St Thomas** was rebuilt and extended in 1856 but contains a Norman font.

HARLEY [Shrewsbury and Atcham]

SJ5901: 2 miles (3km) NW of Much Wenlock

With timber-framed cottages clustered round the **church of St Mary**, the village of Harley occupies a pleasant hilltop site above Harley Brook and below Wenlock Edge. The church was rebuilt in 1846 by S.P. Smith, but the medieval tower was spared. The chancel contains a brass memorial to Sir Richard Lacon, who was Sheriff of Shropshire in 1477 and 1486. The writer, naturalist and photographer Frances Pitt (1888-1964) lived at Castle House from 1958.

HARMER HILL [Shrewsbury and Atcham]

SJ4922: 6 miles (10km) N of Shrewsbury

Harmer Hill is a widely spread settlement but the nucleus is around a complex road junction where the A528 meets a number of lesser roads. Modern houses dominate the scene but a few older ones, of both sandstone and brick, still stand. The **church** lies a little to the north. It is built of red sandstone and has a hexagonal chancel. The main landscape feature is further south, the tree-clad, sandstone outcrop of Pim Hill, which gives its name to **Pimhill Organic Farm**, based at Lea Hall. This has been a pioneer in the organic revolution, with Richard Mayall persuading his father Sam to jettison chemicals as early as 1949. Richard Mayall now runs the farm in partnership with his daughter Ginny and in 1990 he received an MBE for his services to agriculture.

One of the roads which converges on Harmer Hill is Lower Road, which leads to Myddle by way of **Webscott**, where a craggy sandstone cliff pocked with abandoned quarries and topped with Scots pines is being taken over by birch and sycamore. Of the few cottages and farms along here none is more picturesque than **The Nest**, built into the cliff itself.

Haughmond Abbey

HAUGHMOND [Shrewsbury and Atcham]

SJ5415: 3 miles (5km) NE of Shrewsbury

Haughmond is not exactly a village, nor a hamlet even, but a scattering of farms overlooked by Haughmond Hill, a flat-topped hill clothed in woodland and plantation which conceal a quarry. Scots pines crown the rocky top, where there is also an Iron Age fort.

Below the north-western edge of the hill is **Haughmond Abbey**, the exact origins of which are unknown, though it probably began as a fairly humble house of Augustinian canons. Early in the 12th century it attracted the patronage of the wealthy FitzAlan family of Clun and soon gained the status of an abbey. Henry II appointed his former tutor as abbot c1154 and from then on Haughmond enjoyed considerable prosperity, which is reflected in its fine buildings. These are ranged round two courtyards cut into the hillside in a series of terraces.

Most of what survives belongs to the late 12th century and the 14th century. The arches in the chapter house are decorated with wonderful carvings of saints and there is also a superb wooden ceiling, probably dating from early in the 16th century. The abbot's private rooms feature a richly decorated bay window and there are more carvings of saints in the cloister. In the remains of the abbey church are the tombstones of two former patrons, John FitzAlan, who died in 1272, and his wife, Isabel de Mortimer.

The abbey was suppressed in 1539, after which the abbot's hall and the adjoining rooms were converted into a private house. After a fire during the Civil War the ruins were pillaged for building stone and then a farmer built himself a house in the former kitchen, stabling his horses in the chapter house. The site was occupied until 1933 but is now looked after by English Heritage.

Less than a mile to the west of the abbey, **Sundorne Castle Farm** incorporates the remains of Sundorne Castle, a battlemented building designed by George Wyatt in the early 19th century.

HEATH [South Shropshire]

SO5585: 8 miles NE of Ludlow

An isolated community on the lower western slopes of Brown Clee Hill, Heath comprises a sparse scattering of farms around the renowned **Heath Chapel**. This simple building stands alone in a field and is the purest example of Norman church architecture in Shropshire. The arch round the door is enriched with chevron and roll mouldings, and inside a Norman tub font stands raised on two blocks. The box pews, pulpit, reader's desk, squire's pew and communion rails are all 17th century. The church is surrounded by the extensive earthworks of a **deserted medieval village**, with the remains of house platforms, streets, enclosed fields and fish ponds.

HIGH ERCALL [Wrekin]

SJ5917: 7 miles (11km) NE of Shrewsbury

Though an attractive village, High Ercall suffers from its position at a busy road junction. There are some interesting buildings, including **Ercall Hall**, built in 1608 for Sir Francis Newport by Walter Hancock (more famous for designing Shrewsbury's Market Hall). It was later fortified and garrisoned in the Civil War, holding out against a lengthy siege before the Royalists surrendered in 1646. The curious arcade of four arches visible in the garden at the rear of the hall is probably part of the original manor house built by the de Arkles, the family after whom the village is named.

The 11th-century **church of St Michael and All Angels**, with its massive 15th-century tower, was damaged in the Civil War and shot marks can still be seen. It was restored in 1865 by Street. An 18th-century sundial in the churchyard gives the time not only in High Ercall, but also in Rome, Jerusalem and Plymouth, New England. Not far from the church is the Gospel Oak, once a venue for religious meetings but now a popular gathering place for young people. On the main road is a former toll-house,

Tollgate House, and a range of brick **almshouses** founded by the Earl of Bradford in 1694.

Less than a mile to the north is the hamlet of **Walton,** where there lived a white wizard in the 19th century, the benign Thomas Leigh. He is said to have died after a rival wizard, Jack o'the Weald Moors, cast a spell on him.

HIGHLEY [Bridgnorth]

SO7483: 6 miles (10km) SE of Bridgnorth

Situated on a ridge between Borle Brook and the west bank of the River Severn, Highley is a settlement of great antiquity which probably originated as a clearing in what was then a much more extensive Wyre Forest. Like its counterpart on the east bank (see Alveley) it has long been associated with quarrying and coal mining. The latter began in the Middle Ages but didn't become large-scale until the 19th century and peaked only in 1957, when Highley Colliery was employing 1000 men. It closed in 1967 and the last of the quarries closed in 1969, leaving a scarred landscape full of spoil heaps. Since then the former industrial sites at both Highley and Alveley have been transformed into the popular **Severn Valley Country Park,** which straddles the river. Highley itself has become a commuter village.

At the end of the 19th century Highley expanded enormously as new mines were opened and most of the current village dates from this period. By far the most attractive corner of the village is the churchyard, where **St Mary's Church** is beautifully complemented by its timber-framed neighbour, **Church House,** which was the home of the village priest until the 1620s. St Mary's was first mentioned in a 12th-century document, and much of the present nave and chancel probably date from that period. The 16th-century nave roof has 33 oak bosses carved with Tudor flowers and other devices.

Highley Station is by the river, actually

at the hamlet of **Stanley**. This was a busy place for centuries, long before the railway was built in 1862, with barges and trows carrying coal, stone and timber. The **Ship Inn** was licensed in 1770, and originally catered for boatmen, miners and quarrymen. Today, it's popular with walkers, anglers and railway enthusiasts. For many of the latter, Highley Station is the finest on the Severn Valley Railway.

HILTON [Bridgnorth]
SO7795: 4 miles (6km) NE of Bridgnorth

Pleasant undulating country provides the setting for the small village of Hilton, which stands close to the confluence of Hilton Brook with Stratford Brook. There is an attractive mixture of brick, sandstone and timber-framed houses, together with a pub and a post office. The **Manor House** is the most imposing building in the village, with its five bays and pedimented doorway.

HINSTOCK [North Shropshire]
SJ6926: 5 miles (8km) S of Market Drayton

Blighted by the presence of the A41 and the A529, Hinstock could not be called a peaceful village, despite the attractive farmland which surrounds it. Red-brick houses straggle alongside the A41 but the village centre is based around St Oswald's Church, which dates mostly from the early 18th century. There is also a Wesleyan chapel where John Wesley himself is said to have preached.

HODNET [North Shropshire]
SJ6128: 5 miles (8km) SW of Market Drayton

A largely main-road village above the River Tern, Hodnet is famous for the gardens which surround **Hodnet Hall**. It's a substantial and very attractive village which was once a town: in the reign of Henry III it was granted a market charter, but it never quite made the grade. Hodnet is derived from a Celtic word meaning "peaceful valley" so it is a long-established

settlement, pre-dating the Roman occupation, though there are no obvious signs of this today. The earliest structure still apparent is to be found in the grounds of Hodnet Hall, where earthworks indicate the site of a Norman **motte and bailey castle** built by Baldwin de Hodnet c1082. However, it's possible that the mound on which **St Luke's Church** stands was once the site of a prehistoric fort. St Luke's is a large sandstone building of considerable interest, including a 14th-century octagonal tower – unique in Shropshire. Though the church was thoroughly restored in 1846 it retains some Norman work. Inside there are monuments to such prominent local families as the Hills, Vernons and Hebers. There is also a small collection of rare books. Reginald Heber (1783-1826), who wrote a number of popular hymns, was rector at St Luke's for a time before moving on, ultimately to become Bishop of Calcutta.

Anthony Salvin built Hodnet Hall in the neo-Elizabethan style for the Heber-Percys in 1870. The gardens, which are open to the public, were laid out over a 30-year period in the 20th century by Brigadier A.G.W. Heber-Percy, and are arranged around a series of lakes fed by underground springs. Adjacent **Home Farm** has possibly the finest timber-framed barn in Shropshire, built in 1619. **The Old Vicarage**, built for Reginald Heber, stands north-west of the church and was the birthplace of novelist Mary Cholmondeley (1859-1925).

The **Bear Inn** is apparently haunted by the unfortunate Jasper, a 16th-century merchant who died of cold when the landlord threw him out for being unable to pay for a night's lodgings. As he lay dying he cursed the landlord, who died of a heart attack the same night.

HOLDGATE [South Shropshire]
SO5689: 8 miles (12km) SW of Much Wenlock

Set on a knoll above Corve Dale, Holdgate is a tiny farming hamlet which was once of more importance. It is named after the Norman Helgot, who was given the manor after the Conquest and built a motte and bailey castle, which was one of the few Shropshire castles mentioned in the Domesday survey of 1086. His son, Herbert FitzHelgot, entertained Henry I here in 1109. The castle was later sold to Robert Burnell (see Acton Burnell). In 1280 Burnell built a new stone castle in the bailey of the old wooden one. All that remains now is a high, tree-clad mound, and a tower which was incorporated into **Holdgate Farm**, built within the former bailey after the castle had fallen into decay in the 17th century. Slight earthworks, revealing where the houses of the much larger medieval village stood, mark the fields on the other side of the lane.

Holy Trinity Church has a 12th-century nave, 13th-century chancel and tower, a richly decorated south doorway (possibly by the renowned Hereford School of craftsmen) and various features from later periods. On the exterior south chancel wall is a sheela-na-gig, a pagan fertility figure, and inside is a 12th-century font, one of the finest in the county, with elaborate carvings.

HOOK-A-GATE [Shrewsbury and Atcham]

SJ4609: 3 miles (5km) SW of Shrewsbury

The Shrewsbury suburb of Bayston Hill is ominously close, but for the time being Hook-a-gate remains a small village in sheep country above the Rea Brook, with a few old cottages, a brick chapel, a large Georgian house and three pubs. In Victorian times there was a soap and candle factory in the village, while at Welbatch, just to the south, there was a clog-making factory, which closed down at the end of the 19th century. For a time in the late 18th and early 19th centuries local mineral water was bottled and sold as Hanley's Spa Water.

HOPE [South Shropshire]

SJ3401: 4 miles (6km) SW of Pontesbury

With Stiperstones to the east and Bromlow

Callow to the west, the villagers of Hope are assured of fine views, while the steep, well-wooded Hope Valley is itself very lovely. The **church of Holy Trinity** was built in 1843 by Edward Haycock and stands in parkland approached over a little footbridge. This was once lead-mining country and the area is still riddled with old mines, while spoil heaps are everywhere, some of them absorbed into the landscape, others less so. There are numerous smallholdings along the valley and on neighbouring Hope Common, many of which originally belonged to the lead miners. A little to the south of Hope is **Gravels**, where 19th-century mine workings are overlooked by a gash in the hillside which reveals the site of Roman mining activities.

HOPE BAGOT [South Shropshire]

SO5874: 5 miles (8km) E of Ludlow

Occupying a secluded position below Titterstone Clee Hill, the lovely village of Hope Bagot is approached along deeply cut lanes. A tree-shaded churchyard full of wild flowers surrounds the small Norman **church of St John the Baptist**. The tower is of uncertain date, but is possibly 13th century, while the porch is thought to be made from the timbers of a 14th-century lychgate. A Norman chancel arch is the main treasure and there are Norman windows and doorways. Some authorities consider the arch over the entrance into the vestry to be Saxon. A tablet in the chancel recalls Benjamin Giles "snatched away from his parents, in consequence of a fall from his horse, by the irresistible call of the King of Terrors". A brook runs past the churchyard, at the entrance to which is a path leading to an ivy-shrouded holy well under a great yew tree, believed to be over 1600 years old. The well water was formerly believed to restore lost eyesight.

There are some fine Georgian houses nearby, including **Hope Court** and the **Old Vicarage**.

Church of St John the Baptist, Hope Bagot

HOPE BOWDLER [South Shropshire]

SO4792: 2 miles (3km) SE of Church Stretton

A remote, stone-built village to the south of the Stretton Hills, Hope Bowdler takes its name from one of the local words for a valley, and from Baldwin de Bollers, the Norman lord of the manor during the reign of Henry I. Wild Edric (see Stiperstones) was the lord of the manor until the Conquest. **St Andrew's Church** is a Victorian rebuilding of 1863, by S. Pountney Smith, and is approached along a yew avenue and through an attractive lychgate with a good example of a coffin rest. There is a prehistoric field system on the slopes of Hope Bowdler Hill.

HOPESAY [South Shropshire]

SO3883: 3 miles (2km) W of Craven Arms

Tucked away in a secluded valley below steep slopes, Hopesay is a delightfully peaceful village. Sadly, there is said to be nobody of local origin living in the village today, and there is no shop, pub, school or bus service. Many of the older houses are surprisingly large and grand for so small a community, so presumably it has long been seen as a desirable place to live. It is believed that several of the smaller houses were originally built for servants.

Hopesay Farmhouse, in the village centre, is the oldest surviving building, apart from the church, and is a mixture of timber-framing and stone. **St Mary's Church** is of Norman origin, with a distinctive arched doorway of about 1160, a nave and chancel of c1200 and a splendid, chestnut-panelled nave roof that is probably 15th century. The broad, low tower dates from around 1200, looks defensive in purpose and is very reminiscent of the one at Clun.

There is a substantial Iron Age fort, concealed by conifers, on top of **Burrow**, whose steep slopes rise to the west of the village. There is also a prehistoric settlement on **Wart Hill**, to the north-east. To the east is **Hopesay Hill**, a glorious expanse of rough, brackeny land with marvellous views. Unlike neighbouring hills, it escaped enclosure and has survived as open sheepwalk. It was bequeathed to the National Trust in 1952.

HOPTON CANGEFORD [South Shropshire]

SO5480: 4 miles (6km) NE of Ludlow

About as tiny as any hamlet can be, Hopton Cangeford shelters under the south-west slopes of Brown Clee, its alternative name of Hopton-in-the-Hole probably inspired by its position at the junction of three valleys. There are a few cottages and a brick church, which was built in 1766 but made redundant in 1983 and is now in private ownership. About a mile to the south-west is **Downton Hall**, the 18th-century home of a prominent local family, the Rouse-Boughtons.

HOPTON CASTLE [South Shropshire]

SO3678: 5 miles (8km) SE of Clun

Three valleys meet below wooded hills and provide a fine setting for the small village

Hopton Castle

of Hopton Castle, distinguished by the solid keep of a Norman **castle** and a fine timber-framed house which was once the rectory. The **church of St Mary** dates from 1870-71 and was designed by T. Nicholson. The castle was built by the de Hopton family in the late 11th century and rebuilt in the 14th century. During the Civil War it was held for Parliament but taken by the Royalists after a three-week siege. Most of the defending garrison was killed and the bodies dumped in the moat.

A mile to the south-east a few cottages cluster round a railway station on the Heart of Wales line at **Hoptonheath**.

HOPTON WAFERS [South Shropshire]

SO6376: 3 miles (5km) W of Cleobury Mortimer

The hamlet of Hopton Wafers clings to a slope above Hopton Brook as the land begins its gradual rise towards the top of Titterstone Clee Hill. Despite its rural setting, Hopton's past economy was based as much on coal mining, quarrying and iron forging as on agriculture. The Botfields of Hopton Court were among the leading mine owners in Shropshire for a time.

The **church of St Michael and All Angels** was rebuilt in 1827 but the medieval tower was retained. The church contains a very handsome memorial to Thomas Botfield. A group of cottages stands opposite St Michael's, attached to **Hopton Manor**, a late 18th-century brick house. A little to the north, aloof from the village in secluded parkland (possibly landscaped by Humphry Repton), is **Hopton Court**, a large, brick house built by Thomas Botfield in 1776 as an extension to an existing house on the same site. Further additions made to the house in 1812 are said to be by John Nash. The garden contains an unusual greenhouse, its framework cast at Coalbrookdale.

HORDLEY [North Shropshire]

SJ3830: 3 miles (5km) SW of Ellesmere

A small village, Hordley lies in gentle arable and dairy country between the River Perry and the Shropshire Union Canal, on the edge of reclaimed marshland known as Baggy Moors. The **church of St Mary** was restored in the 19th century and in 1967 but retains its Norman nave and chancel.

HORSEHAY [Wrekin]

SJ6706: 2 miles (3km) SW of Telford Centre

On the western edge of Telford, Horsehay lies on high ground which was purely agricultural until 1754 when Abraham Darby II (see Coalbrookdale) rented land here and constructed a blast furnace. Within a few years there were brick works and pottery kilns, and in 1838 the Coalbrookdale Company began the manufacture of ceramic pottery. But Horsehay's industrial prosperity was short-lived and by the 1860s forges, furnaces and factories were closing. More recently the area has been subject to opencast coal mining but this has finished too and the old workings have been landscaped. There are a few factories in operation today and there are shops, pubs and a Methodist church to cater for the residents. **Horsehay Pool**, which powered Darby's ironworks, is now a lovely tree-fringed lake alive with waterbirds. A row of 27 terraced houses borders the pool to the west, originally built by the Coalbrookdale Company to house its Horsehay workers.

HUGHLEY [Shrewsbury and Atcham]

SO5698: 5 miles (8km) SW of Much Wenlock

Hughley is a pleasant farming village isolated in flat green fields below Wenlock Edge, and best known to many people because of Housman's (see Ludlow) reference to "Hughley steeple". In fact, there is no steeple, only a timber-framed belfry. The **church of St John the Baptist** is mostly of the 13th and 14th centuries.

There is a Jacobean pulpit and a magnificent 15th-century chancel screen which Pevsner suggests is the finest in the county. The best of the village houses is the timber-framed **Old Hall** of c1600. Up above Hughley, on Wenlock Edge, is **Major's Leap**, where Major Smallman, a Royalist Civil War soldier, is said to have escaped his parliamentary pursuers by leaping on horseback from the top of the Edge.

IGHTFIELD [North Shropshire]

SJ5938: 4 miles (6km) SE of Whitchurch

A small village in gentle pastoral country, Ightfield is a pleasant place with a reasonable range of facilities, including a shop, a school and the **church of St John the Baptist**. The church was built in the Perpendicular style in the 14th century and restored in 1865 when the chancel was rebuilt. An avenue of trees leads from the church to **Ightfield Hall**: legend has it that they were planted by the devil.

IRONBRIDGE [Wrekin]

SJ6703: 3 miles (5km) S of Telford Centre

The little town of Ironbridge is built of mellow brick, with attractive buildings clinging in tiers to the north side of the Ironbridge Gorge, overlooking the River Severn. Though it has become a major tourist centre it has not lost its charm and retains a tangle of steep, narrow streets and patches of woodland reached by a short walk uphill from the river frontage.

The Severn Gorge has a long industrial history because of the availability of coal, iron ore, limestone and timber and the proximity of the River Severn for transport. The Buildwas monks were smelting iron in charcoal forges as early as 1200 and iron was made at Coalbrookdale from at least 1500. But here, as everywhere else, production was limited by the fact that the smelting of iron was dependent on timber, which first had to be made into charcoal. When, in 1709, Abraham Darby discov-

The iron bridge

ered that coke could be used for smelting (see Coalbrookdale) the Industrial Revolution was born. Suddenly, iron could be cheaply produced in large quantities, and it was Darby's grandson, Abraham III, who constructed the world's first iron bridge. Cast in 1779 and opened in 1781, it still spans the Severn close to Coalbrookdale, at the place we now know as Ironbridge.

The construction of the bridge led to an increasing use of iron in many areas of engineering and the gorge became heavily industrial, only to decline eventually in the face of competition from elsewhere. For a time, however, it was the foremost iron-making area in the world and was celebrated for its innovations: not only the first iron bridge, but also the first iron boat, the first iron rails, the first steam locomotive. Once decline set in, however, it was dramatic, and looking at bustling, prosperous Ironbridge today it's hard to believe that for half the 20th century this was practically a ghost town. It had been decaying and increasingly abandoned since the late

19th century and only in the 1960s did the creation of Telford New Town provide the necessary impulse to tackle the problems of the gorge. In 1968 the Ironbridge Gorge Museum Trust was founded and millions of pounds of grant aid was poured in to revitalise the area. Most of the industrial scars have now healed and the Severn Gorge is green once more, but those industrial relics which do survive have been transformed into a collection of museums which usually prove fascinating even to those who are normally bored by museums. Ironbridge Gorge is now a UNESCO-designated World Heritage Site.

The **Iron Bridge** itself is a graceful structure and remains the focal point of the little town. Its combination of strength and elegance is an appealing one, and its setting is worthy of it. Closed to traffic since 1934, it is open to pedestrians and there is an information centre in the former toll-house on the south side of the river.

Facing the bridge is the imposing **Tontine Hotel** (c1785), and nearby is the former **Market House** (c1790), with five distinctive segmental arched arcades. A steep flight of steps and a tunnel under the graveyard lead up to **St Luke's Church**, built of brick in 1836 to the design of Thomas Smith of Madeley.

Upstream from the bridge is the former Severn Warehouse, an embattled, exuberantly Victorian, brick building which now houses the **Museum of the River**. Ironbridge was a substantial port, with goods carried downriver on the famous Severn trows. In the 1830s there might be up to 150 vessels on the river between Ironbridge and Coalport at any one time. Ironbridge was less industrialised than neighbouring Coalbrookdale or Jackfield; its function was more as a trading centre. Nevertheless, the most famous furnaces in the entire gorge are just downstream of Ironbridge – the Madeley Wood or **Bedlam Furnaces**, built in 1757 and closed in 1832.

As well as sheltering Britain's best-known industrial monument, Ironbridge has also nurtured a few famous names. Billy Wright (born 1924), who captained England 90 times in the 1950s, was born in Wolverhampton but learnt his footballing skills on the streets of Ironbridge as a child. On Church Hill, a Victorian house called The Orchard was once the home of Captain Matthew Webb. He was born in Dawley and became the first man to swim the English Channel.

Dividing Ironbridge from Coalbrookdale is wooded **Lincoln Hill**. A network of paths through the woods was designed by ironmaster Richard Reynolds as "Sabbath Walks" to provide healthy Sunday recreation for his workers. The hill itself was eaten into by a great quarry, which extends so far underground that tours of its limestone caverns were enormously popular with 19th-century day-trippers. Bands played in the illuminated caverns and thousands came on excursion trains from the Black Country and Birmingham.

JACKFIELD [Wrekin]

SJ6802: 1 mile (2km) E of Ironbridge

Just downstream from Ironbridge, Jackfield is not so well known as its neighbour but is a fascinating settlement with a long history. It first came to prominence as a port, from which coal was shipped down the Severn, following the construction of a wooden railway from Broseley in 1605. The village developed around the area where the railway met the river and soon industry, mainly pottery manufacture, moved in. But it was as a port that Jackfield really prospered, and by 1756 there were 100 Severn trows based here, transporting coal and other goods down river. The trows were carried downstream by the current, but were hauled back upstream by gangs of bow-hauliers; rough, tough men for whom Jackfield catered with numerous pubs and brothels. By 1811 there was a horse towpath from Coalbrookdale to Gloucester, enabling horses to take the place of the bow-hauliers, but if Jackfield's economy suffered from their loss it made up for it with increasing industry, as furnaces, forges and engineering works were built by the river. The cannon used against the French at Waterloo were made here at Calcutts Ironworks. In the second half of the 19th century the local economy was boosted by the development of encaustic tile works. The leading producers were Maw and Company and Craven Dunnill, both of which exported their produce all over the world. Today, the Craven Dunnill factory, built in 1871, is home to the **Jackfield Tile Museum**, while **Maws Craft Centre** is housed in the surviving buildings of what was Maws and Company, once the largest encaustic tileworks in the world. It was constructed in 1883 by brothers George and Arthur Maw, whose tiles are now sought after by collectors. The factory closed in 1969 and was partly demolished, but what remains is full of interest in its own right, as well as being the home of around 20 craft workshops.

The former Severn Valley Railway ran through Jackfield and its trackbed is now a footpath. There are many reminders of the railway, including an old level crossing gate said to be the widest in Britain. Jackfield also has a variety of interesting buildings to admire, from terraced cottages to late 17th-century mansions such as **The Calcutts**, and **The Tuckies**, which was the home of ironmaster William Reynolds from 1800 to 1803. The **church of St Mary** stands nearby and was built in 1863 to a design by Sir Arthur Blomfield, using bricks of red, yellow and blue with stone dressings.

KEMBERTON [Bridgnorth]

SJ7204: 2 miles (3km) SW of Shifnal

A small village on a slight hill above the River Worfe, Kemberton enjoys fine views over the surrounding mixed farmland. At the highest point of the village stands the **church of St John the Baptist and St Andrew**, on what is an ancient site. The church itself, however, has been rebuilt six times, most recently in 1882, while the tower was added in 1908. There was once a large colliery nearby but it closed in 1967 and Kemberton is largely a commuter village now.

KEMPTON [South Shropshire]

SO3583: 4 miles (6km) NE of Clun

Kempton is a tiny place of farms and cottages sheltering in the valley of the River Kemp, a tributary of the Clun. It is most notable for **Walcot Park**, which was one of several properties belonging to Robert Clive (1725-74), better known as Clive of India (see Moreton Say).

KENLEY [Shrewsbury and Atcham]

SJ5600: 4 miles (6km) W of Much Wenlock

Spread out along a ridge, the mainly stone-built hamlet of Kenley benefits from fine views. The Norman **church of St John** stands on a circular mound with a number of ancient yew trees. The rector here at the end of the 18th century was **Archibald Alison** (1757-1839), the author of *Essays on the Nature and Principles of Taste* (1790) and a good friend of Thomas Telford, who was a frequent visitor to Kenley. Alison's son, eventually **Sir Archibald Alison** (1792-1867), was born here and became a respected historian, biographer and lawyer, as well as Sheriff of Lanarkshire.

KETLEY [Wrekin]

SJ6711: 2 miles (3km) E of Wellington

Now very much part of Telford, Ketley is of Anglo-Saxon origin and remained a rural village until 1757 when Abraham Darby, Richard Reynolds and Thomas Goldney built an ironworks by the Ketley Brook. By 1806 it was the second largest ironworks in Shropshire and was internationally known for its innovatory techniques. In 1787 William Reynolds constructed a canal to Oakengates which incorporated the first inclined plane to be used successfully on the British canal system. By the middle of the 19th century, however, Ketley was in decline, though Glynwed still has a large factory there. Ketley today is a motley collection of old and new, with modern developments jostling for position with old brick chapels, landscaped spoil heaps and walls built of glassy-looking slag from the old iron furnaces. The **church of St Mary** was built in 1838. Just to the south-east is **Ketley Bank**, which retains a little more character and is pleasantly leafy in places. **Bank House**, built in 1721, was the home of Richard Hartshorne, who died in 1733. He was a leading coalmaster who supplied coal, coke and iron ore to Abraham Darby.

KINLET [Bridgnorth]

SO7280: 4 miles (6km) NE of Cleobury Mortimer

The present village of Kinlet is a pleasant but unremarkable roadside huddle of buildings in mixed farmland just to the north of

Wyre Forest. The original Kinlet was further north, near to the **church of St John the Baptist**. The church is now in the grounds of **Kinlet Hall**, built of brick by Francis Smith of Warwick in 1727-9 for the then owners of the estate, the Childe family. The surrounding parkland was landscaped at the same time and the Childes decided the village spoiled the view. They had it demolished and at a later date a new village was built to house their estate workers. They were not over-impressed with the church either, but fell short of destroying it, contenting themselves with planting a small wood to partially hide it. Today only the tower protrudes from the trees, and an ivy-clad tunnel provides an entrance to the church, which has a Norman nave with 14th-century transepts and chancel, and an unusual timber clerestory added in the 15th century; all were restored in 1892. The church contains a fine collection of monuments to local landowners such as the Childes, the Blounts and the Baldwins. In the north transept is a most imposing Elizabethan monument to Sir George Blount and his wife. He won the title of Terror of Scotland for his exploits in cross-border battle but he kneels tranquilly enough here, a Bible in his hands. The couple's son and daughter kneel between them.

KINNERLEY [Oswestry]

SJ3320: 6 miles (10km) SE of Oswestry

Kinnerley is an unremarkable village in gentle countryside. The **church of St Mary** perches on top of a mound and is a Georgian rebuilding of 1774 by Thomas Farnolls Pritchard. The tower is 15th-century Perpendicular. A disused chalybeate spring called Lady Ida's Well is to be found a little to the north. The eponymous Lady Ida was a former Countess of Bradford. Just to the south of Kinnerley, at Belan Bank, are the remains of a Norman motte and bailey castle. The adjoining settlement of **Dovaston** has some pretty cottages, a pub and a United Reformed Church built of brick.

KNOCKIN [Oswestry]

SJ3322: 5 miles (8km) SE of Oswestry

A village of some character on the Weir Brook, Knockin has brick and timber-framed houses, a good range of facilities and a wooded mound which is all that remains of a motte and bailey castle which was plundered for its stone, mainly to build the churchyard wall. The castle may have been built by Henry II; certainly it was a royal fortress during his reign. It was later given to the le Strange family but was abandoned at an early date. The **church of St Mary** is a 12th-century foundation. Although it retains its Norman nave and chancel, it was over-zealously restored in 1847. Adjacent **Knockin Heath** is a scattered but attractive community, with a few old cottages, a Methodist church and plentiful areas of woodland. Knockin was formerly in the ownership of the Earl of Bradford, whose estate provided employment for many local people. Nowadays most villagers commute to work in Oswestry and Shrewsbury.

KNOWBURY [South Shropshire]

SO5775: 4 miles (6km) E of Ludlow

A scattered village, unremarkable except for the fortunate position it enjoys on the southern slopes of Titterstone Clee Hill, Knowbury has the benefit of fine views and is surrounded by small, irregular fields, many of them enclosed with unusually dense and obviously very ancient holly hedges. Given its pastoral setting, one would expect Knowbury to be an agricultural village, but it actually developed more as an industrial community. In the late 17th century, iron ore was mined at Knowbury and transported to Bringewood near Ludlow where it was smelted in charcoal furnaces. Later, local furnaces were established and quite an important ironworks developed in the 19th century. Coal mining and limestone quarrying provided other employment for the population and there were also clay pits, a tile works and a brickyard in the 19th and early 20th centuries. With so much industry, squatting flourished and some of the cottages and smallholdings are still owned by descendants of the squatters, many of whom came from the Black Country and South Wales. Small heaps of coal and iron slag are still visible in places beside footpaths and tracks.

Knowbury used to be split between the parishes of Caynham and Bitterley, and it wasn't until 1839 that it acquired its own **church of St Paul**. The parish of Knowbury came into existence the following year when the church was consecrated.

Knowbury House is the home of Major Adrian Coles who founded the British Hedgehog Preservation Society in 1982.

KYNNERSLEY [Wrekin]

SJ6716: 4 miles (6km) NE of Wellington

Kynnersley is a village of mainly brick houses on a slight rise in the Weald Moors, close to Strine Brook. It is surrounded by large, fertile fields, put to both arable and pasture and drained by a complex system of ditches.

Kynnersley suffered a disastrous fire in 1791, after which much of it was rebuilt in brick. Many of the local houses are of a distinctive, dormered style known as Duke of Sutherland cottages. However, it does retain a few timber-framed houses that predate the brick ones, and the **church of St Chad** stands on a raised, probably prehistoric, site. It dates from the 13th century, with 19th-century alterations and a tower added in 1722. Nearby is a raised triangular patch of ground called The Whym, where criminals used to be hanged from a tree, after first being tried in the Court Room in the Manor House. Timber-framed, 16th-century Whym Cottage has an orchard which is said to have served as the burial ground for those so executed.

A mile to the north, Wall Farm lies within the earthen banks of a large **Iron Age camp** where flint arrowheads, a Celtic bead, Roman coins and other artefacts have been found. This is one of the largest surviving lowland camps in the country, most others having been ploughed out. It is believed by some authorities to have been used as a transit camp for stock during seasonal movements from the western hills to the lowland pastures, though there is also ample evidence of its defensive function. Wall Farm itself is said to be haunted. Since 1994 part of the farm site has been managed for its conservation value under the Countryside Stewardship scheme.

LANGLEY [Shrewsbury and Atcham]

SJ5300: 5 miles (8km) W of Much Wenlock

A remote hamlet below Acton Burnell Hill, Langley is notable only for **Langley Chapel**, which was built in 1564, a time at which very few new churches were erected. A small, simple and enormously atmospheric building with a weatherboarded belfry, it is now in the care of English Heritage. The interior layout and furnishings are pure 17th century, having survived entirely unspoilt. The chapel served Langley Hall, whose impressive gatehouse still stands nearby, and other fragments of which are incorporated into a later farmhouse. Hummocky ground next to the farm indicates the site of long-gone medieval buildings. It was the demise of the hall and the dwindling of the local population that preserved Langley Chapel, for it would not otherwise have escaped the attentions of the 19th-century restorers.

LAWLEY [Wrekin]

SJ6608: 2 miles (3km) W of Telford Centre

An industrial village on the edge of the Telford conurbation, Lawley is surrounded by the detritus of opencast mining. Quite recently one of the huge pits swallowed up the already scanty remains of New Dale, a model village built in 1759 by the Darbys of Coalbrookdale for their Lawley workforce. It contained the earliest examples of back-to-back housing in the country and (despite the bad reputation of back-to-backs) represented a great improvement over previous housing standards for industrial workers. Much of it was demolished in the 1960s and in 1987 the opencast mine finished the job, but not before an archaeological dig had been mounted. There is now little of interest in the village. The **church of St John** was built in 1865 by John Ladds in red and yellow brick.

LEA [South Shropshire]

SO3589: 2 miles (3km) E of Bishop's Castle

The tiny hamlet of Lea is just a cluster of farms around a road junction in the shadow of the Long Mynd, but it is notable for **Lea Castle**, a ruined tower house which dates from the 13th or 14th century, though a modern farmhouse now adjoins it. A fairly insignificant ruin, it does retain some interesting details, such as a portcullis groove above a doorway. In 1645 the tower was besieged and taken by parliamentary forces.

LEA CROSS [Shrewsbury and Atcham]

SJ4208: 6 miles (10km) SW of Shrewsbury

A tiny hamlet close to the Rea Brook, Lea Cross has a few houses, a pub, a shop and the unconsecrated **church of St Anne**, built in 1888 as an act of defiance by the Reverend Hawkes after a quarrel with the vicar at Pontesbury. Nearby **Cruckton** would be another insignificant hamlet were it not for the annual Ploughing Match to which competitors come from all over the country.

LEATON [Shrewsbury and Atcham]

SJ4618: 5 miles (8km) N of Shrewsbury

A scattered hamlet close to the Severn, incorporating Leaton Heath and Leaton Knolls, Leaton has a pleasant situation but

little of interest apart from the **church of Holy Trinity**, designed by S. Pountney Smith in 1859 and provided with a facade described by Pevsner as "crazy". The tower and north aisle were not added until 1872.

LEEBOTWOOD [Shrewsbury and Atcham]

SO4798: 3 miles (5km) NE of Church Stretton

Leebotwood is a widely spread village enjoying a prime situation north of the Long Mynd and west of the Lawley. Much of the village clusters around the main road but the **church of St Mary** is away to the west in a rather isolated but commanding position. A 13th-century building with a Georgian tower, it occupies a circular churchyard with a bank round it – an indication of pre-Christian significance. There are some fine Jacobean box pews inside, probably made by the same local craftsman who provided the 17th-century **Pound Inn** with splendid panelling in the dining room. The inn was built in 1650 and was a popular overnight halt with cattle drovers using the important drove road which came from Montgomery through Bishop's Castle and Plowden to the Long Mynd and the Port Way then north to Shrewsbury via Leebotwood.

LEE BROCKHURST [North Shropshire]

SJ5426: 3 miles (5km) SE of Wem

Lee Brockhurst is an attractive village sheltering at the foot of the wooded sandstone slopes of **Lee Hill**, which is partly owned by the National Trust. The village lies by the main Shrewsbury to Whitchurch road, near a bridge over the River Roden built in 1800 by Thomas Telford. Some of Lee Brockhurst's houses date from the 15th and 16th centuries, while **St Peter's Church** is 12th century with some later work, including Victorian alterations and additions, such as the bellcote. Across the road from the church is a low mound upon which a barn has been erected. The mound is the site of an early castle but nothing further is known about it, although it is known that Roger de Montgomery owned Lee Brockhurst after the Conquest.

LEEGOMERY [Wrekin]

SJ6612: 1 mile (2km) NE of Wellington

A Saxon settlement originally, built in a forest clearing, Leegomery is now a modern suburb of Telford. Housing estates, shops, schools, community centres and other facilities have the benefit of plentiful green space and a fair number of trees. Immediately to the west of Leegomery is the huge Telford Hospital, its rather grim aspect earning it the name of "the prison" locally. To the north of the hospital, **Apley Park** is public open space which includes delightful woodland and once formed the grounds of Apley Castle, which originated as a fortified manor house built by Alan de Charlton in the 14th century. It was replaced in the 17th century but this later building was dismantled after a successful siege by the parliamentarians in the Civil War. In the 18th century another house was built on the site but this was demolished in 1956. The estate was owned for centuries by the Charltons, whose wealth was based on coal mines at Wombridge, an iron forge at Wytheford, a brick works at Wellington, ironstone mines at Wrockwardine Wood and a salt works at Preston-on-the-Weald-Moors, as well as agricultural estates and forestry.

LEIGHTON [Shrewsbury and Atcham]

SJ6105: 4 miles (6km) N of Much Wenlock

A leafy village of 18th- and 19th-century cottages, Leighton stands on a slope above the Severn, with excellent views of the river valley. It was once an industrial centre in a small way, with some coal mining and an iron furnace that was operative from the 16th century. During the Civil War some of the cannon balls and musket shot used by the Royalists were made at Leighton.

The **church of St Mary** was largely rebuilt in brick in 1714 but inside there is a 13th-century effigy of a cross-legged knight holding a shield and sword, his feet on a lion. It was apparently brought from Buildwas Abbey. Adjacent to the church is **Leighton Hall**, built in 1778, and in the grounds is Leighton Lodge, where the writer **Mary Webb** (1881-1927) lived as a small child. She was born Mary Gladys Meredith and married Henry Webb in 1912. Her first novel was published in 1916 and she went on to write several more. Her most famous works are *Precious Bane*, *Gone to Earth* and *The Golden Arrow*, which are imbued with a rich and atmospheric sense of the local landscape. Sadly, fame was not forthcoming in her lifetime; it was only after her death that public acclaim was granted to her. It was sparked by posthumous praise from the Prime Minister, Stanley Baldwin, who, like his contemporary A.E. Housman (see Ludlow), was a Worcestershire man brought up within sight of the Clee Hills. For a few years Mary's books were fashionable but they are not popular today, and are all too easy to make fun of (Stella Gibbons's classic *Cold Comfort Farm* was actually a parody of Mary's novel *The House in Dormer Forest*). Yet few writers have been so much in tune with their surroundings and anybody who loves Shropshire is likely to value her work.

LIGHTMOOR [Wrekin]

SJ6705: 2 miles (3km) N of Ironbridge

Lightmoor is an intriguing settlement, or collection of settlements, in a hilly landscape which still looks attractive even when it becomes apparent that the hills are actually spoil heaps made green again by natural regeneration. There are housing estates, old and new, and various industrial premises, both operative and abandoned. Much of the area was originally squatted, and although many of the squatters' cottages have been bulldozed into oblivion others are still standing, though it's unlikely their original owners would easily recognise them now. The Coalbrookdale Company had several works and furnaces at Lightmoor but brick making is the main industry today.

LILLESHALL [Wrekin]
SJ7215: 3 miles (5km) SW of Newport

The village of Lilleshall has developed close to Lilleshall Hill, an unexpected rocky lump in an otherwise flat, agricultural landscape. The obelisk on top is a Victorian monument to George Granville Leveson-Gower, the first Duke of Sutherland, who was responsible for draining the Weald Moors and building the distinctive cottages which still feature throughout the area.

There is believed to have been a Saxon church at Lilleshall as early as 670 but the present **church of St Michael** is a Norman building of red sandstone with a 13th-century chancel and Perpendicular tower.

There was considerable industry at Lilleshall in the past, for it lies on the northern edge of the Shropshire coalfield. An iron-smelting furnace was already in operation by 1562, one of the earliest in the county. An area of woods and ponds on the northern extremity of the village is a former industrial area of limestone quarries and limekilns. Shropshire's very first canal was built for Earl Gower (father of the Duke of Sutherland) in 1765-68 to transport coal from Donnington Wood to a roadside wharf at Pave Lane, near Newport, and its course can still be traced in places, just to the east of Lilleshall. An inclined plane linking the canal with another that ran to Lilleshall's limestone quarries was built in 1796 at the site now known as Hugh's Bridge. The stable that housed the horses used on the incline still stands, and the incline itself is easily recognisable.

About a mile south-east of the village are the impressive ruins of **Lilleshall Abbey**, an Augustinian house founded c1148. It developed into one of the finest abbeys in the country and owned extensive estates. After the Dissolution the Abbey came into the possession of the Leveson family but it was badly damaged in the Civil War and much of the remaining masonry was subsequently plundered for building stone. What remains is in the care of English Heritage and is very impressive. As at Buildwas Abbey, the most substantial remains are those of the church. The chancel is almost entirely Norman and there is some splendid Early English work. The Norman west front is magnificent and the whole site is enhanced by the ancient yew trees which surround it.

Abbey Wood stretches north-east from the Abbey to Tudor-style **Lilleshall Hall**, now famous as the National Sports Centre. It was built in 1829 by Sir Jeffry Wyatville for the Duke of Sutherland, and is approached along tree-lined Duke's Drive. It is still basically a beautiful house but the changes made to it recently will not be to everyone's taste.

LINLEY [Bridgnorth]
SO6898: 4 miles (6km) NW of Bridgnorth

Linley is a scattered community, encompassing the hamlets of Linley Brook and Linleygreen, while the former Linley Station is some distance away at Apley Forge (see Apley). Linley itself is based around **Linley Hall**, which stands on a slope above the Linley Brook in attractive mixed farming country. The hall, an Elizabethan stone building with a facade of Georgian brick, is now divided into flats. **St Leonard's Church** stands aloof, a small Norman building consecrated in 1139 and not much altered, although Sir Arthur Blomfield's restoration of 1858 was not so sensitive as it might have been. Some of the Norman features are unusual, such as the twin arches decorating the bell-openings on the tower. Above a blocked north doorway is a tympanum with a primitive carving of a Green Man, a pagan fertility figure.

LINLEY [South Shropshire]

SO3492: 3 miles (5km) NE of Bishop's Castle

Linley consists of little more than **Linley Hall**, a farm and a few houses. The setting of Linley Hall is an enviable one, below the slopes of Heath Mynd and The Knolls, with Linley Hill and Norbury Hill just to the north-east. This Palladian mansion was designed in 1742 by London architect Henry Joynes, and was the first of its type to be built in Shropshire. Erected on the site of an earlier house, it remains, outwardly at least, very little altered since the 18th century. Until a few years ago it belonged to a family who came over with the Conqueror and were rewarded with the manor of More, from which they took their name. One 18th-century member of the family, Robert More, was a great traveller and botanist who brought home exotic tree species. He is credited with having planted England's first larch trees in 1783 in the grounds of the hall, where they still stand today. There is

also a magnificent beech avenue high on Linley Hill, planted in either the late 18th or early 19th century, a time when grandiose landscaping schemes were fashionable.

The Mores may be one of Shropshire's oldest families, but they were not the first people to live at Linley. The site of what appears to have been a Romano-British village has been discovered by the River West Onny and the Romans are known to have mined lead in the hills behind Linley Hall. Traces of a furnace where lead was processed have been found, together with remains of an aqueduct. Ingots stamped with the name of the Emperor Hadrian (117-138) have also been discovered.

LITTLE STRETTON [South Shropshire]

SO4491: 1 mile (2km) S of Church Stretton

Little Stretton is a largely timber-framed village in a wonderful setting below the Long Mynd. A number of footpaths lead directly to the hill, and there is a small brook with a ford and a stone bridge. The timber-framed, thatched **church of All Saints**

All Saints' Church, Little Stretton

is modern, built in 1903, but the other buildings are much older, including the picturesque **Manor House** of around 1600.

LITTLE WENLOCK [Wrekin]

SJ6406: 3 miles (5km) NW of Ironbridge

Little Wenlock is a rather remote village on a hill below the Wrekin. It seems to have been a daughter settlement of Much Wenlock, established by the abbey. For most of its existence it has been dependent on opencast mining for its livelihood. Coal has been mined here since at least the beginning of the 16th century and was transported to iron foundries in Shirlett Forest. At the beginning of the 18th century Abraham Darby I laid a wooden tramway to transport coal down to his works at Coalbrookdale. This was succeeded, probably in 1767, by an iron tramway known as the ginny rail, which is believed to have been the first to be built with cast-iron rails. Mining no longer plays a significant part in the village economy, but some people still dig up coal in their gardens. A plant for washing opencast coal for use in industry has been installed at Coalmoor just outside the village.

The **church of St Lawrence** stands on a mound in the village centre and is partly 12th century. The tower was built in 1667 and in 1865 a brick nave and chancel were added and the tower enlarged. There are few other buildings of interest, except perhaps the partly Elizabethan **Old Hall**.

LLANFAIR WATERDINE [South Shropshire]

SO2476: 5 miles (8km) NW of Knighton

A small cluster of buildings squeezed between the road and the River Teme, Llanfair is only just in England. Steep hills crowd it on all sides and it should be no surprise to learn that Lord Hunt, leader of the first successful Everest expedition, lived near here for many years. When he was cre-

ated a peer in 1966 he chose to become Baron Hunt of Llanfair Waterdine.

The name of the village is partly Welsh and partly Old English and translates as "the church of St Mary in the river valley". The river is spanned by an attractive stone bridge and there is a surprising range of facilities for such a small village, including the **church of St Mary**, rebuilt in 1854 to a design of T. Nicholson, replacing a much older and far more appealing church. A little of the old woodwork is preserved inside, including some fine carvings on the altar rail.

LLANYBLODWEL [Oswestry]

SJ2422: 5 miles (8km) SW of Oswestry

A small village, Llanyblodwel lies by the River Tanat (a tributary of the Vyrnwy) in bosky country close to the border. Until 1573 it belonged to Wales and until the 1880s church services were performed in Welsh. The **church of St Michael** was found to be in a dangerous state by the Reverend John Parker when he took over the living in 1845. He offered to superintend its repair but ended up having the entire church more or less rebuilt to his own design. Perhaps it is fortunate that he was a vicar and not an architect: Shropshire could not happily accommodate too many such churches. Pevsner describes it as "absurd" and it is certainly different, with a bullet-shaped tower and spire, but many people find it charming. It is the interior which is most exuberantly eccentric, with a colourful jumble of patterns and texts covering almost every surface. It must be difficult to concentrate on a sermon with so many distractions screaming for attention. The woodwork is equally elaborate. The church is only one of several buildings of interest in this remote village, which has an unusual former school, built of stone and now converted into a private house. It, too, was designed by John Parker, as was the vicarage. A three-arched sandstone bridge of 1710 spans the river, completing an attractive picture formed by a group of timber-framed buildings, including the **Horseshoe Inn** of 1445.

LLANYMYNECH [Oswestry]

SJ2620: 6 miles (10km) S of Oswestry

Llanymynech is a fairly large village bisected by the national boundary and occupying a narrow neck of land between the Montgomery Canal and the River Vyrnwy. Above it to the north towers much-quarried Llanymynech Hill, along which run both the national boundary and Offa's Dyke. The hill has been quarried and mined since prehistoric times and is riddled with shafts and tunnels. The Romans worked lead, copper, zinc and limestone here, turning the latter into mortar for use in the building of Viroconium (see Wroxeter). In the 17th and 18th centuries limestone was the main product of the hill, some of it for use in iron smelting, some for agricultural purposes and some for mortar. Demand was high and large amounts were transported on the canal, a branch of the Shropshire Union. Some limestone is still quarried on the west side of the hill today, at Blodwel Quarry, but the steeper slopes overlooking Llanymynech, and the top of the hill, are now used for different purposes. There is a golf course and also an important **nature reserve** rich in limestone-loving wild flowers and jointly managed by the Shropshire and Montgomeryshire Wildlife Trusts. The old limestone workings are also accessible and full of interest. The main features include a ruined engine house, a restored winding drum (used to control the descent of the wagons) at the head of an incline, some traditional limekilns and the revolutionary Hoffman kiln, renowned as the most efficient of all time. Unfortunately, it was not built until about 1880, when Shropshire's second Iron Age was already almost at an end. The kiln closed in 1914 and was restored in 1995.

The village of Llanymynech is a rather grey place, with little of particular interest, though the Victorian buildings dominating the High Street are an eloquent reminder of the prosperity brought by the limestone. The **church of St Agatha** was built in 1845 to a neo-Norman design by Thomas Penson and is another of those described by Pevsner as "crazy".

LLYNCLYS [Oswestry]

SJ2824: 4 miles (6km) S of Oswestry

Little more than a hamlet based around a crossroads and a dismantled railway line, Llynclys has a handful of houses and a pub. The railway was a mineral line that linked the local quarries with Oswestry. Just to the south-west of the hamlet is Llynclys Hill, the northern extension of Llanymynech Hill. The limestone here is of poorer quality than at Llanymynech, which might explain why Llynclys Hill was named on an 18th-century tithe map as Scabby Rock Hill. Much of it is common land and there is a scattering of cottages built originally by squatters, most of whom would have been miners or quarrymen. There is a nature reserve, **Llynclys Common**, managed by Shropshire Wildlife Trust, where a rich limestone flora (including eight species of orchid) is under pressure from invading scrub. Human volunteers labour to keep it clear, helped by the grazing of sheep and ponies. Just to the north of the village is the lake ("llyn" in Welsh) from which it takes its name. Known as Llynclys Pool, it has attracted a variety of legends, including one that tells of a drowned city beneath its waters.

LONGDEN [Shrewsbury and Atcham]

SJ4406: 4 miles (6km) SW of Shrewsbury

A substantial but unremarkable village, Longden has modern housing, a post office, a pub, a Primitive Methodist Chapel of 1870 and the **church of St Ruthin**, which is mainly of the 19th century, though it also incorporates some 17th-century work.

There are several farms round the village, but there used to be mining in the area too, with a colliery at Moat House, about a mile to the north.

LONGDON ON TERN [Wrekin]

SJ6115: 3 miles (5km) NW of Wellington

A scattering of mostly unremarkable houses and farms alongside the road, Longdon is superficially of little interest. However, just to the north of the road, marooned in fields, is a cast-iron **aqueduct**, designed in 1794 by Thomas Telford (though it was begun by Josiah Clowes) to carry the now abandoned Shrewsbury Canal over the River Tern. It is often claimed to be the first ever aqueduct to be made of cast iron, though this is disputed. There was a wharf by the canal at Longdon; it has gone now but was situated close to the **church of St Bartholomew**, a 1742 brick rebuilding of an earlier church. Further rebuilding took place in the 19th century. Next to the church the remains of **Longdon Hall**, a Tudor mansion, have been incorporated into a farmhouse.

LONGFORD [Wrekin]

SJ7218: 1 mile (2km) W of Newport

Longford Road heads west out of Newport towards Longford Moors, part of the extensive Weald Moors drained for the Duke of Sutherland. Longford itself lies strung out along the road to the south of the Strine Brook and consists of little more than two ruined churches and **Longford Hall**, together with its associated buildings. The hall itself lies hidden in wooded parkland and was built for the Leeke family in 1794-7 by J. Bonomi. An imposing house with seven bays, giant pilasters and Tuscan columns, it currently serves as boarding accommodation for Adams' Grammar School, which is based in Newport. Next to the road are the former stables and coach-house built around a courtyard and nearby is the redundant **church of St Mary**, built between 1802 and 1806 of red sandstone. It was erected alongside its tiny 13th-century predecessor, of which very little remains, though enough to serve as a Talbot mortuary chapel, with a striking monument to Thomas Talbot (died 1686). Further west is **Longford Farm Mill**. This curious building has the brick tower mill encircled by a range of arches, built for some unknown purpose. The mill ceased operation in the 1930s.

LONGNOR [Shrewsbury and Atcham]

SJ4800: 6 miles (10km) S of Shrewsbury

Just to the north of the Stretton Hills, the village of Longnor enjoys good views and a pleasant setting on the edge of **Longnor Park**. A mixture of old and new, it has some black and white houses, the most notable of which is **Moat House**, still with some water in the moat and probably dating from the 14th century. The **church** is a small and unspoilt example of Early English style, with 18th-century furnishings inside and the unusual feature of an external stone stairway leading to the interior gallery. It was built c1260 as a private chapel for a fortified manor house and stands next to an area of hummocky ground which may mark the site of the original village. This was moved by the Corbett family as it interfered with their vision for Longnor Park, which was landscaped to complement **Longnor Hall**, built for Sir Richard Corbett in 1670. The deer park contains some fine trees, including two famous ones known as the **Black Poplars of Longnor**. A native but uncommon tree, the black poplar is rarely seen in Shropshire, but these two are among the largest in Britain.

LOPPINGTON [North Shropshire]

SJ4729: 2 miles (3km) W of Wem

A compact village in gentle country near the River Roden, Loppington is a pleasant place with an unpleasant reminder of a bar-

barous pastime: in front of the Dickin Arms is the only known **bullring** in Shropshire still on its original site. The so-called "sport" of bull baiting was practised here until around 1835. Bear baiting took place too; in 1825 it was part of the festivities following the marriage of the vicar's daughter.

The **church of St Michael** is mainly 14th century, though traces of an earlier building were discovered during restoration in 1870. It was garrisoned by Parliament in the Civil War and damaged by fire when captured by the Royalists. Parts were subsequently rebuilt in 1656-8. Nearby **Loppington Hall** is an 18th-century house of red brick with a Tuscan doorway. It was the home of the Dickin family who gave their name to the pub. The village pond is a former tan-pit, where hides were treated before being finished for sale.

LOUGHTON [South Shropshire]

SO6183: 6 miles (10km) NW of Cleobury Mortimer

A tiny hamlet by a crossroads in remote country below the Clee Hills, Loughton is set on a small hill with attractive views over the surrounding farmland. It comprises a handful of houses and farms and a tiny **church** on a pre-Christian site. The church dates largely from 1622, though it replaced a much older one, of which some 12th-century masonry survives. In the churchyard is the large, hollow **Loughton Yew**, one of the oldest in the county. Carbon dating by Cambridge University in 1986 suggested an age in excess of 1000 years. Hollow it may be, but it looks healthy enough to last another 1000 years or so. This was the first tree in the world to be carbon dated.

LUDLOW [South Shropshire]

SO5074: 8 miles (12km) SE of Craven Arms

There is nowhere quite like Ludlow and superlatives are soon exhausted in any attempt to describe it. Though only a small town, it is crammed with a total of 469 listed buildings, so it should be obvious that only the barest outline can be given here. Beautifully situated, its medieval street pattern survives almost intact, but its history goes back much further than that. There are Bronze Age sites nearby and it may be that the parish church stands on the site of a prehistoric burial mound – the Ludan Hlaw (Luda's Grave) from which the name Ludlow derives. Others, however, consider it to be a Saxon burial mound and it is likely that there was a Saxon settlement on the site of present-day Ludlow, which may well have originated as a crossing place of the River Teme.

But the town's history really began about 20 years after the Norman Conquest when Roger de Lacy built **Ludlow Castle** on a fine defensive site high above the confluence of Teme and Corve. A planned town was laid out in a grid pattern outside the castle gates and was soon a thriving centre. The castle was later greatly extended and town walls were begun in 1233, enclosing the castle within their circuit, and making Ludlow one of just over 100 towns in England and Wales to be fortified with a full circuit of walls.

Life must have been uncertain, given the ever-present threat of Welsh raids and the continual power struggles of the Mortimers and their fellow Marcher lords. Certainly, the story of Ludlow in its early years is a colourful catalogue of war, rebellion, intrigue, betrayal, daring deeds and romantic legends, far too full and complex to be recounted here. Stirring times notwithstanding, the business of trade was more important, and Ludlow grew rich trading in wool and cloth before gaining additional administrative and political importance during the Wars of the Roses, involvement in which was inevitable after the Earldom of March passed to the Duke of York's son, Edward. The Lancastrian Henry VI took Ludlow in 1459 but in 1461 Edward, based at the Mortimers' former stronghold of

Ludlow Castle

Wigmore, marched to victory at Mortimer's Cross and then took the throne as Edward IV. Ludlow Castle now became Crown property and in 1472 it became the seat of the Council in the Marches of Wales, which was charged with the administration of this turbulent area. For 200 years Ludlow was the capital not only of the Marches but virtually of Wales too. Edward IV's two sons were sent to live at Ludlow Castle, but on his death in 1483 they were taken to London and murdered, achieving posthumous fame as the "Princes in the Tower".

Other Royal children were also brought up at Ludlow. Henry VII sent his sons Arthur and Henry to the castle, but Arthur died there in 1502, of natural causes, soon after his marriage by proxy to Catherine of Aragon. The Prince's body was taken to Worcester Cathedral for burial but his heart was interred in Ludlow Church. Catherine was later married to his brother, the future Henry VIII, an event that would subsequently provide Henry with the opportunity to break with Rome and establish the Church of England. Henry's daughter Mary lived at Ludlow for a time too.

Ludlow Castle was the last in Shropshire to hold out for Charles I in the Civil War, not surrendering until June 1646 when the parliamentarian cannons on Whitcliffe Common finally battered it into submission. The king's nephew, Prince Rupert, was its commander for a time, and much later, during the reign of Charles II, he returned to become Lord President of the Council in the Marches. There was, however, no longer much need for the Council so it was abolished in 1689 and Ludlow Castle left to decay. It was acquired by the Earl of Powis in 1811, and essential repairs were made.

Today, still owned by the Powis family, it's open to the public and is one of the country's more substantial ruined castles. Numerous 12th-century and 14th-century walls and towers survive and it is dominated by the early 12th-century gatehouse-keep, a relatively rare type. The magnificent view from the top of the keep fully illustrates why this commanding site was chosen by Roger de Lacy for his castle. There is also a range of Elizabethan buildings erected in 1581 for Sir Henry Sidney, President of the Council in the Marches. Perhaps the most unusual feature of Ludlow Castle, however, is the chapel of c1140, which possesses a very rare circular nave.

Naturally, such a romantic castle has a similarly romantic ghost, that of Marion de la Bruere, a 12th-century lady whose lover used to visit her secretly by night. On what proved to be his last visit he was accompanied by armed men who took control of the castle. Deeply shamed, Marion stabbed him to death with his own sword and then threw herself from the battlements.

Even after the Council in the Marches was abolished the town continued to prosper and became a fashionable social centre for wealthy county families in the 18th and 19th centuries. Glove making was now the main industry, reaching a peak in 1814, when 660,000 gloves were produced. Today, Ludlow still thrives as energetically as ever, mainly through light industry, administration and tourism, and as a market centre for a large part of southern Shropshire and northern Herefordshire. It is renowned for the superb festival it stages for a fortnight every summer, the highlight of which is the twice-daily performance of a Shakespeare play in the ruined castle. This recalls the fact that it was at Ludlow Castle in 1634 that John Milton's celebrated masque *Comus* was given its first performance. Ludlow Festival is run by volunteers, but ticket sales are apparently high enough to make it the third most popular festival of its type in the country.

When Ludlow is viewed from a distance, church and castle dominate the skyline together and it's easy to see that **St Laurence's Church** is the most majestic in Shropshire, with very nearly the stature of a small cathedral. Despite this, the church is scarcely visible from the town centre, so hemmed in is it by buildings. The original

Norman church was first rebuilt in 1199 and the unusual hexagonal porch (one of only two in the country) was added a few years later, along with a chancel. Further alterations and additions followed in the 14th century but most of what exists today is 15th-century Perpendicular in style and built with profits from the wool trade. The huge tower, magnificently arrogant in its lack of proportion to the rest of the church, is the most obvious manifestation of the Perpendicular and has a wealth of turrets, finials, buttresses and battlements. Inside, the soaring arches give an initial impression of severity but closer inspection reveals a complexity of detail such that the church requires a book to itself. Briefly, however, it is most notable for its richly carved screens, its stained glass and the collection of 32 superbly carved 15th-century misericords in the chancel. There are many fine monuments and furnishings inside, and a memorial stone to **A.E. Housman** is to be found on the exterior wall near the north door. Housman (1859-1936) was a distinguished classical scholar, a Professor of Latin and a Fellow of Trinity College, Cambridge. More importantly, he was a poet, best known for his slim but evocative volume known as *A Shropshire Lad* (1896). Housman was himself a Worcestershire lad but it was the Clee Hills which dominated the western horizon from his childhood home near Bromsgrove and he formed a romantic attachment to the neighbouring county which resulted in the timeless verse which will forever identify him with Shropshire.

Overlooking the churchyard is the **Reader's House**, a stone and timber-framed building of considerable charm, parts of it dating from the 13th century. The "reader" was an 18th-century term for the rector's chief assistant and this was his home. On the other side of the churchyard are **Hosyer's Almshouses**, founded sometime between 1462 and 1482 by John Hosyer, a wealthy draper, and rebuilt in 1758 by the Shrewsbury architect Thomas Farnolls Pritchard, who worked on several projects in Ludlow. Beyond the almshouses is the former **Cottage Hospital**, originally a college built in 1393-4 by the Palmers' Guild to accommodate its chaplains. The Guild, a religious organisation founded in the 13th century, was a dominant institution in late-medieval Ludlow and owned considerable property. It was dissolved in 1551, when its property and many of its functions were taken over by the town corporation.

Nearly all Ludlow's older buildings are beautiful, but the most flamboyant in town is the magnificent **Feathers Hotel** on Corve Street, once the home of Rees Jones from Pembrokeshire who served as an attorney at the Council in the Marches. Built c1603, it was enlarged and refronted by Rees Jones in 1619 and became an inn in 1670. It is just conceivable that there may be finer timber-framed buildings in England, but it is hard to imagine anything more captivating. The oldest pub in town, however, is not the Feathers but the **Bull Hotel**, just across the road. It was an important coaching inn but its history goes back much further. This is true of so many of Ludlow's buildings, the majority of which appear to be Georgian but are often much older, their timbers concealed behind an elegant brick or stucco facade added in the prosperous 18th century.

This is not true of the **Butter Cross**, however, where what you see is exactly what was built in 1742-4, when it was intended to function as the town hall, though it has also been a school and a museum. A stone building, with Tuscan columns, pediment, semicircular window, parapet, clock turret and cupola, it has enormous character, not at all diminished by the fact that the open ground floor is occupied by stalls on market days. It stands almost in the centre of town, at the top of **Broad Street**, which is described by Pevsner as "one of the most memorable streets in England". It is a majestic street, spoilt only by the inexplicable provision of car parking. The 13th-century **Broad Gate** itself, one of seven which once guarded the town walls, still stands, with the addition of an attractive castellated house built over it in the 18th century. Beyond the gate, Lower Broad Street leads down to the river, with more fine houses and the **Wheatsheaf Inn**, built in 1668 and distinguished by a Gothic window with an ogee heading.

Ludlow's longest streets are Corve Street and Old Street, which meet at the Bull Ring. The area to the west used to be part of an enormous market place, much of which has long since been built on. The timber-framed island building which stands in the Bull Ring is the **Tolsey**, which housed the quaintly named Court of Pie Powder, where any disputes arising at the market could be settled immediately. The curious name comes from the French *pied poidre*, meaning "dusty feet", implying you go straight to the court for judgement, feet still dusty from the market square.

We have already seen how the top end of Corve Street is dominated by the timber-framed Feathers Hotel. After that, however, Georgian brick has the upper hand until the lower end of the street is reached and timber-framing takes over again. There are some stone buildings too, such as **Foxe's Almshouses**, built in 1593 but heavily restored. Near the bottom of the street the River Corve is spanned by 18th-century Corve Bridge. Just a little to the north-east, but out of the town centre, stands the Roman Catholic **church of St Peter**, built on Henley Road in 1936 in a Byzantine/Romanesque style by Rivolucri, its most striking feature a huge dome.

Returning to the town centre again, Castle Square is a natural focal point that really comes alive on market days. The castle is at the west end of the square and there are fine buildings on every side, one of the best of which is **Castle Lodge**, its 14th-century ground floor of stone overhung by

16th-century timberwork. The house has a long, interesting and well-documented history but had a narrow escape in the 1990s when it came onto the market as a potential office block. Fortunately, it was bought by a Mr and Mrs Pearson who were determined to preserve it and they have embarked on a programme of sensitive repair and restoration, with the necessary funds being raised by opening the house to the public and to film crews for use in period dramas.

Next to Castle Lodge is the top of Mill Street, another important survivor of the Norman grid. The building just round the corner is the **Assembly Rooms**, built in 1840, which now houses an arts centre. The adjacent tourist information centre shares premises with **Ludlow Museum**, where the displays focus on the history of the town and the internationally important geological discoveries made in the area. Mill Street contains many fine examples of Georgian facades, including the **Guildhall**, built in the 15th century but refronted by Pritchard in 1776.

At the south-west corner of Castle Square is a street called Dinham, which leads down to Dinham Bridge (1823) spanning the Teme. The most imposing building on Dinham is undoubtedly **Dinham House**, a plain brick mansion of nine bays, with a long list of illustrious past residents, including Lucien Bonaparte, brother of Napoleon, who lived here in 1810. The oldest building on Dinham is the former **Chapel of St Thomas of Canterbury**, which is partly 12th century.

While Ludlow's more obvious attractions are easily found, there are endless lesser treasures to discover, hidden in little streets and courts such as Harp Lane, Pepper Lane, Raven Lane, Brand Lane, Fish Lane and Quality Square. In fact, every street in the town centre is worth exploration.

On the other side of the River Teme, linked to Ludlow by Ludford Bridge and Dinham Bridge, is **Whitcliffe Common**, an area of woodland and grassland which offers magnificent views of Ludlow against the backdrop of the Clee Hills. A charter of 1241 granted all second generation Ludlovians the right to graze two cows or horses or six sheep on the common and to let their pigs forage on it at acorn time. Few bother to exercise such rights today, but Whitcliffe is an immensely popular place for Ludlovians to walk their dogs and admire the stunning views of their incomparable town. The views were much improved in 1999 after a Commons Enhancement grant provided funds for a much-needed thinning of Whitcliffe's trees, using shire horses to remove the felled timber. In the winter there is an added attraction as Whitcliffe is the only place in the county which is graced by a flock of hawfinches almost every year. Hornbeam mast is the favourite food of this elusive bird and Whitcliffe's numerous "beeches" (as most people assume them to be) are actually hornbeams, generally an uncommon species so far north. Interest of a different sort is provided by the ditches, which reveal where Cromwell's men dug artillery trenches as they prepared to besiege the castle in the 1640s.

Ludford is a tiny, picturesque hamlet which was formerly in Herefordshire and is missed by most visitors to Ludlow, though it is only just the other side of 15th-century Ludford Bridge. The small cluster of buildings includes the **church of St Giles**, which has a Norman nave and chancel of c1300, and stands close to almshouses, **St Giles's Hospital**, founded in 1216. **The Old Bell** is a timber-framed house of 1614, which was once a pub, and **Ludford House** is an impressive building which is either late Elizabethan or early Jacobean. Stone and timber **Ludford Mill** sits by the riverbank, facing **Teme Mill** on the other side. At **Ludford Corner** a plaque on a cliff records the work of Roderick Murchison, the great geologist who, partly thanks to the amazing variety of rocks in Shropshire, established the order of rocks in his Silurian system, pub-

Top: modern architecture in Telford contrasts with The Feathers in Ludlow.
Below: the town of Ironbridge is named after its most famous structure.

Telford
Centre

Traditional
shop in
Whitchurch

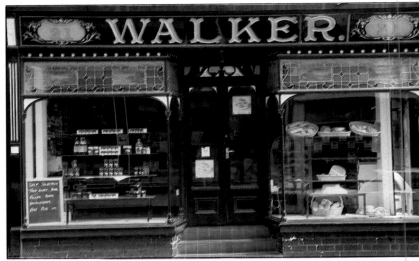

The Cliff
Railway at
Bridgnorth

Viroconium
Roman town,
Wroxeter

Shrewsbury
Castle

Ludlow from
Whitchurch

Cottage at
Ashford
Bowdler

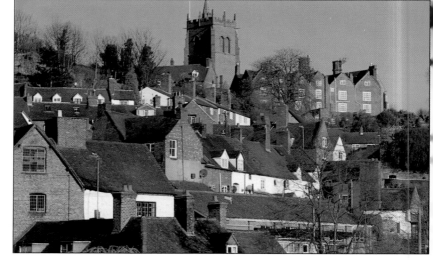

Bridgnorth

Hen Dinas,
Oswestry

lished as a book of that name in 1839. This put such Shropshire names as Ludlow and Wenlock prominently on the geological map. The "Ludlow Bone Bed" was found in 1990 in the rocks above the plaque and revealed fossils of the first land animals, tiny mite-like creatures that lived 400 million years ago.

LYDBURY NORTH [South Shropshire]

SO3586: 3 miles (5km) SE of Bishop's Castle

Set below the slopes of Oakeley Mynd on the edge of the Kemp valley, the substantial village of Lydbury North was already a busy market town long before Bishop's Castle came to prominence in the 12th century. There are still traces of earthworks which probably date from the 9th or 10th century and may have been built to defend against the Danes who were pushing up the River Severn at this time. Bishop's Castle soon overtook Lydbury, however, which lost its market and administrative status. Today, many of the villagers commute to Bishop's Castle. The large Norman **church of St Michael and All Angels** is a reminder of grander days. Its massive tower dominates the village from its position on a raised mound and it has two long transepts, the Plowden Chapel and the Walcot Chapel, both named after prominent local families.

On the far side of the River Kemp is **Walcot**, a brick mansion built for Robert Clive (see Moreton Say) c1763 by Sir William Chambers. The surrounding parkland has many fine trees and a lake made by damming the river. It attracts large numbers of wildfowl, especially Canada geese. The Clive family moved from Walcot to Powis Castle in 1933.

LYDHAM [South Shropshire]

SO3391: 2 miles (3km) NE of Bishop's Castle

In the Anglo-Saxon period Lydham was regarded as a town. Like many such, it never realised its full potential and is now just an unremarkable village strung out along the main road. The village centre is grouped around the **church of Holy Trinity**, which superficially appears to have been built in the 13th century but substantially restored in 1642 and again in 1885. There is some evidence, however, that the 13th-century church was a rebuilding of a Saxon one, which seems likely enough if Lydham was a Saxon town. Domesday Book certainly records a priest here in 1086. The double-belled gable at the west of the church is most unusual. Behind the church is the mound of a Norman motte and bailey castle but the approach to it appears to be private.

Just to the south of the village is **Lydham Manor**, surrounded by private parkland containing a number of very fine trees, including the **Lydham Manor Oak**. Estimated to be 600-800 years old, it is the second largest oak in the country, though its present rate of growth puts it on course to become the largest in a few years. Other trees grow from its bole, including hollies and elders, and it is an entire habitat in its own right.

MADELEY [Wrekin]

SJ6904: 1 mile (2km) NE of Ironbridge

Though now part of Telford, the former industrial township of Madeley still exists in its own right, sandwiched between modern housing estates. Even so, it benefits from a fair amount of green space and the **Blists Hill Open Air Museum**, where a former ironworks is now at the centre of an award-winning recreation of a 19th-century industrial town (see Coalport).

By 1300 Madeley was already a flourishing township belonging to Wenlock Priory. Small-scale coal mining began early on and by 1711 sophisticated deep mines were in operation. An underground network of tunnels was developed, complete with wooden tramways along which wagons were hauled on the first stage of their journey to the River Severn, where the coal was loaded onto boats for export. Between 1780 and 1870 Madeley prospered so rapidly that its population doubled twice and the old centre was rebuilt. The High Street, however, still reflects the plan imposed in the 13th century by Wenlock Priory, and the octagonal **church of St Michael**, rebuilt by Thomas Telford in 1796, stands on the pre-Christian raised site occupied by its predecessors. There is much of interest in Madeley, including a number of good brick houses, notably the beautiful **Old Vicarage** (c1700). Particularly interesting is the **Anstice Memorial Club and Institute**, built in 1869 in a grand Italianate style and claimed to be the first working men's club in the country. More impressive is **Madeley Court**, a little way north of the town centre, an Elizabethan mansion of grey limestone that has recently been restored. It belonged to Sir Robert Broke (see Claverley) a respected lawyer and Speaker of the House of Commons. It was a descendant of his, Sir Basil Brooke, who built the Old Furnace at Coalbrookdale where Abraham Darby first experimented with the use of coke for iron smelting. In 1709 Darby took up residence at Madeley Court and lived there until his death in 1717.

MAESBROOK [Oswestry]

SJ3021: 5 miles (8km) S of Oswestry

A scattered village in low-lying country near the River Morda and the River Vyrnwy, Maesbrook is prone to flooding, despite the earthen banks constructed for protection. The **church of St John the Baptist** was built in 1878, and there is also a Methodist church of 1844.

MAESBURY MARSH [Oswestry]

SJ3125: 3 miles (5km) SE of Oswestry

Flat fields of sheep and wheat provide the setting for Maesbury Marsh, a small village beside the Montgomeryshire branch of the Shropshire Union Canal. Maesbury developed as a canal port in the early 19th cen-

tury and is the best example of its type in the county. The Navigation Inn still has the stables used by the towing horses, and a crane (thought to be the only surviving example of a 15-cwt crane) stands by the old wharf. The village houses, which include boatmen's cottages and a canal agent's house, are mainly brick but **St John's Church** is built of white-painted corrugated iron, topped by a little weatherboarded belfry.

MAINSTONE [South Shropshire]

SO2787: 3 miles (5km) SW of Bishop's Castle

A remote hamlet in gorgeous countryside close to the border, Mainstone is a small cluster of farms and houses in the deeply cut valley of the River Unk There is a Primitive Methodist Chapel of 1891 but, oddly enough, the parish **church of St John the Baptist**, also known as "the church on the dyke", is nearly a mile to the west. It shelters deep in Cwm Ffrydd, next to Offa's Dyke in the tiny hamlet of Churchtown, with just a couple of cottages to keep it company.

The name Mainstone is derived from the Welsh *maen* meaning "stone". The stone in question is supposedly the smooth granite boulder that now sits inside St John's Church beside the pulpit. What it is doing there nobody knows, though there is a tangle of legends surrounding it. The church was restored in 1887 but some older features were preserved, notably a magnificent Elizabethan oak roof.

MARCHAMLEY [North Shropshire]

SJ5929: 5 miles (8km) E of Wem

A most attractive small village on a hill, Marchamley has a good mixture of brick and timber-framed houses, their gardens enclosed by sandstone boundary walls. The **Old Manor House**, its timbers infilled with brick, is dated 1658. Hawkstone Park is just to the west (see Weston under

Redcastle) and the surrounding farmland is put to both pasture and arable.

MARCHE [Shrewsbury and Atcham]

SJ3311: 5 miles (8km) NW of Pontesbury

Marche Farm, Marche Hall, Marche Manor and Marche Manor Farm cluster round a bend in Marche Lane to make up the hamlet of Marche. It might not sound like much, but the quality of the buildings is remarkable. **Marche Manor**, in particular, is superb, a beautifully situated timber-framed house which dates from 1604 and has all the charm of its period. Less than half a mile north-east of Marche Manor, and accessible by public footpath, is a prehistoric earthwork, its purpose unknown.

MARKET DRAYTON [North Shropshire]

SJ6734: 8 miles (12km) SE of Whitchurch

An attractive market town by the Staffordshire border, Market Drayton has a long history, having probably started life as a prehistoric camp guarding a strategic crossing point of the River Tern. St **Mary's Church** now stands on the elevated site thought to have been occupied by the camp. It is a large building, mostly of the 14th century, but some earlier Norman work survives, though the church suffered such heavy restoration in 1884 that it appears overwhelmingly Victorian.

Next to the church Clive Steps lead to the former **Grammar School**, founded in 1558 by Sir Rowland Hill, a local man who became Lord Mayor of London. This was the school attended by Robert Clive (see Moreton Say) until his expulsion.

In 1245 Henry III granted Drayton its market charter and marketing has been its main role ever since, serving a large area of Shropshire, Staffordshire and Cheshire. Food is the main focus, of course, and Market Drayton's speciality is gingerbread, created by a Mr Thomas in 1817 and still made to a secret recipe. Also popular are pies based on a recipe associated with Robert Clive and sold at the Clive and Coffyne (a coffyne is a pie case).

The High Street is the heart of town, with the other main streets radiating from it. Market Drayton is built mostly of brick but there are also some striking black and white buildings, especially on Shropshire Street, where **Sandbrook Vaults** (1653) is particularly impressive, as is the **Star Hotel** (1669) on Stafford Street. But the majority are Georgian brick, foremost being the **Corbet Arms** and the **Trustee Savings Bank** on High Street, **Ryland House** on Great Hales Street, and **Red House**, just one of many splendid examples on Shropshire Street. Cheshire Street has much to offer too, including the **Butter Cross**, a small, open-sided market hall of 1824 with Tuscan columns, a pediment and a bellcote with two fire bells. On market days (Wednesdays) Cheshire Street vanishes under a flood of colourful stalls.

Little Drayton has now been swallowed up by its larger sibling but it was for centuries an independent community. Today it is essentially a residential suburb, but mixed in among the modern housing are some mellow Georgian and Victorian cottages. Near the centre is **Christ Church**, built in 1847 in red sandstone to the design of S. Pountney Smith and J. Smith.

Shropshire Wildlife Trust manages a former water-meadow as a riverside nature reserve at **Walkmill Marsh** on the southern edge of Market Drayton, and there is a good range of wildlife to be seen along the Shropshire Union Canal, which passes to the east of town.

On the Newport road, on a small hill overlooking the River Tern, is the site of **Tyrley Castle**, probably built by Ralph de Boteler, Baron of Wem, in 1247. Only the mound is still there; a farmhouse has replaced the castle. The surrounding countryside has a good number of impressive houses such as **Tunstall Hall** (c1723) to the north-east and **Buntingsdale Hall** (c1730) to the south-west.

MARTON [South Shropshire]

SJ2802: 7 miles (11km) SW of Pontesbury

A hilltop village in attractive country close to the border, Marton overlooks the wide valley of Aylesford Brook, a tributary of the River Camlad. To the north-east is Marton Pool, where a prehistoric dugout canoe was found buried in the mud some years ago. It is now in Shrewsbury Museum. Although still large enough to be used for sailing and fishing, Marton Pool has been considerably reduced in size by drainage.

Marton has a fair range of amenities to cater for the residents of its timber-framed cottages and modern bungalows. There are pubs, a shop and the **church of St Mark**, built of stone in 1855. The fact that this is border country is emphasised by the remains of motte and bailey castles here and there beside lonely farmhouses: there is one less than a mile to the east of Marton at Wilmington and another just to the south at Wotherton.

Marton Crest was the birthplace of **Dr Thomas Bray** (1656-1730), a clergyman and philanthropist who founded a parochial libraries system which developed into the Society for Promoting Christian Knowledge (SPCK), whose bookshops are now a familiar feature in our towns.

MELVERLEY [Oswestry]

SJ3316: 8 miles (12km) SE of Oswestry

Melverley is a small village caught in a loop formed by the Severn and the Vyrnwy, close to their confluence, a position which makes it vulnerable to flooding. It is notable only for **St Peter's Church**, a beautiful and very rare example of a timber, wattle and daub church. It seems that by Saxon times there was already a chapel at Melverley but in 1401 this, or possibly its successor, was destroyed by Owain

St Peter's, Melverley

Glyndŵr. Almost immediately work started on a replacement and by 1406 a new church was standing on the site, the same church we see today. It remains substantially unaltered except for interior embellishment, added windows and some necessary repairs. All the original beams, made from local oak, are fixed together with wooden pegs; no nails were used at all. There is a Saxon font, which must have stood in the original church, while the altar and finely carved pulpit are Jacobean. With the Vyrnwy below its west wall and the Severn close by, this lovely church has often been cut off by rising water, sometimes for as much as a month. The fields on the other side of the Vyrnwy are in Wales, the river forming the national boundary at this point.

MEOLE BRACE [Shrewsbury and Atcham]

SJ4810: 2 miles (3km) S of Shrewsbury

Once part of a vast royal forest, the former

village of Meole Brace is now just another suburb of Shrewsbury, but the old centre retains some charm, with Victorian and Georgian houses. In the 12th century the village acquired a castle, erected by the Norman lord of the manor, de Bracey, but it was burnt down in 1669. It stood in what are now the gardens of Meole Brace Hall. **Holy Trinity Church**, built 1867-8 of red sandstone, has some widely acclaimed stained glass by Edward Burne-Jones and William Morris, making it one of the most important churches of its period. It was here that Mary Webb (see Leighton) was married in 1912, having lived in the village since 1902.

MERRINGTON [Shrewsbury and Atcham]

SJ4721: 6 miles (10km) NW of Shrewsbury

A hamlet set in quiet countryside, Merrington stands on a slight rise with pleasant eastward views to the sandstone ridge of Pim Hill. There is a mixture of old and new houses and bungalows – one of the latter was for many years the home of the late Percy Thrower, one of Britain's best-known gardeners. A little to the west is **Merrington Green**, where Shropshire Wildlife Trust manages a nature reserve registered as a medieval common by the borough council. The common has a good mix of habitats - woodland, scrub, grassland and ponds. In the past it was mined for its clay, to supply brick and pipe works at Leaton and Old Wood, both now closed. During the Second World War it also provided a base for an American army camp, followed by a German prisoner-of-war camp. Today, it is a tranquil and beautiful place, supporting abundant wildlife.

MIDDLETON [South Shropshire]

SO5477: 2 miles (3km) NE of Ludlow

A tiny farming hamlet, Middleton perches above Ledwyche Brook, enjoying an excellent view of Titterstone Clee Hill to the

east. A sandstone Norman **chapel**, consisting only of nave, chancel and bellcote, and restored in 1851, stands close to **Middleton Court**. Just to the south of Middleton Bridge the course of a dismantled railway can be seen; this was the mineral line which linked the Clee Hill quarries with the main line at Ludlow.

MIDDLETON IN CHIRBURY [South Shropshire]

SO2999: 5 miles (8km) NE of Montgomery

Scarcely even a hamlet, just a sparse scattering of farms and cottages, Middleton is strung out along the western slope of Stapeley Hill. It is an enviable situation, except perhaps in a hard winter. The most notable building is Edward Haycock's **church of Holy Trinity** (1843), renowned for its abundance of fine carvings made by the Reverend Waldegrave Brewster between 1877 and 1890. More memorable than the church, however, and perhaps nearly 4000 years older, is **Mitchell's Fold**, a Bronze Age stone circle (English Heritage) on top of Stapeley Hill, which is traversed by a prehistoric ridgeway. There are 15 surviving stones but it is believed there were originally 30. Like other such structures, its purpose can only be guessed at, but there are plenty of legends attached to it. One of the commonest themes, which occurs with several variations, concerns a fairy cow which provided an unending flow of milk during a famine, filling any container presented to it, until a witch milked it into a sieve, eventually causing the exhausted beast to collapse and disappear into the ground.

There are several other prehistoric monuments on Stapeley Hill, including a standing stone, cairns and other stone circles, notably **Marsh Pool Circle**.

MIDDLETON SCRIVEN [Bridgnorth]

SO6887: 5 miles (8km) SW of Bridgnorth

Beautiful rolling country provides a fine

setting for the hamlet of Middleton Scriven, which occupies a ridge between Crunells Brook and Horsford Brook. The **church of St John the Baptist** was rebuilt in Early English style between 1843 and 1848. There are two old yew trees in the field across the road, as though the church was rebuilt in a different position, though there is no other evidence to confirm this. Nor is there any apparent explanation for the name of **Old Castle Farm**: if there was a castle here it has long since disappeared. Across the road from the farm a tiny, abandoned quarry once yielded local building stone.

MILSON [South Shropshire]

SO6372: 3 miles (5km) SW of Cleobury Mortimer

Hilly pastoral country dotted with old orchards enfolds the tiny village of Milson, including the Norman **church of St George** with its squat 13th-century tower and 14th-century timber-framed porch. Nearby **Church House**, part brick and part timber, is the most impressive village house. A short distance to the south-east of Milson, **Moat House** stands on the site of a fortified medieval house.

MINSTERLEY [Shrewsbury and Atcham]

SJ3705: 2 miles (3km) SW of Pontesbury

A large village with some industry, Minsterley is, nevertheless, an attractive place with timber-framed **Minsterley Hall**, pleasant cottages, a stream running through the village centre and plenty of amenities. Both lead and coal used to be mined nearby and there is a working quarry just to the east, but the local economy is mainly agricultural.

The most noteworthy building in Minsterley is the **church of Holy Trinity**, if only because it looks like no other. It must have come as quite a shock to conservative Salopians when first built. A curious

brick structure, it was erected in 1689. Externally, its most striking feature is the west end, where the doorway is decorated with a profusion of semi-classical, semi-baroque stone carvings of skulls, crossbones and cherubs. The architect was William Taylor from London and it was built for the 1st Viscount Weymouth, a prominent local landowner and a member of the Thynne family, whose best-known representative today is the flamboyant Marquis of Bath who owns Longleat in Wiltshire.

Few churches were built in the late 17th century (except in London), making Minsterley something of a rarity, and doubly so by virtue of its extraordinary style. The interior is remarkable for its collection of maidens' garlands, wooden-framed crowns adorned with paper ribbons and flowers (see Astley Abbotts). The Minsterley garlands were all made between 1726 and 1794 and it is one of the largest collections in the country, probably second only to that at Abbotts Ann in Hampshire.

MINTON [South Shropshire]

SO4390: 2 miles (3km) SW of Church Stretton

One of the most charming hamlets in Shropshire, Minton is a peaceful place in sheep country on the lower slopes of the Long Mynd. The setting is magnificent and Minton is interesting because it is a rare survival of a typically Anglo-Saxon settlement with farmhouse, cottages and manor house grouped round an irregular green. There is a mound behind the manor house, which may be a Norman motte or an earlier Saxon fortification, perhaps re-used by the Normans.

MONKHOPTON [Bridgnorth]

SO6293: 6 miles (10km) W of Bridgnorth

A small village, Monkhopton clusters beside a brook in well-wooded undulating country replete with cattle, sheep and cereal crops. **St Peter's Church** has a Norman nave and chancel but the tower dates from 1835. Opposite is **Monkhopton House**, a brick building of the 17th century. In the Middle Ages Wenlock Priory was one of the largest landowners hereabouts. This is reflected not only in the village name, but also in the names of several other outlying farms and hamlets: Monkhall Grange (a grange was usually a monastic farm), Lower Monkhall, Upper Monk Hall, Masons Monkhall and Harpers Monkhall.

MONTFORD [Shrewsbury and Atcham]

SJ4114: 5 miles (8km) NW of Shrewsbury

This small, isolated farming hamlet once formed part of the huge Powis Estate (based on Powis Castle near Welshpool). Square-towered, sandstone **St Chad's Church** occupies a dominant position on high ground above the river, with fine views to the Breidden Hills. It dates from 1737-8 and was designed by a Shrewsbury man, William Cooper. It was badly restored in 1884. Just outside the church is the grave of Charles Darwin's parents, Robert and Sussanah.

MONTFORD BRIDGE [Shrewsbury and Atcham]

SJ4315: 4 miles (6km) NW of Shrewsbury

Montford Bridge is an unremarkable village except that a bridge has spanned the Severn here since the early Middle Ages, though the present three-arched sandstone bridge was built in 1792 by Thomas Telford as part of his famous Holyhead road. It was his first major bridge in Shropshire. The ancient river crossing was once a traditional meeting place for negotiations between English and Welsh leaders in times of conflict. In 1283 Dafydd ap Gruffydd, the last true Prince of Wales, was brought here in chains by his own countrymen and handed over to the English. He was convicted of treason at a Parliament called by Edward I (see Acton Burnell) and subse-

quently dragged through the streets of Shrewsbury, tied to a horse's tail, before being hung, drawn and quartered.

Less than a mile upstream (south) is Preston Montford, where the Field Studies Council has a residential field centre at **Preston Montford Hall**, a handsome, 18th-century brick house.

MORE [South Shropshire]

SO3491: 2 miles (3km) NE of Bishop's Castle

The village of More is small and utterly charming, with beautiful timber-framed houses clustering round 13th-century **St Peter's Church**. The church occupies a circular raised churchyard with huge stones in its enclosing wall, suggesting this was once a pre-Christian religious site. The More chapel on the north side of the church was added in the 17th century but was rebuilt, along with much of the rest, in 1845. The squat, sturdy Norman tower has a stepped pyramid top similar to more famous examples at Clun and Hopesay.

Close to the village is the site of **More Castle**, a Norman motte and bailey structure now marked only by a series of earthworks and ditches. Other earthworks nearby may be house platforms, indicating that the village has either moved or shrunk since the Middle Ages. The castle site is in a field known as Moatlands, contained within a loop formed by a tributary of the River West Onny. The ground is damp and poorly drained, which may explain the village's name (Old English *mor* means "a moor, marsh or fen"). After the Conquest the manor of More was given to a Norman called Richard, who adopted the village name as his own (see Linley).

MORETON CORBET [North Shropshire]

SJ5623: 8 miles (12km) NE of Shrewsbury

The surrounding countryside is flat and uninspiring, the presence of Shawbury Airfield means Moreton Corbet is not always a peaceful village, and its main street is not particularly noteworthy. It does, however, possess one of the most important and dramatic ruins in the county, now in the care of English Heritage. This is **Moreton Corbet Castle**, and it's actually a fusion of two separate ruins. The older one is that of the original Moreton Corbet Castle, its Norman keep of c1200 still standing. The more recent ruin is the Moreton Corbet Castle built around 1579 for Sir Andrew Corbet and family, which is not really a castle so much as a magnificent house. Though basically Elizabethan, it has strong classical influences, its Tuscan and Ionic columns, ogee gables, projecting bays and mullioned windows all combining perfectly. Moreton Corbet was besieged by Cromwell's troops in 1644 and they were responsible for its destruction. They spared the **church of St Bartholomew**, which stands close by, completing a splendid group. The church has a Norman chancel, a south aisle of 1330-40 and work from several later periods. There is an impressive collection of Corbet memorials inside, and some excellent modern glass.

An interesting local tradition tells of John Dutton, controller of the household in 1635, who was a scarcely believable 8ft 4ins tall (not far off 3m), and an ancestor of the (much shorter) "Shropshire Giant", Thomas Dutton (see Stoke on Tern).

MORETON SAY [North Shropshire]
SJ6334: 3 miles (5km) W of Market Drayton

Tucked away in a quiet situation in gentle dairy country near Market Drayton, Moreton Say is a pleasant village with a mixture of old and new houses. The **church of St Margaret** was built of stone c1200 but has been encased in Georgian brick, the tower added in 1769. Across the road, **Church Farm** is also in disguise, a coat of rendering covering what was originally a row of three 14th-century, timber-framed cottages.

Moreton Say is best known as the place where **Robert Clive** (1725-74) was born and buried. He was actually born at **Styche Hall**, an Elizabethan timber-framed house a mile north-east of the village centre (in the 1760s this was replaced by the present brick house built by Clive for his parents and since converted into flats). He was a troubled youth, subject to depression, and when he attended school in Market Drayton he also proved himself an enterprising young thug, running a protection racket and generally terrorising the town.

In 1743 Clive joined the East India Company in Madras as a clerk, mainly because his family wanted rid of him. However, he made a name for himself in the field of military exploits when he and a small force held Arcot against a Franco-Indian army for 53 days in 1751. In 1753 he returned to England a hero but was soon back in India, where, after further military successes, he virtually ruled Bengal on behalf of the East India Company, as well as acquiring a personal fortune and a drug habit. In 1760 he returned home, again to a hero's welcome, and in 1761 entered Parliament as member for Shrewsbury. In 1762 he became Baron Clive of Plassey and in 1764 returned to India as governor and commander-in-chief of Bengal. He rooted out corruption in the East India Company, restored military discipline and established British supremacy throughout India. Inevitably, he made powerful enemies and when he returned to England in 1767 he found himself facing parliamentary questions about his handling of affairs. In 1773 he was vindicated but committed suicide soon after. He was buried at Moreton Say in an unmarked grave, for 18th-century law did not permit suicides to be interred in consecrated ground.

MORVILLE [Bridgnorth]
SO6794: 3 miles (5km) W of Bridgnorth

A village of considerable beauty and interest on the banks of the Mor Brook, Morville was a flourishing place before nearby Bridgnorth was even thought of.

Domesday Book records in 1086 that Morville had as many as 17 dependent villages and hamlets. The **church of St Gregory** was already of some importance by this time too, and in the 12th century it established many daughter chapels in the surrounding countryside. The present church is mostly Norman, the nave and chancel dating from 1118. In 1138 Shrewsbury Abbey established a dependent cell at Morville and tradition suggests that what is now the village pub, the Acton Arms, was then the Abbot's lodgings and is haunted by the ghost of Richard Marshall, sometime Abbot of Shrewsbury.

Morville Hall was built (or rebuilt) in 1546 for Sir William Acton, owner of a local ironworks. The village was remodelled to improve the view for the benefit of the Actons. In the 18th century the hall was again rebuilt but it remains a minor masterpiece. It now belongs to the National Trust but admission is only by written appointment with the tenants.

Immediately to the north of Morville is **Aldenham Park**, standing at the end of a long, tree-flanked avenue, with elaborate wrought-iron entrance gates fronting onto the road. There was a house here in 1383 but it was rebuilt in 1691 by Sir Edward Acton, and further alterations were made in the Victorian period. The Acton family produced some distinguished men, including Sir John Acton, who became Prime Minister of Naples (see Acton Scott), and **John, first Baron Acton of Aldenham** (1834-1902), a respected historian and founder-editor of the *Cambridge Modern History*.

MUCH WENLOCK [Bridgnorth]

SO6200: 7 miles (11km) NW of Bridgnorth

Much Wenlock is an immensely picturesque little town with a wealth of beautiful buildings in stone, brick and timber. Though small, it has a long and important history. Its name suggests Celtic origins – Wenlock is believed to derive from *gwyn-loc*, Celtic for "white monastery". A Saxon town developed in conjunction with a monastic foundation and by 1224 Wenlock had gained the right to hold a weekly market and an annual fair. Edward IV granted a special borough charter in 1468, giving the town jurisdiction over 17 parishes and the right to return two MPs, a right relinquished only in 1885. (Borough status was lost in 1966, despite Edward's charter declaring it to be "in perpetuity".) Decline set in during the 19th century, due chiefly to the development of industry at Broseley and Ironbridge, resulting in a new regional focus of influence. The consequent lack of development was to Wenlock's benefit, resulting in the unspoilt townscape that still largely survives today.

The focus of the town is the Square, dominated by the timber-framed **Guildhall**. The lower part of the building probably dates from 1540 and the upper storey, which contains a panelled court room and council chamber, from 1577. The open ground floor served as a market. Across the street is **Much Wenlock Museum**, housed in a former Victorian market hall. Close by is **Holy Trinity Church**, founded c680 as a place of worship for the nuns of Wenlock Abbey. The church was enlarged between 800 and 1050 and the Cluniac monks of Wenlock Priory built the present nave around 1150. There is also work from several later centuries. At the west end is a memorial to indefatigable local benefactor **Dr William Penny Brookes**, who was extremely active in the town, supporting numerous worthwhile projects.

Other notable buildings include the **Gaskell Arms Hotel** (a handsome old coaching inn) and a 17th-century **squatter's cottage** nearby, recognisable by its characteristically huge chimney stack. The custom was that if you could build a house in 24 hours, the building and the land it stood on were yours. In practice it was enough to have smoke issuing from a chimney so a would-be squatter always began

Wenlock Priory

with a large, free-standing chimney stack, onto which the rest of the house could be built at leisure. The pleasing **Corn Exchange** of 1852 was probably built on the site of St John's Hospital, a 13th-century refuge for "lost and naked beggars". **Raynald's Mansion** is an uncommonly fine Elizabethan town house, with gables and tiny balconies. **Ashfield Hall** is a mixture of stone and timbering, a splendid house which has also served as an inn, where Charles I stayed in 1642. Almost opposite, a 17th-century black and white building is another former inn and now houses **Barclay's Bank**. One of the oldest buildings in town is **St Owen's Well House**, which is of cruck construction. St Owen was a French monk of the 6th century who visited Much Wenlock.

The most important building is just outside the town centre. **Wenlock Priory**, an English Heritage property, which is in ruins today, was once a prosperous and powerful religious centre and a place of pilgrimage.

The ruins are those of a Cluniac priory built in the 12th and 13th centuries, but the original religious house on this site was an abbey founded c680 by Merewalh, the son of King Penda of Mercia. He placed his daughter Milburgha in charge as Abbess in 682. Under her guidance the foundation flourished mightily and she was credited with miraculous works.

Milburgha's abbey was damaged or destroyed c874, possibly by a Danish raiding party, but in the 11th century Earl Leofric of Mercia built another religious house on the same site, which was in turn succeeded by a Cluniac priory founded by Roger de Montgomery after the Conquest. However, most of the existing buildings are not Earl Roger's. They are almost entirely Early English and represent the work of Prior Humbert in the 13th century. There is only a little Norman work remaining, though what does survive is superb, especially the decorative arcading in the chapter house and the carvings in the lavatorium. It is the church, however, that dominates the scene, with its towering gable.

The Priory continued to flourish until the Dissolution, its diverse interests including a Severn toll bridge, coal and copper mines, ironworks and vast agricultural and forest holdings. Adjacent to Wenlock Priory is **Prior's Lodge**, now a private house. Built c1500, it is considered to be one of the best examples of domestic architecture in the country.

In many ways, however, Wenlock's greatest appeal lies not in individual buildings but in its unpretentious and harmonious mix of materials and styles and in the wealth of small but enjoyable details (old street signs, for instance) which are apparent everywhere. There is even a real working farm in the town centre, **Brookhouse Farm**, which is of medieval origin.

Rather surreally, the revival of the Olympic Games is linked with Much Wenlock. Dr Brookes founded the Wenlock Olympian Society in 1850, and by 1860 was organising an important annual track and field event with prizes of laurel wreaths and medals. In 1890 Baron de Coubertin visited the Wenlock Olympics, was greatly impressed and six years later organised the first international modern Olympics at Athens. Wenlock, meanwhile, continues to hold its own Wenlock Olympian Games on a regular basis.

MUNSLOW [South Shropshire]

SO5287: 6 miles (10km) NE of Craven Arms

An attractive village of Wenlock limestone, Munslow enjoys good views of Brown Clee Hill from a pastoral setting in Corve Dale. **St Michael's Church** dates from 1115 and has a squat, square, partly Norman tower, while the chancel is 12th century and the nave is later. The timber-framed south porch is unusual and probably of the 14th century, while some 13th-century ironwork survives on the south door. The church was restored between 1868 and 1870. A remnant avenue of yew trees leads down to the church through Munslow Deans, coming from the top of Wenlock Edge along a bridleway believed to be part of a medieval pilgrims' route linking Wenlock Priory, Ludlow Church and Hereford Cathedral.

The **Crown Inn** was once the Hundred House at which medieval manorial courts were held. The gabled stone house near the war memorial was the birthplace in 1589 of lawyer **Edward Littleton**. He became successively Chief Justice of North Wales, Solicitor General and Chief Justice of England, but achieved as much notoriety as fame because of the way he kept changing sides in the years leading up to the Civil War.

About half a mile to the north, **Millichope Park** clings to the side of Wenlock Edge, the mature parkland with its lake and statuesque trees providing the perfect setting for Millichope Hall, designed by Edward Haycock c1840. A square house of grey stone, it has an Ionic portico and is complemented by the garden buildings, which include a rotunda. To the north of Millichope Park is **Upper Millichope Farm**, a 14th-century stone tower house, a very rare survival. The upper part is timber-framed and was added later.

MUXTON [Wrekin]

SJ7113: 3 miles (5km) NE of Telford Centre

Formerly a village in its own right, Muxton is now part of Telford. Adjoining it to the west is the massive Army Central Ordnance Depot, while Donnington and Donnington Wood adjoin it to the south-west and south. To the south and south-east is the reclaimed Granville Country Park, a former colliery wasteland. Most of what remains of interest in the former village is to be found on Muxton Lane. There are still a few timber-framed houses, one of them with a jettied upper storey. **St John's Church** is still in use, but St Chad's Church (a mission church built of corrugated iron) was dismantled and rebuilt at Blists Hill Open Air Museum.

MYDDLE [North Shropshire]

SJ4623: 4 miles (6km) SW of Wem

Until the late 16th century the village of Myddle was surrounded by forest, but this was cleared between 1550 and 1650 to fuel local glass works and ironworks. Today, gently undulating green fields show few signs of their former tree cover. **St Peter's Church** was rebuilt in 1744 and Gothicised in the 19th century. The tower is older: it looks Perpendicular, but was actually built c1634. Close to the church is the site of **Myddle Castle**, built in 1307 by John le Strange of Knockin. In the 16th century it was owned by outlaw Humphrey Kynaston (see Nesscliffe) and fell into disrepair. Today there is only a slight mound topped by part of a stair turret.

Myddle is best known for *The Antiquities and Memoirs of the Parish of Myddle*, written between 1701 and 1706 by **Richard**

Gough (1635-1723). It gives a rare and intimate glimpse into everyday country life and has become a minor classic of social documentation.

MYNDTOWN [South Shropshire]
SO3989: 4 miles (6km) E of Bishop's Castle

Situated at the end of a "no through road", Myndtown is the tiniest of hamlets, occupying a wonderful position on the western slopes of the Long Mynd. A farm, a few cottages and the Norman **church of St John the Baptist** are the sum total of the settlement, apart from glorious views.

NASH [South Shropshire]
SO6071: 5 miles (8km) SW of Cleobury Mortimer

In a remote location in hilly country below the southern slopes of Titterstone Clee Hill, Nash is a tiny hamlet in dairy and cereal country, with most of its few houses built of brick. The **church of St John the Baptist** is partly 14th century but the north aisle was added in 1865. Beyond the churchyard is **Nash Court**, an imposing brick house built in 1760 by the Arbuthnot family. Just to the south-east of Nash, near Whatmore Farm, stands the pollarded **Nash Oak**, around 500 years old, craggy, gnarled and still flourishing. Further north, **Court of Hill** is a notable brick house of 1683, which incorporates a 13th-century predecessor.

NEEN SAVAGE [Bridgnorth]
SO6777: 1 mile (2km) N of Cleobury Mortimer

A handful of houses, a church and a parish hall are all that make up the tiny agricultural hamlet of Neen Savage as it slumbers peacefully beside the River Rea, close to a ford. The **church of St Mary** has a Norman tower, with battlements added in 1825 after a lightning strike had destroyed a wooden spire. The surrounding countryside is peaceful and pastoral today, but there used to be paper mills and brick works, powered by the River Rea, alternative names for

The Conyngesby Memorial, Neen Sollars

which used to be Nene or Neen. In the 13th century the manor came into the ownership of Adam de Sauvage.

NEEN SOLLARS [Bridgnorth]
SO6672: 3 miles (5km) S of Cleobury Mortimer

Neen Sollars is a small village lost in deeply sunken lanes in hilly, well-wooded countryside close to the Worcestershire border. The 14th-century cruciform **church of All Saints** stands on the site of a Saxon predecessor and dominates the village from an elevated position. Inside there is an exceptional monument to Humphrey Conyngesby "a perfect scoller... and a greate traveyler" who explored much of the world but disappeared without trace in 1610.

There are several black and white cottages in the village, probably now the homes of commuters. To the south there is a weir on the River Rea and a dismantled railway runs beside the river. This was the Bewdley to Tenbury and Woofferton line, operative from 1864 to 1964. A short walk northwards along a wooded riverside footpath provides a view of the **viaduct** which carried the railway across the river. The railway was preceded by a canal, which opened in 1790. It connected Marlbrook (just over a mile south of Neen Sollars but within the parish) to Tenbury and Leominster, and was used to transport coal from mines at Mamble (just over the border in Worcestershire). In 1858 it was sold to the Shrewsbury and Hereford Railway Company which laid a trackbed on part of it. Traces of the canal can still be seen at Marlbrook.

NEENTON [Bridgnorth]

SO6387: 5 miles (8km) SW of Bridgnorth

Though it is a scattered village, the centre of Neenton is on high ground between Rea Brook and Clee Brook, while a number of farms, connected by an unusually dense web of footpaths, are arranged haphazardly nearby. A pub and the **church of All Saints** stand near the highest point of the village, with the church occupying a raised site, probably prehistoric. A pink sandstone building, it was rebuilt it in 1871 in Early English style by Sir Arthur Blomfield. There is a Norman font inside and the east window is thought to be by William Morris and Co c1920 (not by Morris himself, who died in 1896). Stone and brick cottages and council houses complete the village.

NESSCLIFFE [Shrewsbury and Atcham]

SJ3819: 8 miles (12km) NW of Shrewsbury

An unremarkable village straggling along the A5, Nesscliffe is blighted by traffic and offers no immediate incentive to linger, though the **Nesscliffe Hotel** is impressive and the **Old Three Pigeons Inn** dates from 1405. There is, however, more of interest than is at first apparent. To the east of the road is a country park based on the sandstone outcrop of **Nesscliffe Hill**, its canopy of trees concealing not only abandoned quarries and a prehistoric fort, but also the intriguing **Kynaston's Cave**. Humphrey Kynaston of Myddle was a landowner who became a highwayman after being outlawed in 1491 for his involvement in a mur-

der. He became a popular hero, roaming the countryside like another Robin Hood, stealing from the rich to give to the poor. His horse, Beelzebub, is credited with jumping the Severn at Montford Bridge after the bridge had been partially dismantled (simply a matter of lifting the planks which constituted the roadway) in an effort to prevent Kynaston getting across. Henry VIII gave Kynaston a free pardon in 1518 and he spent his last years in peaceful retirement on an estate near Welshpool, where he died in 1534. Kynaston's Cave is reputed to have been his home while he was living as a highwayman. A tree-lined holloway leads from Nesscliffe to a flight of earth and timber steps that climb to the base of a cliff. A further flight of stone steps, hacked out of the rock, leads to the cave, which has openings for a door, window and chimney vent, as well as two small rooms (one of which was Beelzebub's), several storage niches and a primitively vaulted roof. When cave-living lost its charm Kynaston could always go to the pub: a fireside seat in the Old Three Pigeons is claimed to have been his.

NEWCASTLE [South Shropshire]

SO2482: 3 miles (5km) NW of Clun

A fair-sized village of stone houses, Newcastle stands in lovely pastoral country above the confluence of Folly Brook and the River Clun. The uplands of Clun Forest rise to the north and south of Newcastle, with Offa's Dyke snaking past the east end of the village. The **church of St John the Evangelist** was built in 1848 and lies between the village and the dyke. Its most notable feature is an unusual revolving lychgate. To the south-west of the village a Norman motte stands close to the river. The hills around Newcastle are well endowed with prehistoric monuments, and there is an Iron Age fort, Fron Camp, directly above the village on the top of a steep hill called Fron. A prehistoric settlement is discernible across the valley of Folly Brook, on the slopes of Castle Idris. **Lower Spoad Farm**, on Offa's Dyke, is famous for an overmantel in the farmhouse kitchen carved with a hunting scene. Though probably Elizabethan, it looks much older.

NEW INVENTION [South Shropshire]

SO2976: 3 miles (5km) N of Knighton

Sadly, the hamlet of New Invention doesn't live up to its intriguing name, though its setting cannot be faulted. This is a magnificent landscape of steep slopes and rounded tops, classic Clun Forest country where sheep easily outnumber people and Wales is never far away. New Invention shelters beside the River Redlake below several formidable hills, including the one topped by **Caer Caradoc** (see Chapel Lawn). There is a Methodist chapel of 1864 and a handful of houses. As for the "new invention", it is said to be the trick of reversing a horse's shoes to confuse pursuers. Dick Turpin is usually credited with the idea but there is no evidence that he ever passed this way and it would be interesting to discover a more convincing explanation. Perhaps it is simply a corruption of a name considered unpronounceably Celtic by Anglo-Saxon settlers.

NEWPORT [Wrekin]

SJ7419: 7 miles (11km) NE of Telford Centre

Newport is one of Shropshire's lesser known market towns but, despite a slightly run-down air, it is a place of some distinction. It started out as a planned Norman town in the 12th century, when it was granted borough status by Henry I. The Normans planned many towns as purely commercial ventures, and plenty of them failed, remaining villages to this day, or disappearing altogether. Newport was one of those that succeeded, though it has never grown large.

Strangely, perhaps, for an inland town, it was noted for its fish. There were numerous ponds and meres in the area and some of these were important fisheries. Moreover, the Weald Moors lay just to the west of town. It's hard to imagine now, since they have been so efficiently drained, but the Weald Moors used to constitute a vast wetland, all meres and marshes in dry weather, fully submerged in wet weather, sometimes for months on end. Little wonder then that three fishes are featured in the town's coat of arms, or that there was a longstanding obligation to supply the Royal Household with fresh fish whenever the king was in the area.

The **church of St Nicholas** stands on an island position in the centre of town, between the High Street and St Mary Street. The church tower is 14th century but most of the rest was rebuilt between 1866 and 1891. It is constructed of red sandstone and has stained-glass windows by Burne-Jones and William Morris. In 1446 William Glover built **almshouses** in the churchyard but in 1836 they were dismantled and rebuilt in Vineyard Road, where they remain today. The **Puleston Cross** still stands close to the church. It was erected in memory of a 13th-century knight, Sir Roger de Pulestone, who was killed in battle.

When the fisheries dwindled Newport continued to prosper as a market town for the new farmland created by the drainage schemes. Before this, however, in 1665, it suffered a great fire that destroyed much of the town, only a handful of timber-framed houses escaping, such as the **Old Guildhall** (1615) and **Smallwood Lodge**, now a bookshop. Newport was rebuilt over the next few decades, explaining the preponderance of Georgian (and earlier) brick houses, some of them three-storeyed. One of the best is **Beaumaris House** (1724), north of the church. It was the Bear Inn for a time and Charles Dickens was a guest there. A little further north is **Chetwynd House**, the home of a recluse named Elizabeth Parker who is believed to have inspired the character of Miss Havisham in Dickens's *Great Expectations*, published in 1861.

Other notable buildings include the **Royal Victoria Hotel** (c1830), complete with Tuscan porch and pilasters, and **Adams' Grammar School**, founded in 1656 but rebuilt in 1821. The large **town hall** in St Mary Street was built in 1859 to an Italianate design by Cobb. Typically Victorian in its lack of regard for the scale of its surroundings, it nevertheless looks rather fetching in its coat of blue paint. Wellington Road has an imposing classical-style **Congregational Church** and the Roman Catholic **church of St Peter and St Paul** on Salter Lane was built in 1832 with funds provided by Lord Shrewsbury.

The Newport branch of the Shropshire Union Canal cut through the north end of town in the 1830s and though it has long been disused it does still hold water and a few features have survived at the former wharf and basin.

Newport remains a service centre for a large agricultural hinterland (barley, wheat, sugar beet and potatoes are the main crops) but there is also some industry in town and housing estates are spreading fast, even encroaching on the town centre near the canal.

NEWTOWN [North Shropshire]

SJ4831: 3 miles (5km) NW of Wem

Flat, pastoral country provides the setting for the scattered hamlet of Newtown, where there is little of note except for a moated site at **Northwood Hall** and an ugly **church of King Charles the Martyr**, built in 1869 by E. Haycock Junior. It replaced a private house that had been converted into a church during the Commonwealth period (the interregnum between Charles I and Charles II). Inside there are unpleasant paintings of the execution and burial of Charles I.

NORBURY [South Shropshire]

SO3692: 3 miles (5km) NE of Bishop's Castle

A remote and delightful village in a wonderful setting, Norbury shelters at the foot of Norbury Hill just to the west of the Long Mynd. The oldest resident is the **Norbury Yew** in the churchyard, probably well over 1000 years old, of massive girth and still going strong. The **church of All Saints** is youthful by comparison, despite its 14th-century tower. The rest is Victorian, including the spire, but the churchyard is Anglo-Saxon or earlier. The village has a handful of attractive cottages and a handsome pub, the Sun Inn.

NORTON IN HALES [North Shropshire]

SJ7038: 3 miles (5km) NE of Market Drayton

Close to the River Tern, which forms the border with Staffordshire at this point, Norton in Hales is a red-brick village arranged round a small green. A large granite boulder, known as the **Bradling Stone**, stands on the green and is assumed to have been deposited by a glacier. It may once have had some pagan significance for echoes of lost ceremonies can be found in the custom, only recently discontinued, of bumping ("bradling") against the stone anyone found working after noon on Shrove Tuesday. Another discontinued custom is the eight o'clock curfew that operated from Michaelmas Day to Lady Day every year. The **church of St Chad** is partly 13th century, but was rebuilt in 1864-72. The Market Drayton to Stoke-on-Trent railway used to pass through the village, but has long since been dismantled, while the station and station-master's house are both private dwellings now.

OAKENGATES [Wrekin]

SJ6910: 1 mile (2km) N of Telford Centre

Very much part of Telford, the former industrial town of Oakengates nevertheless manages to maintain a semblance of separate identity. It occupies a seemingly hilly landscape but many of the hills are actually landscaped spoil heaps, for Oakengates was heavily exploited in the past for coal and iron ore. Coal mining began early but it was only in the 18th century that the industry began to expand significantly. From 1761 ironmaster Richard Reynolds was working the mines, and in the 1770s iron-smelting furnaces were established. In 1787 a canal connecting ironworks at Ketley with coal mines at Oakengates was begun. The main line railway from Birmingham arrived in 1850 and helped Oakengates develop into a prosperous shopping and social centre. The **church of Holy Trinity** was built in 1855.

St Georges is also considered part of Oakengates. It lies to the east, across the A442, and originated as a crossroads settlement called Pains Lane. This became a mining village in the 19th century and in 1861 the **church of St George** was built, subsequently giving its name to the burgeoning community which became St Georges. The architect of the church was G.E. Street and this is considered one of his more inventive works. It stands opposite the Quarry House Inn and a row of brick cottages. The centre of town is to the west of the church and has a fair range of facilities. St Georges has many modern houses, fortunately leavened with a sprinkling of Georgian and Victorian.

Snedshill is considered part of Oakengates too; in fact, it squeezes between Oakengates and St Georges. It used to be important for ironworks and coal mines, but today Snedshill is trading estates and housing estates. There are some 18th-century cottages, 19th-century terraces and brick-built **St Peter's Church**. The **Snedhill Chimneys**, decorated with tile panels, are a reminder of the days when the Lilleshall Company had a brick and tile works here, as well as blast furnaces and a forge.

Adjoining St Georges and Snedshill to the south is **Priorslee**, where **Priorslee Hall**, an 18th-century house of brick and stone, was built by the Jordan family but later became the headquarters of the Lilleshall Company. Priorslee consists of industrial units and housing developments built around flash pools on what used to be spoil heaps. The **church of St Peter** was built in 1836 and a row of miners' cottages with ornate cast-iron windows survives from 1839. There are few facilities but Telford Centre is very close. For a time the Telford Development Corporation was based at Priorslee Hall.

OLDBURY [Bridgnorth]
SO7091: 1 mile (2km) S of Bridgnorth

Oldbury lies on high ground and is a suburb of Bridgnorth now, but it still has a village feel to it. The **church of St Nicholas** is almost entirely Victorian, though it incorporates a tiny fraction of an earlier church, perhaps the one known to have been set up in 1140 as a daughter chapel of St Gregory's at Morville.

ONIBURY [South Shropshire]
SO4579: 4 miles (6km) NW of Ludlow

Situated close to the River Onny, probably by an ancient crossing place, Onibury is a small village with attractive cottages in stone, brick and half-timbering. **St Michael's Church** is a lovely building, both inside and out, which dates from the Norman period, but also contains work of the 13th, 14th and 15th centuries, though it was restored in 1902 by Detmar Blow who created the ironwork and added the gallery. Both Onibury and the River Onny take their names from a Welsh word for ash trees, but today there are more oaks than ash. Holly trees are unusually common in the area, a fact reflected in the name of a pub – the Hollybush – which once stood at Onibury. The Ilex Studio continues the tradition – "ilex" is the Latin for holly.

The Cardiff-Manchester railway passes Onibury but trains no longer stop. However, the handsome stone station house has found a new lease of life as a café.

Nearby **Stokesay Court** is a grand neo-Elizabethan mansion of 1889 in a well-wooded park with some spectacular rhododendrons. The house was designed by Thomas Harris and belongs to the Allcroft family (see Stokesay). The grounds are occasionally open to the public. Further along the lane is the **Wernlas Collection** where rare breeds of poultry are on display.

OSWESTRY [Oswestry]

SJ2929: 7 miles (11km) SW of Ellesmere

The flourishing market town of Oswestry has a long history. It lies astride a prehistoric trade route, Ffordd Saeson, linking Anglesey and the Severn and used by Irish axe traders. Later, during the Iron Age, the fort of **Hen Dinas**, now known in English as Old Oswestry, was created. This formidable fort is the best of its kind in the Marches. Work began c250BC and it was

built in stages over many years, then abandoned soon after the Roman Conquest. It was later reoccupied after the Romans left and the Anglo-Saxons began flooding across the country. It lies just to the north of the modern town. Offa's Dyke is not far to the west but the lesser known **Wat's Dyke** actually runs through the site. Like Offa's Dyke, this was a rampart and ditch construction and it is believed to have been dug in the reign of Athelbold (716-57), Offa's predecessor. It extends from the Dee Estuary to Morda Brook south of Oswestry.

In 642, long before Wat's Dyke was created, King Penda of Mercia had defeated King Oswald of Northumbria in battle at Maserfelt (soon to become Oswestry). Legend has it that Oswald was killed and his body nailed to a tree. A passing eagle carried off one of his arms but soon dropped it, whereupon a spring gushed forth where it landed. This became **St Oswald's Well** and its supposed restorative powers attracted the sick, while its connection with St Oswald attracted pilgrims. It can be found in Maserfield Road, near the Grammar School.

The Heritage Centre, Oswestry

After the Conquest the Normans built **Oswestry Castle** in a commanding position. The motte is still very much in evidence but little else remains, though the adjacent street layout was partly decided by the position of the bailey defences. The **church of St Oswald** was also built by the Normans, but of their church only very little survives. The massive 13th-century tower was partly rebuilt in the 1690s when a balustrade and pinnacles were added. The rest of the church, which is one of the largest in Shropshire, has work from several centuries but there was a major restoration in 1872-4 under G.E. Street. Among the monuments inside is one to Hugh Yale (died 1616), an ancestor of the Elihu Yale who founded the American university.

Like many other towns, Oswestry was deliberately planned and created in the 12th century by the Norman lord of the manor, in this case William FitzAlan. Oswestry, however, probably already had a market before the Conquest, though the first recorded mention is in a royal charter of the 1190s. A borough charter was granted in 1228 and Oswestry became one of the most important Marcher lordships. The town prospered as a market centre and was for centuries more Welsh than English, despite being a centre of English (initially Norman) government. Not until the 18th century did the English influence prevail but even today Oswestry has a Welsh feel about it (it's surprising how many English people think it is in Wales), especially on market days, when this friendly, bustling town really comes to life.

Though Oswestry prospered throughout the Middle Ages, its border position meant turbulent times were inevitable and it was burnt to the ground by King John in 1215 and later by both Llywelyn ap Iorweth (the Great) and Owain Glyndŵr. It was also burnt accidentally several times in the 16th century and badly damaged by Cromwell, who was responsible for the destruction of the castle, and then burnt again in 1742. As

a consequence there are few old buildings in Oswestry.

Llywd Mansion (1604) on Cross Street is one of the few timber-framed houses to survive the fires. Another timber-framed building is **Holbache House**, which is adjacent to the churchyard and was founded between 1404 and 1407 as a free grammar school, that is, one not attached to a church or monastery, a pioneering concept at the time. It is the second oldest secular grammar school in the country (Winchester was founded 20 years earlier). The founder, Welshman **David Holbache**, was Crown Pleader and Attorney for Wales and War Treasurer to Henry IV. Some of the present structure is believed to date from Holbache's time, but there is an abundance of later work. From 1746 to 1755 the Welsh poet **Goronwy Owen** (1723-1769?) was headmaster. By 1776 the school had outgrown the building and moved to its present site in Upper Brook Street. Holbache House now serves as **Oswestry Heritage and Exhibition Centre**, with an accompanying tourist information centre and café.

Other buildings of interest are mainly Georgian and Victorian, and include Georgian **Wynnstay Hotel** and **Bellan House** in Church Street, the **Municipal Buildings** of 1893 and the former **Nonconformist Chapel** of 1830, which houses council offices now. **Holy Trinity Church** in Salop Road was built 1836-7 by R.K. Penson and **Christ Church**, next to the castle, was designed in 1871 by local architect W.H. Spaull. Now used by the United Reformed Church, it was built for the Congregational Church and is unusual in being designed church-style rather than chapel-style. The result is a Gothic masterpiece or monstrosity, depending on your viewpoint.

When Cambrian Railways came to Oswestry the company built its main offices and workshops there, the population increased enormously and many rows of terraced houses were built for the railway workers. Ironic, then, that Oswestry no longer has a train service. The site of the former station is now the home of the Cambrian Railway Society and **Oswestry Transport Museum**. There is some hope that Oswestry Station might reopen in the near future, together with the line that connected it to the main line at Gobowen.

Oswestry has contributed more than its fair share of famous names to the national catalogue. **Sir Henry Walford Davies** (1869-1941), organist, composer, broadcaster, Professor of Music at Aberystwyth University and Master of the King's Music from 1934-41, was born in Oswestry. So was novelist **Barbara Pym** (1913-80). **Canon William Archibald Spooner** (1844-1930), whose nervous habit of transposing initial letters or half-syllables (metathesis) gave us the term "spoonerism", was educated at Oswestry. But the town's most famous son is **Wilfred Owen MC** (1893-1918), the finest war poet of his generation, who was born at Plas Wilmot, Weston Lane. Owen was tragically killed in France just one week before the Armistice, but the poems that this railwayman's son left behind have played a part in shaping modern attitudes to war.

Just out of town to the north-west is Lord Harlech's **Brogyntyn Hall**, an imposing mansion dating from c1730 and surrounded by parkland. **Castell Brogyntyn** is situated in Brogyntyn Park in woods near a lake. A substantial earthwork, it is believed to have been built by Brogyntyn, a Welsh prince. On the north-east edge of Oswestry is **Park Hall Orthopaedic Hospital**, established in 1921 by Dame Agnes Hunt and Robert Jones and now the possessor of an international reputation for innovation in medical techniques.

Oswestry is still essentially a market town, but it has a fair industrial base too: balloon manufacture is one of the more unusual local industries and the balloon flown by Per Lindstrand and Richard Branson across the Atlantic in 1987 was made in Oswestry.

PANT [Oswestry]

SJ2722: 5 miles (8km) S of Oswestry

An unusually large village, Pant lies below Llanymynech Hill and is almost entirely residential. It used to be a busy port on the Montgomery Canal, handling limestone from the Llanymynech quarries. It was something of a railway village too, with the Cambrian Railways line running alongside the canal and narrow gauge mineral lines plunging down from the quarries. All that has gone now but there is still a bank of limekilns by canal bridge 91.

PAVE LANE [Wrekin]

SJ7516: 2 miles (3km) SE of Newport

Pave Lane is just a tiny hamlet but it achieved importance in the 18th century when it was chosen as the terminus for the Donnington Wood Canal. This was constructed between 1755 and 1757 by Earl Gower, to carry coal from his Donnington Wood mines to a point of sale on the old Newport-Wolverhampton road. There were also branches linking to Lilleshall and elsewhere. The canal closed in 1882 (except for a short section near Trench that closed only in 1929). Today there are a few brick houses, a couple of Duke of Sutherland cottages, a restaurant and a farm. Just to the west of Pave Lane are the slight remains, now almost ploughed out, of a prehistoric settlement.

PEPLOW [North Shropshire]

SJ6324: 6 miles (10km) SW of Market Drayton

Scarcely even a hamlet, Peplow lies in flat country near the River Tern. The main feature is **Peplow Hall**, built in 1725 but later enlarged. Close by stands the **chapel of the Epiphany**, built in 1879 of timber and brick to the design of Norman Shaw.

PETTON [North Shropshire]

SJ4326: 6 miles (10km) SE of Ellesmere

A small hamlet on a quiet lane in gentle

countryside, Petton has little of specific interest other than **Petton Hall**, an Elizabethan-style brick house built in 1892 and surrounded by parkland. It now functions as a school. It must lie close to the site of a much older house because the remains of a moat survive nearby, while an earthen mound within the parkland may suggest prehistoric settlement or some sort of Norman fortification. To the south of Petton Hall there stands a brick **church** built in 1727 and altered in 1870 and 1896. There is some good Jacobean woodwork inside.

PITCHFORD [Shrewsbury and Atcham]

SJ5303: 6 miles (10km) SE of Shrewsbury

Both the village and the surrounding arable countryside are unremarkable, but less than a quarter of a mile to the north of Pitchford is the finest timber-framed house in Shropshire, the magnificent **Pitchford Hall**. Built around 1560 for Adam Otley, a Shrewsbury wool merchant, it is a massive but unpretentious house with upright timbers, diagonal struts and star-shaped brick chimney stacks. It was restored in 1887 and again more recently. When it came onto the market in the 1990s the National Trust reluctantly decided that it could not justify the three million pounds asking price and the estate is now the home of a stud farm.

Approached along a tree-lined avenue, Pitchford Hall lies in mature parkland with lakes, woodland and plantations. Nearly as famous as the hall itself is the **Pitchford Lime**, a pollarded large-leaved lime which was already mature when marked on an estate map of 1692. It is the oldest and biggest large-leaved lime in the British Isles, and its massive branches now have to be propped up by supporting posts. It also contains a **tree house** like no other. Instead of the usual ramshackle construction of old planks and tea chests, Pitchford boasts an 18th-century timber-framed structure with ogee windows and sumptuous interior plasterwork, originally designed by

Shrewsbury architect Thomas Farnolls Pritchard, but recently much restored. The young Queen Victoria climbed up into the tree house when she visited Pitchford in 1832 (she was god-daughter to the owner).

Pitchford Hall must stand on the site of an even earlier house for the adjacent **church of St Michael** has some Norman workmanship, including herringbone masonry in the north wall. Mostly, however, it is Early English and there is 17th-century woodwork inside along with other items of interest, including a notable oak effigy of a cross-legged knight, probably John de Pitchford who died in 1285.

The grassed-over course of a Roman road can be traced across fields to the east of Pitchford. Just to the south of the village it continues as a bridleway and then as a modern road heading for Church Stretton, while to the north it continues, via lanes and footpaths, to a river crossing near Wroxeter (the Roman town of Viroconium). Where the bridleway section crosses a brook just to the south of Pitchford there are traces of engineering work, comprising embankments which are believed to be Roman and a bridge abutment which may be Roman or later. These are just upstream from the modern footbridge.

PLAISH [Shrewsbury and Atcham]

SO5396: 5 miles (8km) NE of Church Stretton

A remote hamlet, Plaish enjoys a beautiful setting in undulating pastoral country between Wenlock Edge and the Stretton Hills. Hereford cattle graze peacefully in the fields among the lightest possible scattering of farms and cottages. The only noteworthy building is **Plaish Hall**; a splendid construction of c1540, this Tudor trendsetter was the first large house (possibly the first house of any size) in Shropshire to be built in brick. Red brick, of course, but both blue bricks and stone quoins have been incorporated to decorative effect. The house is said to be haunted by the ghost of a bricklayer, and no wonder, given the story behind the haunting. Plaish Hall was the home of Chief Justice Leighton (who died in 1607 and is remembered in Cardington Church) who was not entirely satisfied with the quality of his chimney stacks. He promised a convicted criminal, a Mr Sherratt, his freedom if he would build him the best chimney stacks in Shropshire. Sherratt worked for months to produce the superb chimney stacks we see today and all were agreed that they had no equal in the county. But so-called "Justice" Leighton had never had any intention of keeping faith and Sherratt was hanged from one of the chimney stacks he had himself just built. In 1916 a skeleton was found in one of the chimneys and buried at Cardington. Whether this was Sherratt is uncertain. Plaish Hall is also said to be haunted by a grey lady.

A little to the east of Plaish Hall is 16th-century Holt Farm, where a giant pollarded oak is known as the **Holt Preen Oak**. A spring flows from beneath its roots and provided Plaish with drinking water until recently. The spring water used to be piped to Plaish by a waterwheel and pumping engine, replaced by an electric pump after the Second World War. These served until 1984 when Plaish was put onto the mains supply. The spring has never been known to run dry and the water is always very cold, even in midsummer. A water trough stands next to the oak, which is enclosed by a gated stone wall believed to have been built about the same time as the farm. That in itself would put the tree at well over 400 years, and in fact its age is estimated at something between 400 and 600.

PLEALEY [Shrewsbury and Atcham]

SJ4206: 2 miles (3km) NE of Pontesbury

Plealey is a small village in pleasant country where the plain is left behind as the land starts to rise towards the border hills. Mainly residential, it has a mixture of old and new houses and a tiny, white-painted Methodist chapel.

PLOWDEN [South Shropshire]

SO3787: 3 miles (5km) E of Bishop's Castle

It would be hard to find a hamlet with a lovelier position than Plowden, which shelters beside the River Onny in a gorge cut by the river between the Long Mynd and the uplands to the south. This is thickly-hedged sheep country, though well-wooded too in places, while the skies belong to the buzzards which circle above at all times. The course of the dismantled Bishop's Castle railway can still be traced near Plowden, though on the far side of the River Onny. It was always regarded as a bit of a joke but it must have provided one of the loveliest of all railway journeys. There is not much at Plowden itself: a few cottages and farms and the brick **church of St Walburga**, a Catholic church with a presbytery. Just to the south, however, is **Plowden Hall**, timber-framed and beautifully situated in a dip on a hillside. An Elizabethan house, it was probably built by the wealthy Catholic lawyer **Edmund Plowden** (1518-85), who sat in Parliament during the reign of Queen Mary and served Elizabeth I as Treasurer of the Middle Temple. His descendants still own Plowden Hall.

A little to the west of Plowden is another small hamlet, **Eyton**, overlooked by **Billings Rings**, an Iron Age fort on a hill behind Eyton Farm. To the west again, **Totterton**, another farming hamlet, has a fine Georgian house in **Totterton Hall**.

PONTESBURY [Shrewsbury and Atcham]

SJ4006: 7 miles (11km) SW of Shrewsbury

Formerly a village, now more of a small town, Pontesbury has been submerged in new housing since it was designated an overflow centre for Shrewsbury. Some buildings of character do survive, notably **The Old Rectory**, which is of cruck construction and probably the oldest house in Pontesbury. The **church of St George** has a sandstone chancel of c1300 but the rest was rebuilt in 1829 following the collapse of the tower in 1825. Inside, there is a Norman font with a scallop design and a variety of monumental tablets.

Mary Webb (see Leighton) lived in Pontesbury from 1914 to 1916, first at Rose Cottage (now Roseville) in Hinton Lane, and later at Nills Cottages on Nills Hill. She wrote her first novel *The Golden Arrow* at Rose Cottage and *Gone to Earth* was written at The Nills. Both are set in the nearby uplands of Stiperstones and Long Mynd. Pontesbury was the location in the 7th century of a great battle between the armies of Mercia and Wessex and nearby Pontesford Hill has a number of legends associated with it, including the story of a golden arrow lost during the battle. It was this that gave Mary the idea for her novel.

Another author who drew inspiration from the area was **D.H. Lawrence**, who visited a friend in Pontesbury and was so taken with the surrounding landscape that he depicted it in his short novel *St Mawr*, published in 1925.

To the south-east is twin-humped **Pontesford Hill** and **Earl's Hill** – two names but, strictly speaking, one hill with two tops. Most people refer to it (or them) as Pontesford Hill. From certain viewpoints it resembles a sleeping elephant, from others a sleeping lion; from any viewpoint it is extraordinarily distinctive. Earl's Hill, the higher and steeper of the two tops, is protected as a nature reserve by Shropshire Wildlife Trust. It was the first nature reserve acquired by the Trust, back in 1964, and is still one of the finest, with a great variety of habitats, some rare plants and spectacular views. It is crowned with a substantial Iron Age fort established c600BC and has been mined for its lead ore (galena) for centuries. The ore was smelted at Pontesford, which is a settlement just to the north-east of Pontesbury, using coal mined locally in many small pits. Apart from the ruins of a colliery engine house

and an ore-smelting works, there are few signs of past industry in today's agricultural landscape, though it is still possible to trace the course of a mineral line which ran from Pontesbury to the lead mines at Snailbeach further south.

To the south of Pontesbury is a suburb called Pontesbury Hill and south of this is **Nills Hill**. Here there are disused quarries, a prehistoric earthwork called **The Ring** and a marvellous Shropshire County Council nature reserve, **Poles Coppice**, a winning combination of ancient woodland, grassland and abandoned quarries.

PREES [North Shropshire]

SJ5533: 4 miles (6km) NE of Wem

Prees is a Celtic name so the village obviously has a long history, but there is little to indicate that today if you pass through on the main road with its straggle of mundane buildings. A little to the east, however, a cluster of houses round the **church of St Chad** represents the site of the Anglo-Saxon village that developed here. There are some attractive cottages and **Prees Hall**, a fine Georgian house. The sandstone church is mostly 14th century but the tower was added in 1758 and some rebuilding took place in 1864. There are monuments to members of the Hill family inside. An unusual survival in Prees is an 18th-century sandstone **lock-up**, one of only a handful of such buildings still remaining.

Prees stands on a major (originally Roman) north-south road and in the 18th and early 19th centuries it was an important coaching stop, until the arrival of the railway in 1853 killed the coach trade. Prees Station is still open, though not manned. To the north is **Prees Heath**, where an accumulation of truck stops and cafés caters for car and lorry travellers, while **Prees Higher Heath** is a large, mainly residential village with a great deal of modern housing.

PREES GREEN [North Shropshire]

SJ5631: 4 miles (6km) NE of Wem

A scattered village, Prees Green is built mostly of brick, including the Methodist church of 1933. It is a former estate village belonging to the Hills of Hawkstone Park, who employed most of the population. The surrounding landscape was once mossland, and among the earliest of the Shropshire mosses to be drained, when Sir Richard Brereton purchased it in 1539 from the Bishop of Lichfield. Brereton began by enclosing the land and commoners lost their rights on it, though not without a fight. Today, the large, flat fields created since are deeply fertile and mostly put to arable.

PRESTON BROCKHURST [North Shropshire]

SJ5324: 8 miles (12km) NE of Shrewsbury

A main-road village, but an attractive one, Preston Brockhurst has a number of fine houses. Most notable of these is **Preston Hall,** a 17th-century manor house which overlooks the village from slightly higher ground to the west, below Grinshill Hill. A few timber-framed cottages line the road and there are some modern bungalows. Less than a mile to the south is **Acton Reynald,** a large and very interesting Victorian stone house incorporating an earlier 17th-century house built for the ubiquitous Corbets. It now functions as a school.

PRESTON GUBBALS [Shrewsbury and Atcham]

SJ4919: 4 miles (6km) N of Shrewsbury

A small village of Saxon origin on a slight hill in gently undulating country dotted with stands of Scots pines, Preston Gubbals is centred on the **church of St Martin,** cared for by the Redundant Churches Fund. Just part of the chancel and a few other fragments of the original church remain, onto which S. Pountney Smith added a new church in 1866. That church was later demolished and the original church was vested in the Fund in 1975. It has a 17th-century font and an exceptional 14th-century effigial slab. The village also has some timber-framed cottages and a large farm with sandstone barns. The name Gubbals derives from Godebold, the landholder (not the landowner, that was St Alkmund's Church in Shrewsbury) after the Conquest.

PRESTON UPON THE WEALD MOORS [Wrekin]

SJ6815: 3 miles (5km) NE of Wellington

Situated at the southern edge of the Weald Moors, Preston is perilously close to Telford, but looks unlikely to be engulfed just yet. When the former marshland of the Weald Moors was drained in the 18th century a great deal of rich farmland was created, enabling the Weald Moor villages to prosper (see Kynnersley and Eyton). Most of them were rebuilt in brick and Preston was no exception. Even **St Laurence's Church** is a brick building, built in 1739 to replace an earlier church. The chancel was added in 1853. St Laurence's stands next to a small village green, an uncommon feature in Shropshire. A bigger surprise, however, is **Preston Trust Homes,** a spectacular range of almshouses completed in 1725 to fulfil the terms of the 1716 will of Lady Catherine Herbert (daughter of the 1st Earl of Bradford). The almshouses are built in brick, with stone dressings, and arranged around three sides of a quadrangle. One wing was originally used to house young girls who were being trained for domestic service and another wing was reserved for widows "of the better class".

To the south of Preston is **Hoo Hall,** a partly timber-framed house dating from 1612. To the south-west is **Kinley Farm** where in 1833 five Bronze Age axe heads were found. Part of the disused Newport branch of the Shropshire Union Canal can be traced to the north of Preston though there is no longer any water in this section.

PURSLOW [South Shropshire]

SO3680: 5 miles (8km) W of Craven Arms

Beautifully set in the Clun Valley, Purslow is just a cluster of buildings to the south of a crossroads. Purslow Hall and Purslow Hall Farm account for most of the hamlet. The name is believed to mean "Pussa's burial mound" (Pussa lawe) and there is a tumulus near Purslow Hall, which could possibly be Pussa's.

QUATFORD [Bridgnorth]

SO7390: 2 miles (3km) SE of Bridgnorth

With sandstone cliffs overlooking the village on the east and the Severn lapping against its western edge, Quatford just about fits into the gap between the two. It is believed that a camp was established here by Danish invaders in 893, while Lady Ethelfleda may also have built a fortification here in 912, when intent on protecting Mercia from further Danish attack. Quatford was later strategically important to the Normans as well, because it apparently had a bridge over the Severn, and Roger de Montgomery, Earl of Shrewsbury, built **Quatford Castle** in the 1070s. The earthworks of Roger's motte and bailey castle still stand by the river. In 1101 Roger's son, Robert de Belleme, abandoned Quatford and moved north to a more easily defended site at what came to be known as Bridgnorth, building a new bridge and castle there.

The **church of St Mary Magdalene** is across the road from the castle, but much higher up, dramatically positioned on a sandstone crag among pine trees. It still retains the chancel built by Earl Roger in 1084 in fulfilment of a vow made by his second wife, Adelisa, when endangered by a storm as she crossed the Channel to join her husband. She promised that if her life were spared she would build a church on the spot where she and Roger met. The chancel is the only Norman work to survive; the windows and buttresses are 14th century and the Gothic nave and tower were built in 1714, the south aisle and porch in 1857. Just to the east of the church is a very old oak tree, known as the **Forest Oak** because it is believed to be a survivor of the great Morfe Forest. It is also claimed that this very tree provided shelter for Adelisa when she first met with Roger after her journey from Normandy, which would make it a highly unlikely 1000 years old.

To the north of the church an embattled **folly tower** of red brick overlooks the road. And to the north again, just to add an element of confusion, there is another **Quatford Castle**, but this one is a house, complete with battlements and other sham fortifications and splendidly sited among trees above the road and river. John Smallman, a local builder, built it in 1830 for his own use. North of this the settlement of **Danesford** recalls the unwelcome visitors of the 9th and 10th centuries.

QUATT [Bridgnorth]

SO7588: 4 miles (6km) SE of Bridgnorth

Lovely rolling country with superb views across the Severn to the Clee Hills provides a worthy setting for the model estate village of Quatt. London architect John Birch was employed to design the estate cottages in 1870, to a standard that was considered very high for the time. They still look good today. The timber-framed bus shelter must be a more recent addition to the scene but reaches the same high standard. If this is where Quatt's teenagers hang out in the evenings, at least they can hang out in some style. **St Andrew's Church** looks superficially Georgian (actually 1763) but much of it is older, with 12th-century work surviving. In fact, some experts suggest there are traces of Saxon work in the south wall of the chancel and there is a Norman priest's door. Of particular interest inside are the many Wolryche tombs dating from the 17th century. The nearby **Dower House** is a handsome 18th-century brick house of nine bays.

Quatt belongs to the **Dudmaston Estate**, which has remained in the same family for 850 years, though it was given to the National Trust in 1978. Because the donor family still lives there, and because the rooms are not impossibly grand, **Dudmaston Hall** has a warmer, more intimate feel than is usual in National Trust properties, and it is packed with items of interest and beauty, notably its collection of botanical art. It was built of brick about 1730 in Queen Anne style, and altered in the 19th century. It is a fine building but it is for its beautiful grounds that Dudmaston is most famous, with woodland, parkland and tree-fringed lakes. To the south-west of the hall is a wooded valley called **The Dingle**, where cascades, winding paths and rustic seats were created in the "picturesque" style. **Lodge Farm**, with its castellated parapets, also represents the picturesque. Built in 1776, it is an early example of a style which was soon to become the height of fashion. The estate is farmed by tenants and much of it is permanent pasture, though cereals and sugar beet are also grown. There is also a great deal of woodland and plantation, the management of which is regarded as a model of enlightened forestry practice. The National Trust strives to be a good landlord in other ways too: when letting cottages in Quatt it gives priority to local people who have an association with Dudmaston or Quatt.

QUEEN'S HEAD [Oswestry]

SJ3426: 3 miles (5km) SE of Oswestry

A red-brick canalside settlement, now blighted by the A5, Queen's Head derives its name from an old coaching inn on Watling Street. The canal is the Montgomery branch of the Shropshire Union, and the locks of the nearby Aston Flight have recently been restored. On the other side of the canal, **Aston Hall** is a fine house of grey stone built in 1780 to a design of Robert Mylne. It stands in attractive wooded parkland with a lake and formal gardens.

Nearby is a ruined **church**, built in 1742 in brick.

RATLINGHOPE [South Shropshire]

SO4096: 4 miles (6km) NW of Church Stretton

Ratlinghope (pronounced "ratchup") is a tiny hamlet with a long history, as the remains of prehistoric settlements on Ratlinghope Hill and neighbouring Stitt Hill demonstrate. Around the year 1200 the manor was acquired by Walter Corbet, an Augustinian canon, probably of Wigmore Abbey, and by 1209 the Wigmore canons had founded a small priory at Ratlinghope. There are few records of the priory and no visible remains of the domestic buildings but there are traces of earthworks in a field by **St Margaret's Church**, though there's no evidence that this was the priory site. The foundations of the church, which was rebuilt c1788, may be those of the original priory church, as may the lower parts of the walls, but there is considerable doubt about this. It was a lonely place for a priory, but a very beautiful one, hidden away in the tiny valley of the Darnford Brook to the west of the Long Mynd. Even today only a handful of cottages, a farm and a manor house keep the church company. A local legend tells of a ghostly horse-drawn funeral procession said to drive from Ratlinghope up to the Long Mynd when the moon is high. It may have been inspired by sightings of the wild horses that are said to have roamed the area until the 1960s.

RED LAKE [Wrekin]

SJ6810: 2 miles (3km) E of Wellington

Squashed between Ketley and Oakengates close to the centre of Telford, Red Lake nevertheless manages to present a surprisingly rural picture in places. The old village centre is based around the **church of St Mary the Virgin**, which stands among trees next to the vicarage. The church was built of stone in 1838 and was paid for by the 2nd Duke of Sutherland, owner of the

Lilleshall estate, of which Red Lake formed a part. The village initially developed from a squatter community in the 18th century, on land that had already been turned into a post-mining wasteland. In 1812 a new estate manager took over and began to regularise the situation, making the squatters into official tenants. In return for paying rent they got a much higher standard of accommodation, most of the houses being repaired, some remodelled in the characteristic style of so-called "Duke of Sutherland cottages". Men were often loaned the money to buy a cow and land to graze it on and in this way some were able to develop smallholdings. Today the old cottages co-exist with some substantial Victorian houses and plenty of modern infill.

REDNAL [Oswestry]

SJ3628: 5 miles (8km) SE of Oswestry

Rednal is the tiniest of hamlets and occupies a small area of undulating country between the Montgomery branch of the Shropshire Union Canal and the wide, flat flood plain of the River Perry. The only real interest is over half a mile to the west where there is a former canal-railway junction. Nowadays trains simply cross the canal without stopping but there used to be a big interchange complex with a canal basin and railway sidings. The remains of a ruined warehouse still stand, and close to the railway bridge there is a brick and timber building which is thought to have been the terminus of an experimental and short-lived high-speed canal passenger service which ran from Newtown to Rednal. Next to this building the canal is spanned by a roving bridge, a fairly rare type on the Montgomery Canal. It allows a horse to cross from one bank to another without the need to unhitch the towrope.

RINDLEFORD [Bridgnorth]

SO7395: 2 miles (3km) NE of Bridgnorth

A thoroughly delightful hamlet in the se-

cluded valley of the River Worfe, Rindleford's main building is a disused watermill, next to which cluster farm buildings, a cottage and a Georgian house, all of them largely unspoilt. There is a weir on the river and remains of cave dwellings in the sandstone cliffs nearby.

RODINGTON [Wrekin]

SJ5814: 6 miles (10km) E of Shrewsbury

A compact village grouped around a crossroads by the River Roden, Rodington is built mainly of brick, including **St George's Church**. In 1851 this church replaced a much older one, perhaps the same one recorded in Domesday Book in 1086. The **Bull's Head Inn** is claimed to be the second oldest in Shropshire. It used to be a popular cock fighting and bull baiting venue for colliers from Oakengates, Ketley and other coalfield towns, many of whom participated in these so-called "sports". The abandoned Shrewsbury Canal used to cross the River Roden just south of the village, carried by a brick aqueduct that has been demolished. An old canal bridge does survive, however, half-hidden by trees but worth searching out.

RORRINGTON [South Shropshire]

SJ3000: 7 miles (11km) SW of Pontesbury

A small but most attractive village, Rorrington lies below Rorrington Hill and just to the north of Stapeley Hill, an area rich in prehistoric monuments. **Castle Ring**, an Iron Age fort on Rorrington Hill, overlooks it from the east, while the remains of a more recent fortification, a Norman motte, stand on the south-east edge of the village. Lead ore was mined locally in the 19th century but the seam was soon worked out and pastoral farming remains the dominant element in the economy.

ROWTON [Wrekin]

SJ6119: 6 miles (10km) NW of Wellington

A fairly small hamlet, Rowton stands on a

slight rise above the valley of the River Tern. There are few noteworthy buildings and Rowton is best known as the birthplace of **Richard Baxter** (1615-91), one of the founders of the Nonconformist movement and author of *The Saint's Everlasting Rest* (1650). **All Hallows Church** was built in 1881 but incorporates the north and west walls of a medieval chapel of ease to High Ercall.

ROWTON [Shrewsbury and Atcham]

SJ3712: 8 miles (12km) W of Shrewsbury

Rowton is a very scattered settlement which straggles along the Shrewsbury to Welshpool road. Its one building of note is **Rowton Castle**, which shows an early 19th-century face to the world, looking like a typical example of the romanticised "castle" so popular at that time. Its history is more complex, however, for it is believed to stand on the site of a medieval castle razed to the ground by Llywelyn, Prince of Wales, in 1482. This was replaced by at least two later structures, notably a Queen Anne house of red brick, which formed the basis of the present castle, modified in 1809-12 and 1824-28 to create the desired medieval illusion. Striking as the castle is, it does tend to be dominated by the **Rowton Cedar**, a huge cedar of Lebanon which stands next to it and is acknowledged to be one of the largest and most magnificent in the country.

RUSHBURY [South Shropshire]

SO5191: 4 miles (6km) SW of Church Stretton

A charming village, Rushbury stands at the junction of several streams in narrow Ape Dale, below Wenlock Edge. An isolated place today, it was less so in Victorian times, when it had its own station on the dismantled Much Wenlock-Craven Arms railway. Such is progress. The heart of the village is **St Peter's Church**, which has some herringbone masonry (late Saxon or

early Norman) and a Norman north doorway. The chancel and tower are of c1200 and there are the inevitable Victorian additions. Nearby stand a school, schoolhouse and almshouses, built in 1821 at the expense of Benjamin Wainwright. **Rushbury Manor** is a handsome, timber-framed house with a massive stone chimney stack, while facing it is **Church House**, another substantial timber-framed building. Between the church and Manor Farm there stands a motte, presumably the site of a Norman castle. The road heading south-east from Rushbury climbs steeply up Wenlock Edge at the place known as **Roman Bank**, which local tradition insists was guarded by a Roman fort. Just below Roman Bank the Eaton Brook is spanned by a small, single-arched **packhorse bridge**.

RUSHTON [Shrewsbury and Atcham]

SJ6008: 3 miles (5km) SW of Wellington

At first glance there is nothing much to this hamlet, just a haphazard grouping of farms below the Wrekin, but Rushton can boast the oldest rock in Shropshire – a few slightly exposed sections of 700 million-year-old rock known to geologists as **Rushton schists**, even older than the Wrekin itself (though only just).

RUYTON-XI-TOWNS [Oswestry]

SJ3922: 8 miles (12km) SE of Oswestry

The most intriguing thing about this village is its name. Though normally abbreviated as above, the historically correct name is Ruyton of the Eleven Towns and it derives from a 12th-century uniting of 11 townships in one manor. Ruyton is one of those near misses so common in Shropshire: a planned township which never realised its full potential. It was created in the early 13th century by the FitzAlan family and became a borough in 1308, a status it kept until 1886. **Ruyton Castle** was first built c1155 but was probably only a timber structure. A stone castle was built by Edmund FitzAlan, Earl of Arundel, in the early 14th century, at much the same time as he acquired the borough charter. What remains of it stands to the west of the church tower, just the ruins of a small keep, with part of three walls still upright. The sandstone **church of St John the Baptist** was probably built to serve the castle. It has a 12th-century nave and chancel and there is also work from the 14th and 19th centuries. There are several timber-framed houses in the village, a couple of pubs, an Express Foods factory and a circular toll-house next to a bridge built across the River Perry in 1701. The former Ruyton Towers, now **Ruyton Manor**, stands in trees well to the west of the village, half-hidden in the trees clothing Grug Hill. It was built in 1860 of red sandstone with a machiolated, crenellated tower, a tourelle and a turret – a romantic reincarnation of a medieval castle.

Sir Arthur Conan Doyle, most famous for his Sherlock Holmes stories, worked in Ruyton in 1878 as a medical assistant to a Dr Eliot.

RYTON [Bridgnorth]

SJ7602: 3 miles (5km) S of Shifnal

An ancient village on the River Worfe, Ryton is as charming as the gently undulating countryside which enfolds it. **St Andrew's Church** lies on a rise above the confluence of the Worfe with a tributary, and is probably 12th century, though the tower is of 1710 and the chancel of 1720: both were restored in 1886 when the nave was rebuilt and a north aisle added. Adjacent to the church are the scant remains of a Norman motte and bailey.

ST MARTIN'S [Oswestry]

SJ3236: 5 miles (8km) NE of Oswestry

A large, sprawling village by the Welsh border, St Martin's is mostly given over to housing estates. The medieval **church of St Martin** presides over the village from a raised mound and makes a bold statement in spite of (or perhaps because of) its mixture of styles. West of the church there stands a charming range of **almshouses** bearing two dates – 1638 and 1810.

The northern end of St Martin's merges with **Ifton**, where a huge coal mine employed many local men until it closed in 1968. The Miners' Welfare Institute is now the village hall. Nowadays the surrounding countryside is mainly agricultural. The Llangollen branch of the Shropshire Union Canal passes to the south of St Martin's and there is a small canalside settlement at St **Martin's Moor**.

SAMBROOK [Wrekin]

SJ7124: 4 miles (6km) NW of Newport

A commuter village by a tributary of the River Meese, Sambrook has a mixture of old and new housing, with some pleasant sandstone cottages. The **church of St Luke** was built in 1856 to the design of Benjamin Ferrey. **Sambrook Manor** is a modest brick house which displays a plaque over the door with the letters "O.A.F." and a date of 1702. The initials stand for Obadiah and Frances Adams, whose son George inherited the Shugborough estate near Stafford. In 1773 he changed his name to Anson and his grandson became the 1st Earl of Lichfield. Shugborough is still the home of the present Lord Lichfield, the respected photographer.

SELATTYN [Oswestry]

SJ2634: 3 miles (5km) NW of Oswestry

Wooded, undulating country just below the border hills enfolds the small village of Selattyn, which has a few old stone cottages among an abundance of new brick houses. The **church of St Mary** is partly medieval but the tower was added in 1703 and the transepts in the 1820s. A complete restoration was carried out in 1892. To the west of the village the land rises steeply to the top of Selattyn Hill, which is crowned by a tower erected in 1947. Both Offa's Dyke and the Welsh border traverse the western side of the hill.

SHAWBURY [North Shropshire]

SJ5621: 7 miles (11km) NE of Shrewsbury

The airfield at RAF Shawbury, with its associated barracks and housing estates, dominates this Anglo-Saxon village on the River Roden. The RAF first came to Shawbury in 1917 and, apart from a period of absence between 1919 and 1935, has been here ever since. The old village is centred on the **church of St Mary**, built of Grinshill stone in 1140 to replace a Saxon church, of which only the font has survived. The tower and north chapel were added later in Perpendicular style and the porch is 17th century. The church stands adjacent to Moat Field, a public open space around a medieval moat that probably marks the spot of Shawbury's first manor house. Like so many Shropshire manors, Shawbury came into the possession of the Corbets and it was a member of that family who built the impressive **Elephant and Castle Hotel** in 1734. There are some attractive timber-framed houses in the village, though they sit uneasily with a modern shopping centre which, if nothing else, provides a good range of facilities. The RAF is not the only large employer in Shawbury; there is also the Rubber and Plastics Research Association (RAPRA Technology) which is claimed to be the only organisation of its kind in the world.

SHEINTON [Shrewsbury and Atcham]

SJ6104: 3 miles (5km) NW of Much Wenlock

There's not a lot to Sheinton, a small hamlet below Wenlock Edge, but its setting is most attractive, on high ground above Sheinton Brook, a tributary of the Severn which is itself only half a mile away. S.

Pountney Smith rebuilt the **church of St Peter and St Paul** in 1854, but the little timbered bellcote is probably from the 17th century. There is an unusual effigy inside (an extremely short, smiling woman), which is believed to date from c1300.

SHELTON [Shrewsbury and Atcham]

SJ4613: 2 miles (3km) W of Shrewsbury

A pleasant suburb of Shrewsbury, Shelton has Anglo-Saxon origins but very little evidence of its history is apparent today. However, **Shelton House Hotel** is a fine building and the **Royal Shrewsbury Hospital** is impressive too, with a neo-Elizabethan facade designed by Gilbert Scott in 1843. **Christ Church** is also Victorian, designed by Haycock in 1854.

SHELVE [South Shropshire]

SO3399: 6 miles (10km) N of Bishop's Castle

A few farms, a couple of cottages and a church make up the hamlet of Shelve, beautifully set in pastoral country below Stiperstones. **All Saints' Church** was rebuilt in 1839 on the site of its ancient predecessor. All that remains of the original church is the font and some fragments of the sanctuary.

Shelve Hill, to the west of the village, has been partially afforested by the Forestry Commission, the conifers concealing a number of abandoned mine shafts, and there are many more shafts on the surrounding hillsides, as well as spoil heaps and the occasional stark tower of a ruined engine house. This was the centre of Shropshire's lead-mining district and has been mined from the earliest times. The Celts may well have dug for galena (lead sulphide) here; the Romans certainly did, and many Roman artefacts have been found in the old workings. Just half a mile to the north of Shelve is the **Roman Gravels Mine**, one of the largest and oldest in the area. Lead production peaked in the 18th and 19th centuries but the market collapsed at the beginning of the 20th century and mass depopulation was the consequence in villages such as Shelve.

SHERIFFHALES [Bridgnorth]

SJ7512: 3 miles (5km) N of Shifnal

Recent development at Sheriffhales has generally been along the main road, sparing the village centre which lies just to the west. The **church of St Mary** is at the centre of the village, but little remains from the original medieval church. The nave was added in 1661 and the chancel in the 18th century. The nave piers and arches were brought to Sheriffhales from Lilleshall Abbey. Just behind the church a flamboyant neo-Elizabethan lodge stands by the start of a lime-bordered avenue which runs for 2 miles (3km) to Lilleshall Hall. To the west of the lodge is **Sheriffhales Manor**, a timber-framed farmhouse where the Reverend John Woodhouse, in the 17th century, started a college for Roman Catholics and Nonconformists who were barred by their religion from attending other colleges. Among the famous names to study there were Tory statesmen Henry St John, 1st Viscount Bolingbroke (1678-1751), and Robert Harley, 1st Earl of Oxford (1661-1724).

SHIFNAL [Bridgnorth]

SJ7407: 3 miles (5km) from Telford Centre

The M54 bounds it to the north and the railway cuts boldly through the centre of it, rather than sneaking furtively past in the normal way of railways serving small country towns, so Shifnal is certainly well connected and has become a useful regional centre with a good range of shops and services. Development has been considerable in recent years but the centre still retains some charm. Shifnal seems to have begun its growth into a town back in the 14th century, and it prospered until 1591 brought a severe setback in the form of a fire which destroyed most of the houses and badly damaged the Norman church. The town was soon rebuilt and flourishing again, receiving a number of important boosts over the years. In the 18th century, for instance, Thomas Telford routed his Holyhead road through Shifnal, and in the 19th century the railway arrived, providing a rapid link to Shrewsbury, the coalfield towns (now Telford), Wolverhampton and Birmingham.

The comic novelist P.G. Wodehouse (see Stableford) knew Shifnal well and it may have been the model for his fictional Market Blandings. It has changed since Wodehouse's day but there are still many buildings of interest in the town centre, mainly along the High Street. Most of them are Georgian or Victorian, but a few older timber-framed houses survive, such as **Old Idsall House**. The **church of St Andrew** stands towards the southern end of town, a large building of red sandstone. It still has some Norman features but there has been a great deal of alteration and addition over the centuries, not to mention repair and refurbishment. Inside there is a good collection of monuments to 16th- and 17th-century members of the Brigges family. A little to the north is the Roman Catholic **church of St Mary**, built in 1860 by J.C. Buckler.

Not much is known about Shifnal's early history but its economy must have been based largely on agriculture and trade. However, industry came early to the town, though only in a small way, when the Earl of Shrewsbury built a charcoal blast furnace nearby in 1562, one of the very first in the country.

SHIPTON [Bridgnorth]

SO5691: 6 miles (10km) SW of Much Wenlock

A tiny hamlet at the foot of Wenlock Edge, Shipton is blessed with a superb Elizabethan house, **Shipton Hall**, built c1587 in Wenlock limestone for Richard Lutwyche of Lutwyche Hall. He gave it to his daughter Elizabeth when she married Thomas Mytton, and she could hardly have wished for a finer wedding present. It has all the features that make classic Elizabethan architecture so enjoyable – a four-storeyed tower porch, star-shaped chimney stacks and mullioned and transomed windows. More unusually, it also has a round stair turret at the back like Wilderhope Manor and Holdgate Farm. There are good outbuildings too, including a 13th-century dovecote (Shipton Hall replaced a much older house on the same site) and a Georgian stable block with a cupola and tall, arched entrance.

To improve the view from his daughter's new house, Lutwyche had the village of Shipton demolished and rebuilt a short distance away around a small green. A few timber-framed cottages remain but there are now modern houses too. Lutwyche spared the **church of St James**, which stands beside the hall, complete with Norman nave and chancel arch and Early English windows. The chancel itself was rebuilt in 1589 and there is also a little weatherboarded tower with a pyramidal roof. There is a memorial tablet to four members of the More family (see Linley) – Jasper, Mary, Richard and Elinor – who were baptised in the church, sailed on the *Mayflower* to New England in 1620 and all, except Richard, died while still young children. The church was restored in 1955 and again in 1998.

SHRAWARDINE [Shrewsbury and Atcham]

SJ3915: 6 miles (10km) NW of Shrewsbury

Locals call it Shraden, an attractive commuter village with timber-framed cottages and sandstone **St Mary's Church**, which is partly Norman, though much rebuilt. The nave dates from 1649, the chancel from 1722, and there was wholesale restoration in 1893. **Shrawardine Castle** consists only of a mound, part of a ditch and fragments of masonry in a field on the east side

of the village. The earliest castle on this site was probably built soon after the Conquest by Rainald the Sheriff, whom Domesday Book records as holding the manor of Shrawardine. It later became a Royal castle, serving as an outpost of Shrewsbury, and was destroyed by the Welsh in 1215. It was rebuilt after 1220 and what survives today is from that period. The castle was dismantled by Cromwell's troops in 1645, after a siege lasting just five days. Much of the stone was used for repairs to Shrewsbury Castle. Across the Severn is **Little Shrawardine**, where there was another Norman castle, of which only an eroded mound now remains.

SHREWSBURY [Shrewsbury and Atcham]

SJ4912: 9 miles (14km) W of Wellington

Shrewsbury is not the largest town in Shropshire, but it is the county town and has always been the focal point for trade and commerce. In 1300 a census showed it to be one of the 12 most prosperous towns in the country. While this is no longer the case, it still has a healthy economy and is full of interest and beauty. Its claim to be "England's finest Tudor town" is rarely disputed.

It was the River Severn that determined Shrewsbury's siting, its development and, to a large extent, its present character. Some believe the site of the present town to have been originally the Celtic Pengwern (others think Pengwern was at The Berth, near Baschurch) but by 901 we have the first written reference to Scrobbesbyrig – meaning "the fortified place of Scrob". Historians are unsure whether Scrob was a personal name or a reference to a scrub-covered hill, but it's worth noting that Richard's Castle near Ludlow took its name from a Richard le Scrob. Whatever its name meant, Saxon Scrobbesbyrig was built within the natural moat provided by a tight loop of the Severn, completely encircled except for a small gap, making a perfect defensive site. Even the gap was guarded by a ridge, on which a castle was later built.

Soon after the Norman Conquest, King William gave much of Shropshire to Roger de Montgomery, creating him Earl of Shrewsbury. Roger didn't endear himself to the townsfolk when he had 50 houses demolished to make room for **Shrewsbury Castle**, completing the town's defences. The Castle saw action almost immediately, being besieged in 1069 by Wild Edric (see Stiperstones) with a force of Welshmen and locals, augmented by a contingent from Cheshire. The castle held out, though much of the town was burnt before the rebels were repulsed. This was just the start, and for many years Shrewsbury was an important military base for Norman operations against the Welsh. At the same time, however, it was building on its riverside location to become a busy inland port. By the 14th century, despite involvement in border conflicts, it was enormously wealthy and successful in a variety of trades. It was the woollen cloth trade, however, which assumed pre-eminence and it remained Shrewsbury's staple until the end of the 18th century, reaching its peak in the Tudor period, after peace with Wales had finally been achieved. It was the wool merchants and drapers who built many of the spectacular timber-framed mansions which still grace Shrewsbury's streets today.

Following the disruption of the Civil War, and a gradual decline in the wool trade, Shrewsbury reinvented itself as a fashionable centre for leisure and shopping, a role which expanded in the great coaching era, thanks to the town's position on the main London-Holyhead road. When the coaching era was at its height Shrewsbury provided stabling for over 100 horses a night: many people travelled regularly to London, seemingly undeterred by a journey-time approaching 30 hours in 1800. Improved roads had reduced this to 16 hours by 1831, but in 1849, with the arrival of the railway, London was suddenly a mere five hours away and the heyday of the coaches was over.

With the subsequent decline of the railways, Shrewsbury has fallen prey to the usual traffic congestion, but remains an important regional centre. For today's visitor, much of its charm derives from the survival of its medieval street pattern, particularly the abundance of narrow passages known locally as shuts and gullets. And then there is the quality of its architectural heritage, with a total of 660 listed buildings in the town centre alone. Few places have such an astonishing wealth of period buildings and the impact is all the greater because most are crowded together in the centre, within the Severn's tight embrace. There is no room here to do more than mention more than the barest handful.

Shrewsbury Station makes a good starting point for any exploration of the town. Built of Grinshill stone, with battlements, a pinnacled clock tower and oriel windows, this is Victorian "Tudor" at its most enjoyable. Just a few paces away is the castle; not Earl Roger's stronghold but a later one, though built of the same red sandstone. The oldest parts date from the time of Henry II (1154-89). Its greatest importance was in the days of cross-border warfare but it was refortified during the Civil War when Charles I established it as a regional headquarters, only to lose it to the Roundheads in 1645. In later years the castle played a variety of roles and was extensively remodelled by Thomas Telford in the 1790s. It now houses the **Shropshire Regimental Museum**. The grounds are enclosed by walls, of which one of the main features is a folly called Laura's Tower, built by Telford.

Not far from the castle is the timber-framed **Old Council House** which was the residence of the President of the Council in the Marches (see Ludlow) when the Council met in Shrewsbury. Charles I also lived there while recruiting in Shrewsbury

Wyle Cop, Shrewsbury

during the Civil War. Across the road is **Shrewsbury Library**, housed in a Tudor building of Grinshill stone, the original **Shrewsbury School**, founded by Edward VI in 1552, before the School moved across the river to Kingsland in 1882. Notable past pupils include **Charles Darwin** (1809-82) and the Elizabethan soldier-poet **Sir Philip Sidney** (1554-86), whose father served as President of the Council in the Marches. Sidney died of wounds sustained in battle at Zutphen (now Shrewsbury's twin town) in the Netherlands.

Charles Darwin was born at **The Mount**, a large house in Frankwell (now council offices, but open to the public). His maternal grandfather was Josiah Wedgwood, the potter, and his paternal grandfather Erasmus was a prominent physician, poet and freethinker who anticipated his grandson's views on evolution. His father Robert was the leading medical practitioner in town. The young Charles didn't shine at school but after a couple of false starts in different careers he was offered the position of naturalist on *HMS Beagle* which was about to

set sail round the world on a detailed scientific survey. The trip lasted five years, following which Darwin published many scientific books and papers, but it was 1859 before he produced his ground-breaking *The Origin of Species by Means of Natural Selection*. Darwin managed to shock much of the educated world with his theories, particularly, of course, the church establishment, but biologists proved easier to convince. The people of Shrewsbury showed how proud they were of their most famous son in 1894, when they organised and paid for the erection of the statue which still sits outside Darwin's former school.

Shrewsbury is renowned for its medieval churches. **St Mary's Church**, a mixture of many periods but originally a Saxon foundation, is the largest and best preserved of them. It is believed to have been founded by King Edgar c970 on the site of an even earlier church. It was rebuilt in 1150, and again on further occasions, showing signs of almost every architectural style from the 12th century to the 19th. A special feature is its superb glass, especially the magnificent 14th-century east window. It is now redundant and looked after by the Redundant Churches Fund which claims it as its "cathedral". Its 15th-century spire, one of the highest in England, partially collapsed in 1894 but was carefully rebuilt. The vicar was convinced that its collapse was divine retribution, as the townsfolk were at that time organising the erection of arch-heretic Darwin's statue. In 1739 a man called Cadman attempted to fly from the top of St Mary's spire, with predictable results. An entertaining plaque on the tower tells his story.

The ancient centre of Shrewsbury is **St Alkmund's Square**, where there are two more churches of Saxon origin. **St Julian's Church** now houses a craft market and a restaurant, and **St Alkmund's Church** was rebuilt in 1793, using cast-iron tracery from Coalbrookdale in the windows. The 15th-century tower was spared because it resisted all attempts to demolish it. Nearby is a range of timber-framed buildings known as **Bear Steps**, parts of which date back to the 14th century. Neighbouring **Butcher Row** is packed with more good buildings, especially the magnificent **Abbot's House** of 1450, and so are Fish Street, Dogpole, Wyle Cop, High Street, Milk Street and many more. Wyle Cop, in particular, has some treasures, such as **Henry Tudor House**, where the future Henry VII stayed one night on his way to victory at Bosworth, and the **Lion Hotel**, one of many former coaching inns. Charles Dickens stayed at the Lion on at least one occasion.

The tourist information centre is housed in the **Music Hall**, an imposing building of 1840 in The Square at the centre of town. Opposite it is the **Market Hall**, built in 1596 for the sale of woollen cloth. A niche in the north gable holds a statue of Richard, Duke of York (the father of Edward IV) which was moved here from the old Welsh Bridge. A statue of Robert Clive also stands in The Square (see Moreton Say).

Other notable buildings include the ruined church in tranquil Belmont, **Old St Chad's**, and its replacement, **New St Chad's**, which caused a certain amount of consternation when it was built in 1790-92 to the design of George Steuart. Its round nave had some observers commenting that it was more suitable for use as a ballroom, but Charles Darwin's parents had no objection to their son's christening taking place there, although the family worshipped at the **Unitarian Church** on High Street. Not far from New St Chad's, on Town Walls, is the Roman Catholic **Cathedral of our Lady of Help and St Peter of Alcantra**. A large, imposing building, it has a high gable in place of a tower and was built in 1856 in Gothic Revival style by E.W. Pugin.

Rowley's House is a spectacular timber-framed building of the 1590s in which one William Rowley established himself as a draper and brewer. This odd combination was obviously a successful one because by 1618 he was prosperous enough to build the attached mansion, the first brick house in Shrewsbury. Today Rowley's House is open to the public in its new capacity as a museum housing a varied range of collections. Less beautiful, but visible for miles around, is **Lord Hill's Column** at the end of Abbey Foregate, completed in 1816 to commemorate the military achievements of Viscount Hill (see Hadnall) and said to be the tallest Doric column in the world.

Clive House Museum has one of the country's finest collections of Coalport and Caughley porcelain and also depicts 18th- and 19th-century life in Shrewsbury. Clive House is itself a splendid building, outwardly Georgian but medieval underneath, and was the home of Lord Clive for a time. Also notable is the former Royal Salop Infirmary (1826-30, by Haycock) in St Mary's Place, now converted into a shopping centre, **The Parade**. There is a good view of it from **English Bridge**, the most famous of the 10 bridges spanning the Severn as it encircles Shrewsbury. Though the river was bridged at this point by the 12th century, or even earlier, the present bridge was first completed in 1774, though it was subsequently dismantled in the 1920s and completely reconstructed with a reduced gradient and wider carriageway. Its counterpart on the other side of town is **Welsh Bridge**, which was built in its present form in 1795, though there was a bridge here soon after 1100. At the other side of English Bridge, beyond the **United Reformed Church** (1863), is the **Abbey Church of St Peter and St Paul.** Shrewsbury Abbey was founded in 1083 by Roger de Montgomery on the site of an earlier Saxon church just outside the town walls. The Abbey Church which survives today was once part of a much larger complex with a full range of monastic buildings. Following the Dissolution of the Monasteries, the church survived because it was in use as a parish church, and some of the other buildings survived until 1834 when Thomas Telford drove his Holyhead road through the site. The 14th-century refectory pulpit was spared, and now sits incongruously in the middle of a car park across the road. The Abbey Church contains work from several periods but still retains its massive Norman columns and simple arches. The great west tower was built in the reign of Edward III and is the dominant part of the present building, with the west window considered the finest Perpendicular window in Shropshire. Shrewsbury Abbey is the setting for the popular Cadfael novels by Ellis Peters (the pen name of the late Edith Pargeter, a native of Dawley).

Shrewsbury has a surprising amount of green space, especially by the River Severn: in fact, few towns make such good use of their river frontage. **The Quarry** is enormously popular and has been used for recreation since the 16th century. Its centrepiece is **The Dingle**, a formal garden designed by **Percy Thrower** (1913-88), Parks Superintendent 1946-74 and for long

the country's most famous gardener. The famous **Shrewsbury Flower Show** is held in The Quarry every August. Less formally, cows graze beside the River Severn on the other side of Port Hill Bridge, while **Rea Brook Valley** is a Local Nature Reserve managed by the borough council and comprising an area of pastures, flood meadows and scrublands along the valley of the Rea Brook from Meole Brace to Abbey Foregate. On the north-east side of town is **Monkmoor Pool**, a settlement lagoon attractive to birds.

SIBDON CARWOOD [South Shropshire]
SO4183: 1 mile (2km) W of Craven Arms

A charming and secluded hamlet, Sibdon Carwood consists of little more than a farm, a church and a couple of houses. So-called **Sibdon Castle** is not a real castle, just a castellated country house. It is believed to have been built in the 17th century, modernised in the 18th and Gothicised at the beginning of the 19th. **St Michael's Church** is of 1741 but was Gothicised in 1871 to match the house. It's believed to stand on the site of a 12th-century building and Sibdon Carwood is certainly a more ancient settlement than it appears for it was mentioned in Domesday Book.

SIDBURY [Bridgnorth]
SO6885: 5 miles (8km) SW of Bridgnorth

A small village in mixed farming country, Sidbury occupies a hill above Horsford Brook. The **church of Holy Trinity** is early Norman, with some herringbone masonry and the original Norman font. The church was heavily restored in 1878-81 and again in 1912, following a fire. Black and white **Rectory Farm** stands opposite the church and close by is the site of a deserted medieval village. There was a moated castle here which survived the abandonment of the village but was destroyed by Cromwell and later replaced by a house. This was destroyed by fire and only the stable block survives. In 1830 Hall Farm was built on the site.

SILVINGTON [South Shropshire]

SO6279: 4 miles (6km) NW of Cleobury Mortimer

In a glorious position on the brackeny north-eastern slopes of Titterstone Clee Hill, Silvington is a tiny, remote hamlet. Earthworks indicate the position of a moat next to the **Manor House**, a partly medieval, partly stone-built house with some very early lancet windows. The **church of St Nicholas** has a 13th-century tower, nave and chancel, with mainly 14th-century windows and a porch of 1662. Church and Manor House combine to make a thoroughly appealing picture in a location that could hardly be more peaceful and unspoilt. There is another handsome farmhouse across the lane and the partly half-timbered **Upper House Farm** below Silvington Common is another treasure.

SMETHCOTT [Shrewsbury and Atcham]

SO4499: 4 miles (6km) N of Church Stretton

One of a multitude of tiny hamlets which dot the landscape at the northern end of the Long Mynd, Smethcott differs from the others in having both a castle and a church. **Smethcott Castle** is a simple Norman motte and bailey, of which only the earthworks remain. The **church of St Michael** stands next to it and is of the same age but was rebuilt in 1850. It still retains a Norman window, and the priest's doorway may also be Norman. Other than a couple of cottages, there is nothing else near the church and castle. However, a small cluster of farms has developed a little way to the north-east. The original village, which must have been more substantial, judging by its entry in Domesday Book, was obviously abandoned at some stage.

SNAILBEACH [South Shropshire]

SJ3702: 3 miles (5km) SW of Pontesbury

The village of Snailbeach enjoys a superb location at the foot of the hills which form the northern part of the range culminating in Stiperstones. Snailbeach has a number of uninspiring houses, old and new, also a village hall, a Methodist chapel and the **church of St Luke**, built in 1872 as a mission church, and now a daughter chapel of Minsterley parish. The real interest here lies in the ruins of a once flourishing lead-mining community. In 1887 **Snailbeach Mine** was described as "one of the most important lead mines in the Kingdom" and this seems to have been no exaggeration. It employed over 500 people in its heyday, and reached 500 metres below the surface at its deepest point. However, competition from overseas lead mines at the beginning of the 20th century led to the decline of the industry in this country. The mine closed in 1911 and the lower levels were allowed to flood. Small-scale mining for barytes continued in the shallower parts of the mine until 1955, when underground mining finally ceased altogether.

The miners left a legacy of contaminated spoil heaps, unstable workings, open mine shafts and derelict buildings so Shropshire County Council initiated a reclamation scheme to deal with these hazards. Not only was the site made safe, it was also made available to the public. Spoil heaps have been grassed over and now look completely natural, a former mineral railway has been enhanced by tree planting and a trail has been created round the site. The work has been carried out with sensitivity and in 1997 it received an award from the Royal Town Planning Institute. Most of the former mine buildings still stand, including a rock store, a locomotive shed, the main mine complex, a Cornish engine house complex, a smelter chimney, a candle house, a magazine and an ore treatment plant. There's also a small reservoir at the

Upper Works and a mine shaft known as Black Tom.

A short walk uphill from Snailbeach leads to other points of interest. Just to the south, up Resting Hill, there is an isolated mine chimney which was restored in 1999. Continuing south from here the footpath leads past the spectacular cleft of Crows Nest Dingle and provides a view of **Castle Ring**, a prehistoric fort on Oak Hill. The path then continues south towards Stiperstones. Alternatively, a short walk east from Snailbeach leads to **Lordshill**, which comprises a farm, a house and an old chapel which was used in the film of Mary Webb's *Gone to Earth* (see Leighton). The novel ends with the heroine plunging to her death down a mine shaft as she tries vainly to save her pet fox from the Hunt.

STABLEFORD [Bridgnorth]

SO7598: 5 miles (8km) NE of Bridgnorth

An attractive small village in undulating pastoral country by the River Worfe, Stableford consists of a mixture of timber-framed houses and modern bungalows. There is also **Stableford Hall**, a seven-bay brick house with an elaborate stone porch. For many people the main interest at Stableford is **Hay House**, where **P.G. Wodehouse** (1881-1975), the creator of Bertie Wooster and the inimitable Jeeves, lived between the ages of 14 and 21. Wodehouse retained a great affection for the area throughout his life and many houses and villages in Shropshire (and neighbouring Worcestershire) inspired the settings for his novels.

STANTON LACY [South Shropshire]

SO4978: 3 miles (5km) N of Ludlow

The village of Stanton Lacy consists of a church, two farms and a picturesque huddle of houses and cottages in stone, brick and timber set against a delightful green backdrop of hills. The first church here was, according to legend, erected c680 by St

Milburgha (see Much Wenlock). The story is that she was being chased by a Welsh Prince determined to be her lover. Having crossed the River Corve she prayed that the water might become an impassable torrent. Her prayer was answered, the Prince was left stranded and in gratitude she founded the church on the site.

Whatever its origins, **St Peter's Church** is an impressive cruciform building which contains some unmistakable Saxon workmanship. The earliest parts of the church are the north and west walls of the nave and the north transept. These are decorated externally with lesenes or pilaster strips in a "long and short" pattern, typical of mid 11th-century Saxon work, as are the tall, narrow proportions of the nave and transept. The moulding above the north door is also Saxon but reveals a Norman influence and probably does not pre-date the Conquest by many years. The dominant feature of the present church is the tower, which is believed to date from c1330.

St Peter's is an unusually large church for such a small village but the explanation lies in the early prosperity of Stanton, which was the site of a Roman villa and continued to be intensively cultivated throughout the Saxon period. By the time of the Domesday survey it was at the centre of the richest, most productive land in Shropshire. At this time Stanton was held by the de Lacy family, close associates of William I. It was Roger de Lacy who created the town of Ludlow, and for centuries Ludlow Castle was actually part of the parish of Stanton Lacy.

STANTON LONG [Bridgnorth]

SO5790: 7 miles (11km) W of Church Stretton

A farming hamlet enjoying a quiet, remote situation in Corve Dale's lush sheep country, Stanton Long is a small collection of mainly stone farms and cottages, with some brick ones. The simple little **church of St Michael and All Angels** dates from the 13th century and much of it is original, though the timber bellcote is a later addition and an over-zealous restoration was undertaken in 1869.

STANTON UPON HINE HEATH [North Shropshire]

SJ5623: 5 miles (8km) SE of Wem

A nucleated village by the River Roden, Stanton upon Hine Heath is pleasant but unremarkable. There are some attractive old houses, mostly of brick, and stone-built **St Andrew's Church** has a Norman nave and chancel and some herringbone masonry in the north wall, indicating either Saxon or early Norman workmanship. The 13th-century tower is topped with 15th-century pinnacles and supported by heavy buttresses dated 1666. The church sits on a roughly circular mound, suggesting a possible pre-Christian origin for this site of worship. Tucked away to the north of the village is **Harcourt Manor**, formerly called The Woodlands, where the young Mary Webb (see Leighton) lived from 1896 to 1902.

STANWARDINE IN THE FIELDS [North Shropshire]

SJ4124: 7 miles (11km) S of Ellesmere

The hamlet of Stanwardine in the Fields sits on the southern edge of Baggy Moor, a former marshland now drained and turned into productive farmland. It was one of the last major drainage projects undertaken in Shropshire and was not completed until the 1860s. Stanwardine consists of a handful of brick cottages, a timber-framed farm and a Primitive Methodist chapel of 1869.

STANWARDINE IN THE WOOD [North Shropshire]

SJ4227: 5 miles (8km) SE of Ellesmere

There is not much woodland at Stanwardine in the Wood today but the name indicates that this hamlet must have been cleared from the forest in Saxon

times. It was probably just an isolated farm and there is not much more to it today, just two or three farms and **Stanwardine Hall**, an Elizabethan mansion built between 1560 and 1580, probably for Robert Corbet, brother of Sir Andrew Corbet (see Moreton Corbet).

STAPLETON [Shrewsbury and Atcham]

SJ4704: 5 miles (8km) S of Shrewsbury

A linear village, Stapleton lies below Lyth Hill and close to the Cound Brook, among fields of sheep and cereals. Most of the housing is modern, but **Manor Farm** has a fine range of traditional farm buildings, including a timber barn. The medieval **church of St John the Baptist** is red sandstone, except for the tower, which is a greyish stone and was added in 1840. It's an unusual church, with an old undercroft incorporated into it by the removal of a floor. The original church and undercroft were built c1200 but in 1786 the church floor was removed so that the floor of the undercroft became the floor of the church. To the south-east of the church there stands the partially tree-clad motte of what looks to have been a fairly substantial Norman castle, while other earthworks nearby may indicate old house platforms.

STIPERSTONES [South Shropshire]

SJ3600: 4 miles (6km) SW of Pontesbury

Stiperstones the hill is well known, Stiperstones the village less so, but it is a former mining community below the north-western slopes of the hill. The countryside all around is riddled with old lead mines and spoil heaps, especially at Perkins Beach, Tankerville, Pennerley and The Bog. Derelict stone buildings are scattered here and there: some of them were mine buildings, others were miners' cottages. Stiperstones village is a motley collection of dwellings, old and new, with a shop, a pub, a school and a Methodist chapel. **The**

Bog was once a mining village too, based around a lead mine which opened in 1740. When the last mines closed in the 1920s most people began to leave. It was a gradual process but by 1970 they had all gone and the old cottages were demolished. In the 1980s the county council reclaimed the area, much as has been done more recently at Snailbeach. There are still plenty of reminders of the mining to be seen and the former village chapel now houses a field centre.

The hill called Stiperstones is part of an important National Nature Reserve and takes the form of a long ridge of rugged heather moorland with a jagged dragon's crest of quartzite pinnacles. This extraordinary landscape has its origins in the last Ice Age, when the ridge stood out above the glaciers and was subject to intense frost shattering, creating a mass of scree surrounding a number of residual tors. Some of the scree is still exposed, while elsewhere thin, acid soils have developed, supporting a sparse but specialised flora and fauna. Stiperstones has attracted many myths and legends; naturally, the usual witches and devils occur, but so does **Wild Edric**, a Saxon nobleman who briefly resisted the Normans. Edric did actually exist and it was inevitable that anybody who rebelled against Norman rule would become a folk hero to the downtrodden Saxons. Successive generations wove increasingly unlikely stories around his memory, but the central story concerns the imprisonment of Edric and his followers in the lead mines beneath Stiperstones and their emergence on horseback to tackle the enemy on those occasions when England is in danger.

STIRCHLEY [Wrekin]
SJ7006: 1 mile (2km) S of Telford Centre

Stirchley is just another part of Telford now but it started life as an Anglo-Saxon farming settlement and continued to be largely agricultural until the 18th century when coal mining began. Iron furnaces came next

and a very different Stirchley began to take shape. In the 1960s another momentous change came about when the development of Telford led to the reclaiming of what had become post-industrial wasteland. Stirchley is now almost entirely given over to housing estates but it has plenty of green space and the old pre-industrial centre still survives at Stirchley Village, where the redundant **church of St James** overlooks the scene from high ground. It retains a Norman chancel and some original windows but was partially rebuilt in brick in 1741 and extended in 1839. There are several other pleasant old buildings, the best of which is **Stirchley Hall**, a gabled building of great character, built (or rebuilt) in 1653. It has been added to since and is now divided into flats. Also associated with Stirchley are areas such as Randley, Brookside and Hinkshay, all of which retain some interest, even though modern housing is the dominant theme. There is plenty of green space, several pools, a Field Study Centre at Hinkshay and abundant industrial remains, such as **Stirchley Chimney**, part of a crucible furnace built in 1873, and over 60 metres tall.

STOCKTON [Bridgnorth]
SO7299: 5 miles (8km) N of Bridgnorth

The village stands on a ridge in attractive country above the Severn and constitutes **St Chad's Church**, the rectory (1702) and a cottage. St Chad's has a Norman chancel but has undergone considerable restoration, mainly in 1860. This little group of buildings stands at one of the entrances to Apley Hall, which is also in the parish (see Apley).

STOKE ST MILBOROUGH [South Shropshire]
SO5682: 6 miles (10km) NE of Ludlow

An attractive village on the lower slopes of Brown Clee, Stoke St Milborough enjoys excellent views and a peaceful setting. St

Milburgha, who obviously led an exciting life (see Much Wenlock and Stanton Lacy), was responsible for another miracle here after she collapsed in an exhausted heap following a two-day chase by yet another unwanted suitor. She lay close to death from thirst but was saved when a spring suddenly burst forth from the ground. The spring still exists and is known as **St Milburgha's Well**. Stoke St Milborough probably originated as a daughter settlement of Much Wenlock and it had daughter settlements of its own, as many as six in 1086 according to Domesday Book. Such settlements were initially speculative ventures which might or might not succeed. New land was settled but the "colonists" remained dependent on the mother village for financial, administrative and religious support until such time as they could stand on their own feet and become established villages in their own right. The **church of St Milburgha**, with its embattled tower, occupies a dominant position in the village and owes much to the 13th and 14th centuries. The timber-framed porch was added in 1707.

STOKESAY [South Shropshire]

SO4381: 1 mile (2km) S of Craven Arms

A castle, a church, a farm and two or three cottages make up the hamlet of Stokesay, which nestles in lovely countryside dominated by wooded hills. Originally called Stoke, the manor was held before the Conquest by Wild Edric (see Stiperstones) but was then given to the de Say family. In 1068 Picot de Say (see Clun) built a house and a church. In 1280 the manor was sold to a wealthy wool merchant, Laurence of Ludlow, who set about rebuilding and fortifying the house, once he had obtained a "licence to

crenellate" from Edward I. The result was the almost impossibly picturesque **Stokesay Castle**, not really a castle at all but a fortified manor house. The architectural style owes more to fashion than to any real need for fortification, and Stokesay could not have withstood prolonged assault.

Ten generations of Laurence's descendants lived at Stokesay and a superb timber-framed gatehouse, embellished with fine carvings, was added in the Elizabethan period. In the reign of Charles I Stokesay came into the ownership of the Craven family and was used as a supply base for the King's forces when they were based at Ludlow in the early stages of the Civil War. It was surrendered to the Roundheads without a siege when it came under attack.

By the 19th century Stokesay Castle had

The Tudor gatehouse at Stokesay Castle

fallen into decay and was being used as a barn. Happily, in 1869 it was sold to John Darby Allcroft, a Worcester industrialist and MP, who set about restoring it. The years of neglect had not been too harmful and Stokesay Castle is the best preserved and probably the oldest example of its kind in England. It is now in the care of English Heritage. Almost every feature of this magical place is special, but the Great Hall is a particularly rare survival, almost untouched since medieval times and containing its original staircase, an open octagonal hearth and an innovative timber roof. There is also a fine solar which is accessible only by an exterior stair and contains Elizabethan panelling and a sumptuous fireplace. The most castle-like part of the house is the south tower, which is of a most unusual shape, partly octagonal, and has lancet windows.

The adjacent **church of St John the Baptist** was largely rebuilt between 1654 and 1664, following damage in the Civil War. This makes it more important than is immediately apparent, because very few churches were built or restored during this period. The south doorway is the only feature to have survived from the original Norman church.

On the far side of the River Onny, the land rises abruptly in the shape of wooded Whettleton Hill, on the summit of which an Iron Age fort, **Norton Camp**, overlooks Stokesay Castle. The camp guarded the southern tip of Wenlock Edge and was defended by substantial ramparts and ditches, which now form the boundaries of adjoining fields to the east and south.

STOKE ON TERN [North Shropshire]

SJ6428: 4 miles (6km) SW of Market Drayton

The village of Stoke on Tern stands in flat farmland close to the River Tern, with the sandstone **church of St Peter** aloof from the village. It was built in 1874-5 to replace a Norman church. Inside there are alabaster effigies from the original church, to members of the ubiquitous Corbet family. Across the river there is a delightful timber-framed house called **Petsey**, dated 1634. To the south-east of the village stands **Stoke Manor**, adjacent to which the remains of a moat mark the site of **Stoke Castle**, which belonged to the Corbets of Adderley and was held for Parliament during the Civil War. At Manor Gate stands a cottage which was the birthplace of the so-called "Shropshire Giant", Thomas Dutton, who was born in 1853. He stood 7ft 3ins (2.5m) and was renowned for his great strength. He is buried in the churchyard at St Peter's.

STOTTESDON [Bridgnorth]

SO6782: 4 miles (6km) N of Cleobury Mortimer

On high ground in the attractive country between the Severn Valley and the Clee Hills, Stottesdon is a village of old cottages and farmhouses mingling with modern houses and bungalows. The **church of St Mary** is one of the most important in the district. It is a Norman building and inside the tower, above what was originally the west doorway, is a carved tympanum. This is probably Norman too, but Pevsner suggests that the lintel and tympanum frame may be Saxon. The church also contains an elaborately carved Norman font that is reckoned to be the best in Shropshire. It dates from c1160 and is almost certainly by a member of the renowned Hereford School of sculptors.

STOWE [South Shropshire]

SO3173: 2 miles (3km) NE of Knighton

Tucked away in a narrow valley cut into Stow Hill, there is not much to Stowe but it is a delightful hamlet. The **church of St Michael** is basically 13th century but with a good deal of later work, including two unusual Art Nouveau mosaics created c1900. Below the church stands the rectory and that's about it, apart from wonderful views across the River Teme to Wales.

SUTTON MADDOCK [Bridgnorth]

SJ7101: 3 miles (5km) SE of Ironbridge

A cluster of mostly nondescript buildings by the main road constitutes the larger part of Sutton Maddock. But there is more to the hamlet, with a church, farm and hall standing aloof at the end of a "no through road" which runs west towards the Severn. There are also further farms and houses off two lanes to the east and another cluster at Sutton Common just to the north. **Sutton Hall** is a brick Georgian house of some stature in beautifully landscaped grounds. The **church of St Mary** stands on a circular mound which indicates antiquity but the church is largely a rebuilding of 1888. The tower is older, however, dated at 1579. The village was originally just Sutton but acquired its suffix when it came into the possession of Madoc, a member of the ruling family of Powys. Later in its history it belonged to a family called Brooks, whose crest features a badger, a symbol now depicted on some of the village houses. Live badgers are probably quite scarce in the surrounding countryside, however, which is flat and put to arable crops – not good badger country.

TASLEY [Bridgnorth]

SO6994: 1 mile (2km) NW of Bridgnorth

Only just beyond the reach of encroaching Bridgnorth, Tasley is a tiny ridge-top hamlet overlooking the town. It has always been a mainly agricultural community but there have been some abortive attempts at industry. There was a brick works for a while but today only Brickyard Cottages reveal the site of this lost industry. After the Second World War attempts were made to mine coal but without much success and nearby Coalpit Plantation is the only obvious clue today. The **church of St Peter and St Paul** was built in 1840 in yellow brick to

the design of Josiah Griffith on the site of a Norman church destroyed by fire. It contains a Norman font, a 15th-century screen and a Jacobean pulpit.

TELFORD [Wrekin]

SJ6908: 3 miles (5km) SE of Wellington

Like Ludlow, Telford is a deliberately planned town, but whereas Ludlow was planned on a small scale over 900 years ago, Telford was planned only in the 1960s and is already the largest town in Shropshire, with nearly twice the population of the county town, Shrewsbury. Telford is a collective name for those coalfield towns (Dawley, Madeley etc.) which were lumped together to form Telford New Town, with housing developments, factories and trading estates filling in the gaps between them and linkage provided by a motorway-like road system, together with cycleways, footpaths and pedestrian underpasses. The more interesting or important of the towns which make up Telford are dealt with separately under their individual names so all that is included here is Telford Town Centre, together with a handful of suburbs.

When the Dawley Development Corporation began work in 1963, it had only a post-industrial wasteland where decay and deprivation were the norm. It was given extensive powers under the New Towns Act and its purpose was to revitalise an area in severe economic decline and develop it as an overflow for Birmingham and the Black Country. In 1968 the name was changed to the Telford Development Corporation and the scope of the project enlarged. In fact, the Corporation's task was the largest urban land reclamation project ever undertaken by a single authority.

The former coalfield industries have been successfully replaced by more advanced technological industries and Telford is promoted not only throughout the UK but also throughout the world as an attractive place for companies to relocate.

Many (including around two dozen Japanese companies) have chosen to do so, and vast new housing estates have been built to house their workforces. Whatever one might think of the urban sprawl that has been created, it's impossible to deny that enormous changes have taken place, many of them for the better. Ironbridge, for instance, was rescued from dereliction to become the charming, thriving little town of today. If other areas have not benefited so obviously we can at least hope that lessons have been learned which will prove invaluable in guiding future development, though that will not be the province of the Telford Development Corporation, which was disbanded in 1991.

Telford Centre is entirely modern, a temple to glass, plastic, steel and concrete. Apart from a huge undercover shopping centre given over almost entirely to multiples, it includes office blocks, a civic centre, entertainment complexes, a hotel, the Wrekin District Council offices, a rather isolated rail station and a desperately dismal, down-at-heel bus station, in which Arriva's sleek modern vehicles look strangely out of place. A network of footpaths links everything and there has been an attempt to retain areas of green space. Of the office buildings of the 1960s and 1970s there is little to be said; some of those erected in the 1980s and 1990s are less brutal. In the very centre of town, at Telford Square, pleasant seating areas surround a pool, at one end of which is an imaginative sculpture of Thomas Telford, created by André Wallace in 1988.

Telford Town Park is quite a surprise; a definite cut above the average municipal park. Near the shopping centre it has a range of amenities for children and such traditional features as flower beds and a bandstand, but further afield it takes on an entirely different character. Remnants of early industry and natural regeneration combine to create a most interesting and, in places, entirely natural-seeming landscape

of woods, pools and grassland. The canals and railways which once ran through the site have now been either reclaimed by nature or turned into footpaths and cycleways, and the former brick pits of Randlay Brick Works are now pools teeming with wildlife. There is also a ruined Norman chapel brought here in 1971 from Malinslee (where it was in the way of a car park) and re-erected beside Withy Pool. In its original incarnation it is believed to have offered rest and refreshment to travellers passing through the Wrekin Forest, which once covered what is now Telford.

Adjoining Telford Centre to the north-east is Hollinswood, the site of a former ironworks but now largely residential. On the western fringe of the centre is Malinslee, an Anglo-Saxon settlement where coal was mined in the 18th and 19th centuries. Something remains of the old village, with its red-brick houses and the **church of St Leonard**, built in 1805 from a yellowish stone. To the north of Malinslee is Old Park, where coal and iron ore were mined. By 1806 the Old Park Company was operating the second largest ironworks in Britain. It closed in the 1880s and now the spoil heaps are grassed over and being covered by new housing estates. Adjacent to Old Park is The Rock, a tiny settlement with a few squatters' cottages and two adjacent Primitive Methodist chapels, of 1861 and 1877. A bleak modern development called Overdale lies just to the north.

Perhaps lessons have been learned from the earlier developments, for in 1998 plans were revealed for an entirely different sort of development on a site at Lightmoor. Provisionally called New Bournville, it will be a rambling development built on the same ethical and architectural principles as George Cadbury's original Bournville in Birmingham. Instead of the usual high-density housing, prospective residents are promised abundant green space and enough amenities to engender a real sense of community. It is hoped that some of the social values of the original Bournville can be imported and the estate will be managed by a trust, offering a variety of accommodation to meet all needs. The so-called "Robin Hood" principle will operate, with two thirds of the properties sold on the open market to allow the remaining third to be made available to tenants at below market rates.

(See also Aqueduct, Broseley, Coalbrookdale, Coalport, Dawley, Donnington, Horsehay, Ironbridge, Ketley, Leegomery, Madeley, Oakengates, Red Lake, Stirchley, Wombridge and Wrockwardine Wood.)

TERNHILL [North Shropshire]

SJ6332: 2 miles (3km) SW of Market Drayton

Ternhill is a relatively new development, not exactly a village as such. It is dominated by an RAF station and an army camp, Ternhill Barracks, which was the subject of an IRA attack in 1989 when one of the accommodation blocks was blown up. There was no loss of life. The most interesting building in Ternhill is **Tern Hall Hotel**, set in beautiful grounds and built in 1911 as a country house by Colonel Coghill, a local sportsman and fisherman.

TIBBERTON CUM CHERRINGTON [Wrekin]

SJ6820: 4 miles (6km) W of Newport

Tibberton is a large village set in a flat landscape by the River Meese. There are a few black and white cottages (at least one of which dates back to 1611) but Tibberton is characterised more by new housing these days. The **church of All Saints** lies on a bank above the River Meese and was built in 1842 of red sandstone to a Gothic design by J. Baddeley, replacing a 12th-century church. There is also a Primitive Methodist chapel of 1842. Tibberton has always been an agricultural village (though there are more commuters than farm workers now) but it also had a paper mill, said to be the

last in Shropshire when it closed down in 1932.

Cherrington is half a mile west of Tibberton, a rambling village on the northern edge of the Weald Moors. **Cherrington Manor** dates from 1635 and is a superb timber-framed house which dominates the hamlet. There are also some cruck-framed houses, probably of the 15th century and very rare in this part of the county.

TILLEY [North Shropshire]

SJ5027: 1 mile (2km) S of Wem

Just beyond the clutches of Wem's southern suburbs, Tilley is a peaceful hamlet with a handful of attractive houses. Timber-framed **Tilley Hall**, with two projecting gabled wings guarding a recessed centre, is dated 1613. **Tilley Manor** is similar but the timbers are partially obscured by rendering. The River Roden passes close to the hamlet and the surrounding fields are flat, some of them reclaimed from marshland and now providing fertile land which is used for both stock and cereals. From nearby **Tilley Green** a "no through road" leads to **Trench Hall**, a fine brick house with stone dressings and the unusual feature of two pediments at roof level. Adjacent **Trench Farm** is where **John Ireland** (died 1808), the biographer of Hogarth, was born and brought up. The Restoration dramatist **William Wycherley** (see Clive) also spent much of his childhood at Trench Farm, which was owned by his father.

TILSTOCK [North Shropshire]

SJ5437: 3 miles S of Whitchurch

Dairy farming used to be the main land use around the village of Tilstock, but an outbreak of foot-and-mouth disease in 1967 changed the landscape for ever. The fields are mostly arable now, with sugar beet, potatoes and wheat important locally. There are abundant new houses in the village and a range of facilities. Brick-built **Christ**

Tilley Hall

Church (1835-6) has cast-iron window frames, a slender tower with a steeple, and a delightful interior.

TONG [Bridgnorth]

SJ7907: 3 miles (5km) E of Shifnal

Pleasantly set in attractive countryside, Tong is not a large village but it is packed full of interesting features. Most famous of them is the **church of St Mary and St Bartholomew**, which was founded c1410 by Elizabeth, widow of Sir Fulke de Pembrugge. It replaced a Norman church and served a chantry college that she also founded to house monks to pray for the souls of her three deceased husbands. The chantry does not survive but the church is a striking Gothic building, all battlements and pinnacles, Perpendicular in style, cruciform in shape, with a tower that starts off square and becomes octagonal and is then topped by a spire. There is an enormous, almost overwhelming, number of monuments inside, especially to the Vernons, a prominent local family. The alabaster effigies are particularly fine. The Vernon Chapel of 1515, also known as the Golden Chapel, is a small but perfectly formed chantry with fan vaulting on which some of the original gilding survives. The church has Jacobean and Georgian furnishings and was restored in 1892 by Ewan Christian.

Charles Dickens stayed at Tong and described both church and village in *The Old Curiosity Shop* (1841), which features the character Little Nell. Outside the church is a grave often said to be that of Little Nell, a fictitious claim first made many years ago by an enterprising verger who realised that showing "Nell's grave" to tourists would be a lucrative source of income.

During construction of the M54 a Bronze Age axe (c700BC) was found near Tong but the present village was an Anglo-Saxon settlement and already of some importance when it came into the possession of Roger de Montgomery after the Conquest. The first castle here was built c1127 by Richard de Belmais, Bishop of London. It was a simple structure, added to by the La Zouche family some years later, and added to again in the 13th century when a new gatehouse was built. In or about 1300 Tong acquired new owners, the Pembrugges, who built a new manor house, obtaining a licence to crenellate in 1381. In 1447 the manor of

Tong passed to the Vernons, who built a new house c1500, which was itself rebuilt in the late 17th century by another family, the Pierrepoints. The Durant family moved to Tong in 1760 and in 1765 all the existing buildings were cleared to make way for an extravagant new house of Moorish-Gothic design built for George Durant by Capability Brown, who was more famous as a landscape artist than an architect. He did also landscape the grounds and various lodges and follies were erected. One of the best known is a curious pyramidal dovecote. The follies survive but the hall was demolished in 1954 by the Earl of Bradford and the M54 now runs through the site. A scattering of remains, mainly foundations, is all that can be seen today.

The Stanley family owned the manor for a time and in 1600 **Venetia Stanley** was born. She became one of the most acclaimed beauties of her age and counted amongst her admirers the dramatist Ben Jonson and the painter Van Dyck. She died suddenly at 33 and a post mortem is reputed to have revealed that her brain had shrunk to the size of a walnut. This was attributed to her having drunk viper wine, whatever that may be, in order to preserve her youth and beauty. Cynics said she was poisoned by her husband, Sir Kenelm Digby, who was well aware that he had himself fathered only a modest selection of her numerous offspring. The Tong women were a colourful lot; another one who made the headlines was **Mary Anne Smythe** (1756-1837), whose father was the agent in charge of Tong Castle. Better known as Maria Fitzherbert, in 1785 she became the mistress and unlawful wife of the Prince of Wales, later George IV.

Apart from the church, other buildings of interest in Tong include timber-framed **Church Farm**, some good brick houses and the unusual **Old Post Office**, which has a Venetian window and a pediment. Adjacent to it is the elegant **Red House**, built in Georgian brick. Adjacent again is a range

of 18th-century **almshouses** and an 18th-century former **vicarage** with Tuscan pilasters supporting a pediment.

Nearby is a mysterious ruin in a field, consisting of sections of walling, a round-headed window and a pointed arch doorway. Its origin and purpose are unknown but it looks to have been of some substance.

TREFONEN [Oswestry]

SJ2526: 3 miles (5km) SW of Oswestry

Set on high ground close to the Welsh border, the village of Trefonen has expanded greatly in recent years so that old grey stone now mingles uneasily with new red brick. **All Saints' Church** was built of stone in 1821-8, but its chancel and apse were not added until 1876. Trenant United Reformed Church was built in 1832. Sections of **Offa's Dyke** survive to north and south of Trefonen.

TUCKHILL [Bridgnorth]

SO7888: 6 miles (10km) SE of Bridgnorth

Tuckhill is a tiny hamlet of houses and farms in a lovely setting on a ridge top by the Staffordshire border. In fact, the border runs through Tuckhill Farm. The **church of Holy Innocents** was built in 1865 to a design of J.P. Saint Aubyn. A thoroughly mediocre building, it has a sort of grandeur conferred on it by the beauty of its setting. It is reputed to have been built to combat Methodism – the present village hall was originally a Methodist chapel.

TUGFORD [South Shropshire]

SO5587: 7 miles (11km) SE of Church Stretton

Tugford is a small village on the lower north-western slopes of Brown Clee Hill on the edge of Corve Dale. Its stone-built cottages shelter by Tugford Brook, where **Tugford Mill** is probably on the same site as a mill recorded in Domesday Book. The simple and delightful **St Catherine's**

Church is Norman with a 13th-century tower and chancel. Inside the arch on either side of the entrance door are two small sheela-na-gigs. These are pre-Christian fertility symbols which are common in Ireland but rare in England. In fact, there are only 18 in the country, and for some reason four of them are in Shropshire (see Church Stretton and Holdgate). Tugford is unusual among Shropshire villages in that it used to have a village green, on which the villagers had common rights. However, in the 17th century squatters built cottages on the green, which were later demolished by order of the manorial court, and the common rights were extinguished in 1815. Part of the former green is now incorporated into the churchyard.

UFFINGTON [Shrewsbury and Atcham]
SJ5213: 2 miles (3km) NE of Shrewsbury

A linear main-road village by the Severn, below Haughmond Hill, Uffington is a small village today but must have been a busy place once. There was a wharf here, serving the Shrewsbury Canal, which was built 1793-97 to link the county town with the Wombridge Canal at Trench. Only a row of cottages marks Uffington Wharf now. The road through the village used to cross the canal on a humpbacked bridge that features in a watercolour painting by Harold Owen, brother of **Wilfred Owen**, the war poet (see Oswestry). Today, the canal has been infilled and the bridge has gone but the Owen connection is still remembered. The family moved from Oswestry to Shrewsbury, where they lived at Monkmoor, just across the river from Uffington. They used to enjoy walking beside the Severn, and would often cross the river to Uffington by way of the cable ferry that operated then. Sometimes they attended evensong at **Holy Trinity Church**, which was rebuilt in 1856 by S. Pountney Smith in Early English style, though its windows contain some 16th- and 17th-century glass from the Netherlands and Germany.

UPPINGTON [Shrewsbury and Atcham]
SJ5909: 4 miles (6km) SW of Wellington

The pleasant village of Uppington sits by Bell Brook in the shadow of the Wrekin and is approached from the A5 along a long, straight lane bordered by mature trees. There are several large brick houses and farms, the splendid timber-framed **Tudor House** and the **church of Holy Trinity**, which stands on a raised mound. In the churchyard is a huge hollow yew tree which must be well over 1000 years old. The church was heavily restored in 1885 but a Norman window, doorway and tympanum with a carving of a dragon reveal its true age (though some think the tympanum is Saxon rather than Norman). A Roman altar by the porch was dug up in 1678 from the ground nearby. The Welsh poet **Goronwy Owen** (1723-69?) was curate of the church from 1748 until 1753.

Theologian **Richard Allestree** (1619-81) was born at Uppington. He achieved fame with his tracts and sermons but his major work was *The Whole Duty of Man*, published at intervals between 1658 and 1670. He became Provost of Eton and Regius Professor of Divinity at Oxford.

UPTON CRESSETT [Bridgnorth]
SO6592: 4 miles (6km) W of Bridgnorth

The remote hamlet of Upton Cressett stands at the end of a "no through road" on high ground above Mor Brook and consists of **Upton Cressett Hall**, the disused **church of St Michael** and the earthworks of a **deserted medieval village.** Upton Cressett Hall (now a farm) was built in 1540 in brick, incorporating the great hall from an earlier building, and the impressive turreted and gabled gatehouse was added about 40 years later. Local tradition has it that the "Princes in the Tower" (see Ludlow) spent a night here (in the earlier house which the Elizabethan hall replaced) on their journey from Ludlow Castle to the Tower of London in 1483.

Nobody knows precisely why the medieval village was not a success but a tax assessment for 1341 reveals that it was already in decline and by the middle of the 16th century what little remained was destroyed when the parkland of the hall was extended. The church survived, of course, and is maintained by the Redundant Churches Fund. The nave and chancel are Norman and there is work from the 13th century. Inside there is a very fine Norman font.

UPTON MAGNA [Shrewsbury and Atcham]

SJ5512: 3 miles (5km) E of Shrewsbury

A pleasant village below Haughmond Hill, Upton Magna is centred around the Norman **church of St Lucy** (an unusual dedication), which has 13th-, 14th- and 15th-century work, including an impressive Perpendicular tower. It was restored in 1856 by G.E. Street. The airy, spacious interior is full of rich but not overly obtrusive detail. Close by are several timber-framed houses including a cruck-framed one. In the late 17th century there was an ironworks nearby, one of several in the Tern valley. It stood by the bridge over the Tern at **Upton Forge**. The links for Telford's Menai Suspension Bridge were forged here in 1825.

WALCOT [Wrekin]

SJ5912: 7 miles (11km) E of Shrewsbury

Walcot is a brick-built hamlet in a damp landscape in the shadow of the Wrekin. The River Tern and River Roden have their confluence here and there used to be a watermill close by, at the present Mill House Farm. A complex of weirs and races associated with the mill adds interest to the scene and there are several pools just to the

north. Half a mile south is **Charlton**, another red-brick hamlet, with the earthworks of **Charlton Castle**. Edward II gave licence to crenellate in 1317 to John de Charlton, Lord of Powys.

WAPPENSHALL [Wrekin]

SJ6614: 2 miles (3km) N of Wellington

At first glance the hamlet of Wappenshall appears to be of little interest: just a handful of brick cottages and a farm amongst arable fields and pastures on the edge of the Weald Moors. However, closer inspection reveals traces of a once busy canal junction at **Wappenshall Bridge**, with warehouses, cottages, offices, stables and the remains of a basin. It was a transhipment point at the junction of the Shrewsbury Canal with the Trench and Newport branches of the Shropshire Union.

WATERS UPTON [Wrekin]

SJ6319: 5 miles (8km) N of Wellington

An attractive village on the northern edge of the Weald Moors, Waters Upton is centred on the red sandstone **church of St Michael**, built by G.E. Street in 1864 on the site of an 11th-century chapel. Opposite the church is a priest's house, apparently used in the Middle Ages by monks from Shrewsbury who stayed here on Saturday nights to be available for Sunday morning mass. Nearby is **The Hall**, formerly the Manor House, built for Shrewsbury haberdasher John Wase in 1703. Behind its elegant Queen Anne facade are parts of a cruck-framed house built centuries earlier. Just to the north of Waters Upton is the confluence of the River Tern, the River Meese and the Platt Brook. Today there is a footbridge across the Tern but at one time there were just huge stepping stones and the place is still called Nobridge.

WATTLESBOROUGH HEATH [Shrewsbury and Atcham]

SJ3511: 10 miles (16km) W of Shrewsbury

Wattlesborough Heath is a straggly sort of

hamlet along the Welshpool road, with little of obvious interest. However, a "no through road" leads north to **Wattlesborough Hall**, a five-bay Georgian farmhouse built of stone. Adjoining it is the high, square keep of **Wattlesborough Castle**, built by the Corbets c1200. A later medieval wing was added by the Leighton family, who lived here until c1711 when they moved to Loton Hall. Back on the main road again, the brick **church of St Margaret of Scotland** was built in 1931 and there is a Methodist church of 1893.

WELLINGTON [Wrekin]

SJ6511: 3 miles (5km) NW of Telford

Wellington is an old market town on the edge of the coalfield, now almost, but not quite, engulfed by Telford (though, administratively speaking, it is part of Telford). It is an unremarkable place, with few buildings of merit or interest. Nevertheless, it is pleasant, bustling and cheerful, its narrow streets, traditional facades and handful of timber-framed buildings giving it the feel of a country market town. Telford seems light years away.

The town is older than it looks, having been founded in the 6th century by the Anglo-Saxons. By 1086 it was still a village but beginning to develop into a regional centre. A market was confirmed by a charter of Henry III in 1244 and new streets and a market square were subsequently laid out. An annual stock fare attracted buyers from as far away as the Netherlands, Italy, Spain and France. Wellington prospered throughout the centuries, developing as a religious and educational centre, as well as a market town. The coming of the railway in 1849 was a useful boost and Wellington remained the chief town in the area, its position on the edge of the coalfield, with farmland on three sides, ensuring it was the regional centre for livestock and wool sales. The decline of the coalfield industries hit it less hard than its neighbours, but

the development of Telford meant big changes. Wellington has somehow managed to hang on to its separate identity and its ancient market is still held on four days a week and still recognised as the best in Shropshire.

The town centre building with the most interest is timber-framed **Old Hall**, which was built in the 15th century for the Keepers of the Wrekin. The town has two Anglican churches: classical **All Saints' Church** was built in 1790 by George Steuart and yellow-brick **Christ Church** in 1838 by Thomas Smith of Madeley.

On the edge of Wellington (Holyhead Road) the National Trust owns **Sunnycroft**, a Victorian suburban villa typical of many thousands built for prosperous professionals and business people but probably unique in having survived largely unaltered and complete with its contents. The grounds contain pigsties, stables, a kitchen garden, orchards, a conservatory, a flower garden and even a Wellingtonia avenue.

Hesba Stretton (real name Sarah Smith) was born in Wellington in 1832, the daughter of a postmaster. She wrote a series of best-selling books, most famous of which was *Jessica's First Prayer*, published in 1866 and the recipient of extraordinary success. Sales ran into millions and it was even translated into Russian and used as a set text in Russian schools. Hesba put her resulting wealth to good use, involving herself in various charitable projects, including the foundation of the London Society for Prevention of Cruelty to Children, which later became the NSPCC. She died in 1911 and her books sank into obscurity. In August 1999, however, Hesba Stretton was rediscovered when Blists Hill Museum (see Coalport) began staging an ongoing soap opera based on her stories.

William Withering (1741-99) was also born in Wellington. A distinguished doctor and scientist, he was co-founder of Birmingham General Hospital but is most famous for his discovery of the use of digitalis (from the foxglove) in treating cardiac disease – though "discovery" is not quite the right word. He was impressed by a Shropshire gypsy who used an infusion of foxglove leaves to cure a patient whom the doctor had thought a hopeless case. He obtained full details of the treatment from the gypsy and published the information in a book of 1785. Digitalis is still a useful cardiac drug.

Wellington's suburbs include Arleston, Admaston, Dothill and Shawbirch and they lie mostly to the north of town (except for Arleston). The M54 bounds Wellington to the south and beyond it lie the Wrekin and its foothill, the Ercall. **The Wrekin** is Shropshire's most familiar hill and has given rise to phrases such as "going all around the Wrekin" and the local toast "to all friends around the Wrekin". It is visible from much of Shropshire (and neighbouring counties) and is often described as the spiritual home of all true Salopians, a sort of focal point and symbol of their home county. It stands in splendid isolation, seeming higher than its modest 407 metres, and is volcanic in origin, a plug of worn-down rock, just a remnant of a vast chunk thrust to the surface by subterranean activity at least 600 million years ago. That puts it among the oldest rocks in the world. The view from the top is extraordinary and the summit is enclosed within the ramparts of an **Iron Age fort** which is believed to have been the main base of the Cornovii, a Celtic people who controlled a fair chunk of what was later to become Mercia. They were subjugated by the Romans and resettled at Viroconium (see Wroxeter) but it is thought many of them moved back to the Wrekin once the Romans had left.

While the **Ercall** is less impressive, it is still a valuable hill, now owned by Shropshire Wildlife Trust. Among geologists it is internationally famous for its superb rock exposures. Its natural history interest is also considerable, with a number of woodland

types, and a wealth of wild flowers and butterflies in the glades opened up by past quarrying. Right on the edge of town, it's very popular with locals and it is often claimed that half of Wellington's population was conceived there.

WELSHAMPTON [North Shropshire]

SJ4335: 2 miles (3km) E of Ellesmere

Welshampton is a main-road village just to the north of the complex of meres near Ellesmere. Its name (together with that of Welsh Frankton) has been taken as evidence that the Welsh border was, for centuries, effectively (if not politically) further east than was previously thought. It is well known that Welsh was the first language in much of the Oswestry area until comparatively recently, and some modern researchers now think that may have been true around Ellesmere too.

The stone-built **church of St Michael** was designed in 1863 by Sir George Gilbert Scott. Buried in the churchyard is an African prince, Jeremiah Lepobona Moshueshue, heir to the throne of Basutoland. He was in England to study at theological college in Canterbury and was staying at the vicarage in Welshampton at the time of his death in 1863, when he was only 24 years old.

WELSH FRANKTON [North Shropshire]

SJ3633: 2 miles (3km) SW of Ellesmere

Welsh Frankton is a brick-built, main-road village in attractive undulating country. The **church of St Andrew** was built in the 1850s and there is also a Methodist chapel. To the north-east, set in parkland, is **Hardwick Hall**, built in brick for John Kynaston in 1693, with projecting wings added c1720. To the south of the village is **Lower Frankton**, at what was once the junction of the Llangollen and Montgomery branches of the Shropshire Union Canal. There was a busy canalside community here until the Montgomery Canal was abandoned. Frankton Locks were restored in 1987.

WEM [North Shropshire]
SJ5128: 10 miles (16km) N of Shrewsbury

Less attractive than Whitchurch, less bustling than Wellington, Wem has nevertheless been a market town since 1202 and possesses a variety of interesting, if unspectacular, buildings. Few of them are very old, because the town was partially demolished in 1643 when a band of 40 Roundheads defeated an attacking force of 5000 Royalists. Further destruction followed in 1677 when 14-year-old Jane Churm ensured herself a place in local history by accidentally setting alight the thatched roof of her home. The resulting "Great Fire of Wem" destroyed nearly 150 buildings in less than an hour.

One that escaped destruction was the **church of St Peter and St Paul**, which has a 14th-century doorway of an uncommon design and a partly 12th-century tower. Much of the rest is Victorian. Next to it stands a mound which was the site of a **castle** built here by the Norman baron William Pantulf in the 11th century. It was apparently a substantial structure but it gradually fell into decay, a process helped by the propensity of locals to remove its stones for other building purposes. Wem had medieval town walls too, but no trace of these survives.

To the west of the church is the former **Market Hall**; originally timber-framed, it was destroyed by the 1677 fire and rebuilt in 1728. Nearby there are some good Georgian houses and some timber-framed houses dating from 1677. New Street has some fine buildings, including a timber-framed one with a projecting porch and **Wem Hall**, a Georgian brick house of considerable stature. Noble Street has much of interest too, including 17th-century **Drawwell House**, which survived the fire and became part of the famous Wem Brewery in 1794. Adjacent to the brewery is **Astley's House**, another timber-framed house which escaped the fire. **John Astley**, portrait painter and friend of Joshua Reynolds, lived there.

Wem is only a small town, but a number of notable people have connections with it. Essayist and critic **William Hazlitt** (1778-1830), whose father was minister of the Unitarian chapel, lived in Noble Street from 1787 until 1799. Another distinguished resident was **William Betty** (1791-1874), a child actor known as "Young Roscius" who achieved a cult following in 18th-century London. But the one of whom Wem is most proud is **Henry Eckford**, who in 1887 developed the modern version of the sweet pea.

To the north of Wem is **Lowe Hall**, a Jacobean house with a 19th-century front. It was the property of the notorious **Judge Jeffreys** of Bloody Assize fame, who became Baron of Wem in 1684 but never lived there.

WENTNOR [South Shropshire]
SO3892: 5 miles (8km) NE of Bishop's Castle

The compact village of Wentnor is enviably positioned on a ridge between the River East Onny and Criftin Brook. The Long Mynd looms just to the east and Norbury Hill to the west. The **church of St Michael** is early Norman with a 15th-century roof but was restored in 1885-6, using the old masonry. On the edge of the village, off Adstone Lane, is a field called Black Graves where victims of the Black Death are said to have been buried. A curious feature of the hill which Wentnor occupies is the shape of the fields which sweep down the eastern side towards Criftin Brook: they are long and narrow, almost like the strip system of the Middle Ages, and perhaps represent some sort of survival from that time. It's not a pattern found on neighbouring hills. On the far side of Criftin Brook, at Wentnor Prolley, is **Robury Ring**, an Iron Age earthwork that now encloses a farm.

WESTBURY [Shrewsbury and Atcham]

SJ3509: 3 miles (5km) NW of Pontesbury

The village of Westbury must have been a busier place in the days when it had a station on the Shrewsbury to Aberystwyth railway, which passes less than a mile to the north. The former Station Hotel has been converted into a house and the cattle market is no more. There's not a great deal at Westbury these days, though it does have a school and a post office. **St Mary's Church** is partly Norman but was much altered in the 13th century when a new chancel and aisle were added. Further changes were made in the 15th century and in 1753, when the tower was built. In 1878 most of the windows were replaced and the north porch and vestry added.

To the south-west of Westbury is **Caus Castle**, built by Roger FitzCorbet who named it after his birthplace (Caux) in Normandy. Not much remains today because it was destroyed during the Civil War but the earthworks and foundations are still there, and a little masonry. Below the castle is a hamlet called **Cause Castle**, all that remains of a planned town established by Robert Corbet in 1198. It grew into quite a flourishing settlement despite the obvious disadvantage of its position in what was effectively Wales. The Corbets were continually skirmishing with the Welsh and Owain Glyndŵr burnt Cause to the ground at the beginning of the 15th century. It was burned again in the middle of the century and by Tudor times it was in decay. In any case, the Tudor Peace and union with Wales rendered the castle, if not the township, redundant.

WEST FELTON [Oswestry]

SJ3425: 4 miles (6km) SE of Oswestry

West Felton is a pleasant village split into two parts by the A5: the modern developments are to the east and the old village to the west, bypassed by the road, but still close enough for rural peace to be a thing of the past. The village was originally Saxon but later developed around the Norman **castle**, of which only a moated motte remains. Next to it is the **church of St Michael**, the earliest parts of which date from c1140. In 1782 the tower collapsed and was replaced by the present one and in 1841 the north aisle and chancel were rebuilt by Sir George Gilbert Scott, with the porch and south aisle added in 1879.

Although located in what has always been a predominantly agricultural area, West Felton used to have a glass factory and also hosted an RAF base during the Second World War. The village is largely inhabited by commuters today.

WESTHOPE [South Shropshire]

SO4786: 3 miles (5km) NE of Craven Arms

A small, though scattered, hamlet (including Middle Westhope and Upper Westhope), Westhope has a lovely setting in Hope Dale below Wenlock Edge. The little church dates from c1650 but the yew tree by its entrance pre-dates it by at least 400 years. **Westhope Hall** stands nearby and was built in 1901 in Tudor style by Sir Guy Dawber. A little to the south is a moated site about which little is known, though we do know that Picot de Say, the builder of Clun Castle, held the manor of Westhope after the Conquest.

WESTON LULLINGFIELDS [North Shropshire]

SJ4224: 9 miles (14km) NW of Shrewsbury

Weston Lullingfields is a community of three hamlets – the other two are Westoncommon and Westonwharf – with outlying farms and houses. It lies on the edge of Baggy Moors, former marshland which drainage has transformed into productive dairy country. The **church of Holy Trinity**, built in 1857 by Edward Haycock Junior, stands at a mid-point between the three hamlets. In 1797 a branch of the

Ellesmere Canal reached Weston, at what became Westonwharf. It was a busy place for a time, with warehouses, limekilns, stables, a weighing machine, a clerk's house and a pub. In 1917 the canal banks were breached and lack of money meant it was abandoned rather than repaired. Most of the canal buildings still stand but now serve other purposes.

WESTON RHYN [Oswestry]

SJ2935: 4 miles (6km) N of Oswestry

There is a great deal of modern development at Weston Rhyn, which is an uninspiring village in itself, though it has a fortunate position close to the lovely valley of the Afon Ceiriog and the border hills. There used to be some industry locally, with coal mining, iron production and paper milling. Today, industry is concentrated across the border at Chirk, where many local people find employment.

On the western fringe of the village is **Quinta Park**, a Gothic house of the 1850s. In the grounds is a bizarre copy of Stonehenge built for Thomas Barnes, cotton magnate and chairman of the Lancashire and Yorkshire Railway. Not far from Quinta is the **church of St John the Divine**, built in 1878.

WESTON UNDER REDCASTLE [North Shropshire]

SJ5628: 3 miles (5km) E of Wem

Weston is an attractive village with a mixture of architectural styles. Before the Conquest it was owned by Wild Edric (see Stiperstones) but the first post-Conquest landholder was Ranulf Peverel. It later passed to the Audley family who in 1228 built what became known as **Red Castle**, either because of the colour of its constituent sandstone or because it was built on the Red Cliff.

The **church of St Luke** was built in 1791, mainly Gothic in style, but with a Georgian tower. It was chiefly paid for by

Sir Richard Hill of **Hawkstone Hall**, which was owned by the Hill family from 1554. The hall stands in **Hawkstone Park**, which was used as a camp for German prisoners of war during World War Two. Red Castle is also within the parkland, which contains a golf course and a sort of 18th-century adventure playground conceived by Sir Rowland Hill. It's a stunning combination of natural and man-made attractions: a wonderfully dramatic craggy landscape with a collection of follies, grottoes, an obelisk, a hermitage, secret paths and tunnels, dramatic viewpoints, passageways hewn from the rock and, of course, the romantic ruin of Red Castle. **Hawkstone Park Hotel** was built in 1790 to cater for those who came to marvel at the park, which later fell into decay and was more or less abandoned for a century or so. It has recently been restored and is open to the public again, with the added attraction of a herd of sika deer.

WHEATHILL [South Shropshire]

SO6282: 5 miles (8km) NW of Cleobury Mortimer

Wheathill is a tiny hamlet lost in pastoral country to the south of Brown Clee Hill. It originally comprised four hamlets – Wheathill, Bromdon, Egerton and Leverdegreene, but only the first two survive. The **church of Holy Trinity** has a Norman nave and chancel and a fine 17th-century nave roof, but most of the rest is 19th century. In 1942 "The Brethren" came to Bromdon. They were a community group originating in Germany who lived and worked together in farming and forestry. They made peaceful, productive lives for themselves here but moved on in 1963.

WHITCHURCH [North Shropshire]

SJ5441: 8 miles (12km) N of Wem

An appealing, unpretentious market town with medieval, Tudor, Georgian and Victorian buildings, Whitchurch is one of the oldest continually inhabited towns in the country and was occupied by the Romans, who named it Mediolanum and valued it for its strategic location at the heart of their road network. There are few traces of the Roman town today, though the modern High Street follows the old Roman road and the basic plan of the town centre owes something to the Romans. A number of Romano-British villa sites have been found in the surrounding countryside, which is pleasantly undulating, green and pastoral.

Whitchurch's history has mostly been fairly uneventful and its main claims to fame have long been cheese and clocks. It was **J.B. Joyce & Co**, the oldest clockmakers in the world, with premises on Station Road, who placed Shropshire firmly on the horological map. Established in 1690, they make magnificent clocks that have gained an international reputation and can be found on cathedrals and public buildings worldwide. There are several examples of Joyce's work in the town, including the church tower clock made in 1849. Joyce's was a family business handed down through eight generations but in 1965 it was taken over by John Smith & Sons of Derby, though the Joyce name was retained. Whitchurch is also a centre of the dairy industry and cheese fairs were a regular feature in the past. Cheshire Cheese used to be exported to Manchester by canal, the narrowboats sheeted up with white canvas to deflect the sun's rays from the perishable cargo. Blue Cheshire remains a popular export today.

St Alkmund's Church was built by William and Richard Smith of Tattenhall in 1712-13, designed by John Barker to replace a medieval church which collapsed in 1711. It is of considerable architectural significance because it pioneers a provincial adaptation of the style then only recently introduced in London by Christopher Wren and his colleagues. An imposing building, it has a semicircular porch on its south side

and a big west tower with balustrade and pinnacles. The interior is majestic, with Tuscan columns and wooden galleries. There is a 17th-century font decorated with a Tudor rose and Prince of Wales's feathers. Among the effigies are monuments to John Talbot, 1st Earl of Shrewsbury, killed at Chantillon near Bordeaux in 1453, and Sir John Talbot, rector and founder of the local grammar school, who died in 1550.

Near the church, **Higginson's Alms-houses** form an attractive row of Georgian cottages (though founded in 1647) with a pedimented gable, and the **Old Grammar School** is resplendent in 19th-century "Elizabethan" dress. There are some good shopfronts on High Street, and a Gothic **town hall** of 1872. On St Mary's Lane a pub called Old Town Hall Vaults was the birthplace of composer **Sir Edward German** (1862-1936), who was born Edward German Jones and is perhaps most famous for the operetta *Merrie England*.

Dodington is probably the best street in town, with many good Georgian houses. One of its finest buildings is the **Mansion House**. Next door, the double-fronted **Dodington House** has had a Georgian facade of stucco rendering imposed on a much older timber-framed building. The disused classical-style **church of St Catherine** was built in 1836 and possesses great elegance. Its clock is thought to be the earliest Joyce turret clock in existence in this country. The **Congregational Church** of 1846 is a most elegant building and the adjacent **Manse** has the best Victorian Gothic bargeboards and finial in town. **Dodington Manor** is much older than it looks – the 1904 restoration hides a house believed to date from c1590.

The Llangollen Canal passes within a mile of the town centre but the Whitchurch Arm, which linked it to town centre wharves, was abandoned in 1944 and filled in. In 1993 a start was made on a major restoration project which has seen the arm partly restored and reopened, forming part of a plan that includes the creation of the only working inclined plane in the country along with a leisure lake and country park.

WHITTINGTON [Oswestry]

SJ3231: 2 miles (3km) NE of Oswestry

A substantial village in flat countryside near the River Perry, Whittington is dominated by its **castle**, built by Fulke FitzWarine c1221. Substantial earthworks remain but the castle fell into disuse after the Civil War and its stone was plundered for road repairs. However, the handsome gatehouse survives intact, its twin circular towers reflected in the moat. It's an impressive sight and a considerable asset to the village.

The great hymn writer (and eventually Bishop of Wakefield) **William Walsham How** (1823-97) was rector in Whittington for 28 years at the **church of St John the Baptist**. The church was built on the site of a medieval church of which nothing remains. The tower dates from 1747, the brick nave from 1804-6, and much of the rest from 1894. The east window is by William Morris and Edward Burne-Jones.

Less than a mile to the east of Whittington is **Halston Hall**, built in 1690 of red brick and extended in 1766. It was the birthplace of one of Shropshire's most colourful characters, **Mad Jack Mytton** (1796-1834). He became MP for Shrewsbury but, not unreasonably perhaps, found the proceedings of the House of Commons too tedious to detain him for long. It is said he managed half an hour before storming out, never to return. He was a drunk and a gambler, given to wild exploits and crazy practical jokes that earned him tremendous affection as well as disapproval. Having wasted a large fortune, he died of a stroke at 38 in a debtors' prison in London but is buried at Halston in a **chapel** in the grounds of the hall. This is one of only two timber-framed ecclesiastical buildings in the county (see Melverley) and is probably 16th century. Raised on a mound and surrounded by yew trees, it has a brick tower and shutters on its clear glass windows. Most of the furnishings belong to the early 17th century.

WHITTON [South Shropshire]

SO5772: 4 miles (6km) SE of Ludlow

The tiny village of Whitton hides its charms deep in the bosky country which lies south of the road between Ludlow and Cleobury Mortimer. **St Mary's Church** stands on a bank high above a sunken lane in the shade of a huge yew tree. Its sturdy stone tower is 14th century, but much of the rest of the church is Norman. There are some thin bricks built into the stonework and these are believed to be Roman bricks, probably salvaged by the builders from the ruins of a villa in the neighbourhood. There are three original Norman windows in the nave, a larger 14th-century one in the south-east corner and an east window by Burne-Jones and William Morris. In front of the church stands the base and shaft of a very old preaching cross with a tabernacle for the reception of the sacred host. The churchyard flora is very rich and indicative of unimproved grassland, and is managed accordingly.

Close to the church are most of the village houses, a mixture of timber-framed and brick cottages, some new ones and some barn conversions. Half a mile to the north **Whitton Court** stands well back from the lane in spacious leafy parkland. A beautiful Tudor house in mellow brick, it has a 14th-century core and a timber-framed wing at the rear. There are 17th-century wall paintings inside. **The Hollins** nearby is a most beautiful, secluded house, built of timber and stone, and believed to have been the Dower House to Whitton Court.

WHIXALL [North Shropshire]

SJ5134: 4 miles (6km) N of Wem

Whixall is not exactly a village, but a thin

scattering of properties over a very wide area. The local soils are deeply fertile and many of the fields are still small and thickly hedged. There used to be many smallholdings but most of these have been returned to grass in recent years.

One of the more interesting houses in this scattered community is **Bostock Hall**, a 17th-century brick farmhouse. There are five churches in the parish. The Anglican one, **St Mary's Church**, was built by G.E. Street in 1867 of red brick. The Llangollen branch of the Shropshire Union Canal runs through the western part of the parish, and just beyond it is **Whixall Moss**, a National Nature Reserve and Shropshire's share of a lowland raised bog that straddles the border. It was saved from destruction in 1991 when English Nature bought it from a company that had planning permission for the extraction of peat for horticultural use. **Wem Moss**, just to the south, is a similarly valuable nature reserve cared for by Shropshire Wildlife Trust.

WILCOTT [Shrewsbury and Atcham]

SJ3718: 9 miles (14km) NW of Shrewsbury

Wilcott is a scattered village with little of interest apart from a Norman motte. A military training area adjoins it to the west and Nesscliff Training Camp is just to the south. During the Second World War the Central Ammunition Storage Depot was sited here and the storage sheds, buffered by earth embankments, still stand. Fortunately, they are scattered and well concealed, making only a limited impact on the landscape.

WILDERHOPE [South Shropshire]

SO5492: 7 miles (11km) SW of Much Wenlock

The tiny hamlet of Wilderhope comprises a farm and **Wilderhope Manor**, which belongs to the National Trust but is leased to the Youth Hostels Association. With its gables and projecting circular stairwell, this is the finest of the old houses along Wenlock Edge. It was built of local limestone about 1586 for Francis Smallman and its appearance has changed little since. Notable interior features include an original spiral staircase and some superb plaster ceilings. Wilderhope Manor forms part of the National Trust's Wilderhope Estate, one of several Trust landholdings on **Wenlock Edge**, which is one of the most distinctive features of the Shropshire landscape. It is best seen from the west, where it appears as an unbroken escarpment running from Benthall Edge to Craven Arms. The Silurian limestone of which it is formed supports a rich flora, although much of the Edge is wooded. The combination of ancient woodlands and flower-rich grasslands is a valuable one but Wenlock Edge is also of great geological importance, of international repute as an example of coral reef deposits. Past industrial activity is also evident along the edge, with limekilns and abandoned quarry workings. A massive quarry at Presthope is still in operation, digging up huge chunks of Shropshire for transport by heavy lorries along narrow lanes to be relaid elsewhere.

WILLEY [Bridgnorth]

SO6799: 3 miles (5km) E of Much Wenlock

Willey is a tiny hamlet in lovely wooded country just to the south of the Severn Gorge. The estate has belonged to the Forester family since 1748. They live at **Willey Hall**, an elegant classical-style house built by Lewis Wyatt for the 1st Lord Forester in 1812-15. Before that they lived at **Old Hall**, a Tudor house of which only a little survives. Close to it is **St John's Church**, with its long, narrow nave and chancel of the 12th century, both with early Norman windows. The embattled west tower is 18th century. A family chapel and aisles were added in 1880 by Sir Arthur Blomfield, making the overall effect of the church Victorian, despite the surviving Jacobean woodwork. **Willey New Furnace** played an important part in the Industrial Revolution for it was here that John Wilkinson established himself as a major ironmaster (see Broseley).

WISTANSTOW [South Shropshire]

SO4385: 2 miles (3km) N of Craven Arms

The village of Wistanstow is built along the course of the old Roman road running north towards Viroconium (Wroxeter) and was established by the Anglo-Saxons after the Romans left. It occupies a pleasant position in the pastoral Onny valley below Wenlock Edge and is built mainly of stone, though there is also some timber-framing. The village takes its name from St Wystan, a Mercian prince martyred in 849. A church was built soon after his death but the present **Holy Trinity Church** dates from c1190-1210, with work from several later centuries. A cruciform structure, it is unusually symmetrical because it has twin transepts and the nave and chancel are virtually the same length. It's an excellent example of the Transitional style that retained Norman features but hinted at the later Gothic styles of the 13th century. Nearby stands the **Plough Inn**, a handsome building famous for its home-brewed beer.

WITHINGTON [Shrewsbury and Atcham]

SJ5713: 5 miles (8km) E of Shrewsbury

The village of Withington lies in a wide, flat valley below Haughmond Hill. During the Great War British servicemen were famously promised "homes fit for heroes". It didn't happen, of course, but at least Withington's ex-servicemen were fairly treated in 1918 when a large part of the manorial estate was sold off to become eight council farms for them. Six distinctive white farmhouses were specially built and the remaining two homes were created from a conversion of the 18th-century **Manor House** and its outbuildings. The sandstone **church of St John the Baptist**

was built by Street in 1874, incorporating fragments of a Norman church. A rector of the earlier church, Adam Grafton, who died in 1530, served as chaplain to both Edward V and Prince Arthur. The Shrewsbury Canal came through Withington in 1797 and there was a wharf where coal was delivered. There were also two lift bridges but they were taken up when the canal was abandoned in 1944. It can still be traced in places in the fields.

WOLLASTON [Shrewsbury and Atcham]

SJ3312: 10 miles (16km) W of Shrewsbury

A tiny village in the shadow of the dramatic Breidden Hills, Wollaston is little more than a handful of farms around a Norman motte and the **church of St John**, which was rebuilt in 1788 and restored in 1885. A brass memorial in the church commemorates **Thomas Parr** (1483-1635), more often known as Old Parr. He was born at nearby **Winnington**, where his recently restored cottage still stands. He was reportedly 152 when he died, and while this may inspire scepticism it appears to be well documented. He was married for the first time at 80 (perhaps that's the secret) to Jane Taylor, who bore him two children, both of whom died in infancy. At 105 he had an affair with Katherine Milton which produced another child. After becoming a widower he married for the second time at 122. In 1635 the Earl of Arundel, visiting his estates in Shropshire, heard about Old Parr and thought Charles I would enjoy meeting this curiosity so he had the poor old chap carted off to London. This came as such a shock to the system that Old Parr died at Arundel's residence the same year and was buried in Westminster Abbey.

WOMBRIDGE [Wrekin]

SJ6911: 2 miles (3km) N of Telford Centre

A suburb of Oakengates, Wombridge has a long and varied industrial history but is now mainly given over to modern housing. By the 16th century the monks of **Wombridge Priory** (founded c1140) were digging for coal and smelting iron ore. The Charltons of Apley Castle and the ironmaster William Reynolds were active here too. Reynolds constructed a long tunnel from his mines at Wombridge to blast furnaces at Donnington Wood. Sand was also quarried and a chemical factory was operative in the 1790s, producing sulphuric acid from iron pyrites in the coal seams. By 1850 half the parish was turning into post-industrial wasteland as the factories and forges closed. The church was torn down in 1869 and the new **church of St Mary and St Leonard** built in stone. Below the churchyard are the remains of the priory.

WOODCOTE [Wrekin]

SJ7615: 3 miles (5km) S of Newport

Woodcote is the tiniest of hamlets, comprising **Woodcote Hall** (1875), a cottage and a 12th-century **chapel** with a fine south doorway. The church was refurbished in the 16th and 17th centuries and most of the windows are 19th century. There are monuments inside to various members of the Cotes family, including Humphrey Cotes, killed fighting for Henry Tudor at Bosworth in 1485.

Woodcote Hall has been frequently rebuilt and the present house is a splendid mixture of neo-Jacobean, neo-Georgian and oriental ogee turrets. It was designed by F.P. Cockerell.

WOOLSTASTON [Shrewsbury and Atcham]

SO4598: 3 miles (5km) N of Church Stretton

Situated on the lower slopes of the Long Mynd, Woolstaston enjoys a beautiful setting and is an unspoilt village which has seen little development. It tends to get cut off by snow in harsh winters, such as 1865 when the Reverend Carr from Woolstaston

Rectory was lost in the snow after taking a service at Ratlinghope. He got hopelessly lost and endured over 24 hours in terrible conditions. He subsequently published a book, *A Night in the Snow*, about his ordeal. **St Michael's Church** underwent Victorian restoration but has a 13th-century nave and chancel and two 12th-century fonts. Next to the church is 17th-century **Woolstaston Hall**, built of brick with stone dressings and a hipped roof. The doorway is believed to be by the same stone carver responsible for Minsterley Church (see Minsterley). At the west end of the village, Castle Bank is the site of a Norman motte.

WOOLSTON [Oswestry]

SJ3224: 4 miles (6km) SE of Oswestry

A hamlet in flat country close to the Montgomery Canal, Woolston is distinguished by **St Winifrid's Well**, one of the most delightful holy wells in the country. It is probably pre-Christian but acquired its dedication when the body of St Winifred, a 7th-century princess, rested here in the 12th century when she was moved from her Denbighshire grave to Shrewsbury Abbey. A timber-framed cottage is set against a hillside above the spring and the water runs through a series of stone basins, forming a little stream. The pretty, timbered building is now a property of the Landmark Trust and the setting, in a wooded dingle, could not be lovelier.

WOORE [North Shropshire]

SJ7342: 7 miles (11km) NE of Market Drayton

Woore is a substantial village in a peninsula of Shropshire caught between Staffordshire and Cheshire. Its position around the crossroads formed by the A51 and A525 ensures that it is blighted by traffic day and night. There are mellow old brick houses here but a large number of new houses have been built in recent years and Woore functions as a dormitory town for Stoke-on-Trent. It's an ancient settlement, already well established by the time of the Domesday survey. From c1552 it had a chapel of ease but in 1830 **St Leonard's Church** was built, though the tower was added later. The white-painted church is Italianate in style and quite charming. The handsome **Swan Hotel** opposite looks about the same age, with three bays and a Tuscan porch, but has 15th-century origins.

Best-selling jockey-turned-author **Dick Francis** rode his first race at Woore, on a National Hunt course that has since been closed.

WORFIELD [Bridgnorth]

SO7595: 3 miles (5km) NE of Bridgnorth

Squeezed between the lovely River Worfe and a sandstone cliff, Worfield is one of the most charming villages in Shropshire. Houses of stone, brick and timber jostle for position along the main street. One of the finest buildings is **Lower House**, a gabled, timber-framed house of two ranges with a turret at their junction. It is probably of the 17th century.

The **church of St Peter**, which dominates the village, is said to have been founded by Earl Leofric (Lady Godiva's husband) in the 11th century but the present church dates from the 13th century. However, much of the detail is 14th century. It has a tall spire of grey stone on top of a red tower. It was heavily restored in 1862 and most of the windows were replaced. For such a small village it is a very large church but the parish is one of the largest in the country, taking in over 30 hamlets, all of which were recorded in Domesday Book and all of which have maintained their separate identity. The old tradition of the passion play was revived at Worfield in 1973 and has taken place at five-yearly intervals ever since. The play was written by local industrialist (also choirmaster and organist) Michael Lloyd, who sadly died in a fire before the first production could take place.

Milling (grain, paper and cloth) and farming used to be the main occupations in Worfield. Farming is still the mainstay of the economy but there are commuters now too. Much of the property belongs to the Davenport estate and tenants present themselves twice a year at the Davenport Arms to pay the rent. **Davenport House** is a substantial brick building in landscaped parkland and was designed by Francis Smith of Warwick in 1726.

WORTHEN [South Shropshire]

SJ3204: 5 miles (8km) SW of Pontesbury

A substantial village, mainly stone-built, Worthen lies on an old drove road not far from the border. Worthen Brook used to power an old mill used for corn, timber, wool and cider at different times, but demolished in 1973 to make way for modern housing. **All Saints' Church** is a Saxon foundation which has a spacious interior with a very wide 13th-century nave. In the middle of the north side is a 12th-century tower with a 15th-century top and 18th-century parapet. The windows and buttresses are 19th century. The brick chancel is of 1761 and the south porch is 17th century. The benches are interesting; a complete set and seemingly medieval.

WROCKWARDINE [Wrekin]

SJ6212: 2 miles (3km) W of Wellington

Close to Telford, but peaceful enough yet, the village of Wrockwardine is surrounded by arable farmland. Very much a red-brick village, it clusters round **St Peter's Church**, which contains work from the 12th, 13th and 14th centuries. With its fine square tower topped with a short brick steeple, the church is a prominent local landmark. Inside there is an ancient font which may be Saxon. Adjacent **Wrockwardine Hall** is an impressive two-storeyed house partly of 1628, and partly Georgian. Other fine buildings include **almshouses**, built in 1841 with a bequest from Edward Chudde of nearby Orleton, and the **Old Vicarage**, with a decorative ironwork porch.

WROCKWARDINE WOOD [Wrekin]

SJ6911: 2 miles (3km) N of Telford Centre

Wrockwardine Wood is a very pleasant, leafy suburb of Telford but for many centuries it was a detached part of Wrockwardine parish. In 1834 it became a separate parish but confusion still reigns. The **church of Holy Trinity** was built in 1833 by Samuel Smith of Madeley. Built of brick, with arched windows, it has a small west tower with a parapet and obelisks. Wrockwardine Wood was known for its coal and iron ore but had other industries too, such as a glassworks. The adjoining suburb of **Trench** was the site of the impressive Trench Incline, which joined canals at different levels. It had become the last working incline in Britain when it finally closed in 1921. Today there's only a slope, with a pub at the bottom, the Blue Pig, this being the name given to furnace slag.

WROXETER [Shrewsbury and Atcham]

SJ5608: 5 miles (8km) SE of Shrewsbury

Wroxeter is a tiny village by the Severn which would be unremarkable but for its superb Roman remains. Wroxeter was the site of **Viroconium**, which, at its zenith, was the fourth largest Roman town in Britain. It began as a military camp AD58 but when the legion was moved to Chester about 30 years later the site was developed as a civil town. Most of the visible remains are of the 2nd-century municipal baths, but the size of these gives an indication of the scale of the town. Also uncovered are parts of the exercise hall, market hall and forum. Still standing is an impressive section of a basilica wall, known as the "Old Work". Aerial photography has demonstrated, by means of crop marks, the presence of streets, houses and fortifications beneath the surface of the surrounding farmland. After the Romans left, Viroconium was abandoned, regarded only as a useful source of building stone while farmers ploughed over its remains. But unlike other Roman cities, such as London, it was never overlaid by rebuilding and the remains of the city, though buried, were relatively undisturbed. In 1996 a three-year project run by the University of Birmingham Field Archaeology Unit began to use the modern techniques of geophysics to explore the site. Without the need for digging, archaeologists were able to reveal the layout of the city with great precision, producing detailed street maps that shatter many earlier theories about Viroconium and revealing details about daily life. The main tool was magnetometry - the measurement of magnetic anomalies in the soil. This revealed a clear plan of the former streets and walls and a surprise - a large rectangular building with an apse, suggesting an early Christian church, a rare feature in Roman Britain. The evidence of aerial surveys had suggested a low-density occupation, a sort of garden city, but magnetometry revealed that it was intensively occupied with maybe three times the population previously thought. Other techniques used on the site include measurements of the electrical resistance of the soil and ground-penetrating radar. The Wroxeter project has become an award-winning test bed for experiments in archaeological geophysics. Viroconium is in the care of English Heritage and there is a museum of artefacts found on the site, though the more precious items are in Rowley House Museum, Shrewsbury.

St Andrew's Church is also of interest. Part of the nave is Saxon and was built with stone from Viroconium. In c1170-80 a new chancel was added, parts of which still remain. The Saxon nave was lengthened in the 13th century and there are windows of the 14th, 15th and 16th centuries. The embattled west tower is also 16th century. The interior is mostly 17th and 18th century but there are handsome 16th-century monuments and a massive font believed to be made from part of a Roman column. The churchyard gateposts are Roman too. St Andrew's is now managed by the Redundant Churches Fund. There are some attractive houses in the village, and earthworks in the neighbouring fields are part of Viroconium's defences.

YEATON [Shrewsbury and Atcham]
SJ4319: 6 miles (10km) NW of Shrewsbury

A compact hamlet by the River Perry, Yeaton has attractive cottages of brick and half-timber but the main interest here is **Yeaton Peverey**, a spectacular sandstone mansion half a mile to the south-east. It is Jacobean in style but was built in 1890-92 by Aston Webb. A little to the north-east is a moated earthwork which must have been the site of a medieval house.

YOCKLETON [Shrewsbury and Atcham]
SJ3910: 5 miles (8km) SW of Shrewsbury

Domesday Book records a thriving agricultural village at Yockleton and little has changed. Milk production is important to the local economy, with cereals, pigs and poultry all well established. The **church of Holy Trinity** was designed by Edward Haycock Junior and consecrated in 1861. Its woodwork and carving were created by a local man, John Evans, who is credited with building the first wooden bicycle, a velocipede. There is abundant new housing development, and few very old houses survive. The only sign of Yockleton Castle, probably built by the Corbets, who acquired Yockleton from Wild Edric after the Conquest, is a motte in a field to the north-east of the church.

Bibliography

Bird, Vivian, *Exploring the West Midlands* (B.T. Batsford Ltd, 1977)

Dickins, Gordon, *An Illustrated Literary Guide to Shropshire* (Shropshire Libraries, 1987)

Garner, Lawrence, *Churches of Shropshire* (Shropshire Books, 1994)

Garner, Lawrence, *Shropshire* (Shire Publications Ltd, 1993)

Gregory, David, *Walks around Telford* (Shropshire Books, 1995)

Jenkinson, Andrew, *Shropshire Countryside* (Minton & Minton, 1990)

Jenkinson, Andrew, *Shropshire's Wild Places* (Scenesetters, 1992)

Jeremiah, Josephine, *The River Severn* (Phillimore & Co Ltd, 1998)

Lias, Anthony, *Place Names of the Welsh Borderlands* (Palmers Press, 1991)

Morriss, Richard K., *Canals of Shropshire* (Shropshire Books, 1991)

Morton, Andrew, *The Trees of Shropshire* (Airlife Publishing Ltd, 1986)

Moulder, Michael, *A Shell Guide: Shropshire* (Faber & Faber/Shell-Mex and BP Ltd, 1972)

Pevsner, Nikolaus, *The Buildings of England: Shropshire* (Penguin Books, 1958)

Raven, Michael, *A Shropshire Gazetteer* (Michael Raven, 1989)

Salter, Mike, *The Castles and Moated Mansions of Shropshire* (Folly Publications, 1988)

Salter, Mike, *The Old Parish Churches of Shropshire* (Folly Publications, 1988)

Shropshire County Council, *Aspects of Shropshire* (Shropshire Books, 1994)

Shropshire County Council, *Shropshire* (Shropshire County Council, 1980)

Trinder, Barrie, *A History of Shropshire* (Phillimore & Co Ltd, 1998)

Waite, Vincent, *Shropshire Hill Country* (Phillimore & Co Ltd, 1989)

Index

Also of interest from Sigma Leisure:

BEST TEA SHOP WALKS IN SHROPSHIRE
Julie Meech

Shropshire "has all the essential qualities that walkers seek" enthuses author Julie Meech.

Discover its spectacular diversity with the thought of a traditional cream tea lingering in your mind.

£6.95

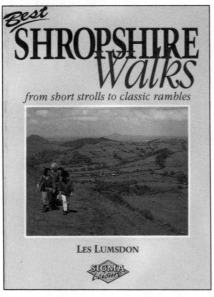

BEST SHROPSHIRE WALKS: short strolls to classic rambles
Les Lumsdon

Walks all over the county, varying from an easy five-miler to walks of 10 miles and more, with visits to local pubs and tiny hamlets.

£6.95